CREATING ATMOSPHERE WIT

How to Use Weather as a Literary Device

by

Benjamin X. Wretlind

In honor of my grandmother, Lucille, who instilled in me a love of weather with a little book one Christmas morning

1919-2012

Nature is so powerful, so strong. Capturing its essence is not easy—your work becomes a dance with light and the weather. It takes you to a place within yourself.

—Annie Leibovitz

TABLE OF CONTENTS

TABLE OF FIGURES

CREATING ATMOSPHERE FROM ATMOSPHERE:
How to Use Weather as a Literary Device

INTRODUCTION

I T'S LATE JULY. I HAVE DECIDED TO SIT OUTSIDE ON THE DECK OF MY house and watch clouds build and obscure my view of Pikes Peak. The temperature is warm, the air humid. My two dogs are in the yard doing their business—apart from barking at the neighbor's dog—and there is just the slightest, if not moist, breeze. It is the calm before the storm, and I am here because I know this.

Something in the moment triggers my amygdala, the part of my brain that experiences emotion. I shift uneasily in my seat and consider the scene as I gather my thoughts. What is this feeling? It can be difficult for me to elucidate in words ambiguous thoughts that swirl in my mind like a thousand squid dancing in a blackened sea. As the clouds build, shafts of rain appear below them. The sun illuminates the tops and sides of the clouds making fine the line between them and the blue sky. A few moments later, a lightning bolt strikes the ground somewhere near the Garden of the Gods. I count the time to the first peal of thunder. Eleven seconds. Still, I am feeling something I cannot describe. Anticipation...maybe?

Flashback to a summer. I am driving through the Kansas prairie on the way to visit my parents' house in Colorado. I have with me in my convertible two of my children, and they are mostly quiet at this point. There is a storm to the southwest, a massive castle of billowing blackness with occasional flashes of angry light. I know from my previous experience that somewhere below that cloud a farm is being assailed, hail larger than silver dollars is raining down on a truck or a tractor somewhere.

Someone is watching intently for a tornado. Children are playing in the puddles while their concerned mother or father or grandparent hastens them inside.

An emergency weather alert breaks through the radio and interrupts my karaoke version of a Mr. Mister song. A computer-generated voice tells me that "THE NATIONAL WEATHER SERVICE IN GOODLAND HAS ISSUED A TORNADO WARNING FOR...CENTRAL SHERMAN COUNTY IN NORTHWEST KANSAS...UNTIL 145 PM. AT 107 PM...THE PUBLIC REPORTED A TORNADO 15 MILES SOUTH-WEST OF GOODLAND...MOVING NORTHEAST AT 40 MPH."

I look to the left and see the storm. That must be it, and if my calculations are correct, we are on track to intercept the monster in just a few miles. I am, in a word, excited. This is what a weather nerd lives for. Not so my two children in the back of the car. Both immediately launch into a game of questions, each one louder than the previous in case I didn't hear it. "Is that coming here?" "Are we going to see a tornado?" "What if it hits us?" "Are we going to die?"

My excitement shifts. I am now in a state of high anxiety as I empathize with my children. They are afraid, and I need to act. Quickly I scan ahead for a shelter, some place I can park while the storm passes over. A convertible with a rag top is not meant to handle Kansas storms, and as raindrops larger than I'd seen in many years pound on the roof and windshield of my car, I squeeze under a freeway overpass. There are about thirty other cars and trucks there, all drivers with the sense to get out of the storm, some luckier than others to have found prime parking. The rear of my car is unprotected and begins taking the brunt of the storm. Hail falls, slamming into the trunk, bouncing off the tempered glass of the rag top. It is little protection against the elements.

I can't help but think of that tornado. Where is it? As my boys sit in silence while the weather rages with a fury that will leave both traumatized for life, I find myself afraid.

"IT WAS A dark and stormy night." We've probably all seen or heard this quote. It's been a joke for years, and even Snoopy's opening line to the novel he couldn't sell. Few can quote its full genius, however.

> It was a dark and stormy night; the rain fell in torrents—except at occasional intervals, when it was checked by a violent gust of wind which swept up the streets (for it is in London that our scene lies), rattling along the housetops, and fiercely agitating the scanty flame of the lamps that struggled against the darkness.[1]

Writer's Digest called this "the literary poster child for bad story starters,"[2] but being someone who loves all things weather, I would have to disagree. And Charles M. Shultz's Snoopy of *Peanuts* fame was not the only place you'll find that quote (or versions of it). Madeline L'Engle started *A Wrinkle in Time* with "It was a dark and stormy night" (although some say she selected this as a nod to the cliché).[3] Near the beginning of *Good Omens*, from Terry Pratchett and Neil Gaiman, the two played with the phrase. "It wasn't a dark and stormy night. It should have been, but there's the weather for you."[4] Even classics are not immune. Alexandre Dumas started one chapter in *The Three Musketeers* with (pardon my French): "C'etait une nuit orageuse et sombre."[5] The more exact translation of this phrase would be "It was a night stormy and dark."

It doesn't end there. In 1982, the annual Bulwer-Lytton Fiction Contest was started that challenged entrants to compose "the opening sentence to the worst of all possible novels."[6] It's been running ever since, and has spawned five different books so far:

It Was a Dark and Stormy Night (1984)
Son of "It Was a Dark and Stormy Night" (1986)
Bride of Dark and Stormy (1988)
It Was a Dark & Stormy Night: The Final Conflict (1992)
Dark and Stormy Rides Again (1996)

The 2021 winner, Stu Duval of Auckland, New Zealand, penned this beauty:

A lecherous sunrise flaunted itself over a flatulent sea, ripping the obsidian bodice of night asunder with its rapacious fingers of gold, thus exposing her dusky bosom to the dawn's ogling stare.[7]

As a weather nerd, I think that's just genius!

We were told as children growing up and learning to write that "you never start a story with the weather." I can still hear one of my high school English teachers slapping her wooden pointer down on a desk to make that argument clear. To that, I say "bah!" Weather can make literary waves. Just look at the following chart and let me know if this is a rule that must (at all costs) be followed.

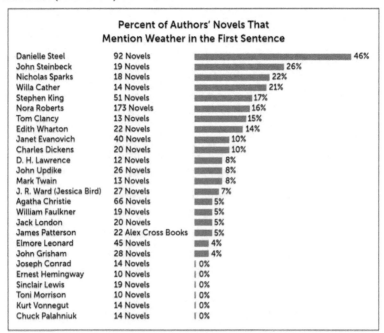

Percent of Authors' Novels That Mention Weather in the First Sentence

Author	Novels	%
Danielle Steel	92 Novels	46%
John Steinbeck	19 Novels	26%
Nicholas Sparks	18 Novels	22%
Willa Cather	14 Novels	21%
Stephen King	51 Novels	17%
Nora Roberts	173 Novels	16%
Tom Clancy	13 Novels	15%
Edith Wharton	22 Novels	14%
Janet Evanovich	40 Novels	10%
Charles Dickens	20 Novels	10%
D. H. Lawrence	12 Novels	8%
John Updike	26 Novels	8%
Mark Twain	13 Novels	8%
J. R. Ward (Jessica Bird)	27 Novels	7%
Agatha Christie	66 Novels	5%
William Faulkner	19 Novels	5%
Jack London	20 Novels	5%
James Patterson	22 Alex Cross Books	5%
Elmore Leonard	45 Novels	4%
John Grisham	28 Novels	4%
Joseph Conrad	14 Novels	0%
Ernest Hemingway	10 Novels	0%
Sinclair Lewis	19 Novels	0%
Toni Morrison	10 Novels	0%
Kurt Vonnegut	14 Novels	0%
Chuck Palahniuk	14 Novels	0%

Figure 1. Share of novels which mention weather in the first sentence worldwide as of 2017, by author.[8]

Mark Twain shunned putting weather in books, even though he shows up in the above table of authors that mention the weather in the first sentence. In *The American Claimant*, Twain writes:

> No weather will be found in this book. This is an at-
> tempt to pull a book through without weather. It being
> the first attempt of the kind in fictitious literature, it
> may prove a failure, but it seemed worth the while of
> some dare-devil person to try it, and the author was in
> just the mood.

> Many a reader who wanted to read a tale through was
> not able to do it because of delays on account of the
> weather. Nothing breaks up an author's progress like
> having to stop every few pages to fuss-up the weather.
> Thus it is plain that persistent intrusions of weather
> are bad for both reader and author.

Ouch. But he continues, and in fact, makes the case for including weather in **any** book.

> Of course **weather is necessary to a narrative of hu-
> man experience.** That is conceded. But it ought to be
> put where it will **not be in the way;** where it will not
> interrupt the flow of the narrative...Weather is a liter-
> ary specialty, and no untrained hand can turn out a
> good article of it.[9]

That's more like it. When I first read about Twain's refusal to put weather "in this book," I thought I would have to abandon all hope and to something else with my time. Maybe I could write a book about all the ways cooking shows up in thriller novels.[a]

For Virginia Woolf, weather was just as necessary for the narrative. In *Between the Acts* she talks about how to write the weather into fiction.

---

[a] I want to do this. There are few thriller novels wherein the food isn't described in excruciating detail, and always fancy. Are all thriller writers wannabe chefs? I've made
this one of my future goals in life to find out. Sad.

> ...set people talking in a room with their backs to the window, and then, as they talk about something else, let someone half turn her head and say "A fine evening," when (if they have been talking about the right things) the summer evening is visible to anyone who reads the page, and is forever remembered as of quite exceptional beauty.[10]

Why would that matter? The aside that Woolf is referring to allows the reader to join with the writer in a shared human narrative. Weather is that permanent connection you as a writer have with the world.

This Book Started on a Hot Summer Day

IN AUGUST 1990, a young man with dreams of becoming a journalist enlisted in the United States Air Force. Because his chosen career was not available, he was placed into a pool wherein he could later select a job based on the needs of the government.[b] For those who are familiar with the recruiting tricks, you know this boy was handed a line and bought it.

While in Basic Training, under the intense and heavy humidity of southern Texas, the day came wherein selections could be made provided the individual's Armed Services Vocational Aptitude Battery (ASVAB) scores were high enough to be granted access. The boy was to rank order his preferences.

On that list were:

- Security Forces
- Fire
- Weather
- Loadmaster
- Public Affairs
- Air Traffic Control

---

[b] Called "Open General" at the time. Yes, call me a sucker if you want, but if I resisted, this book would not have been possible, and my life would have been radically different.

- Communications
- Data Entry

After noticing that "Public Affairs" was on that list, our boy decided luck was on his side. Not only did he have the right score on his ASVAB, but he could also easily pass the performance test that was to be administered. How hard could it be to type 40 words per minute?

Sure enough, the boy passed the performance test (at a staggering 41 words per minute) but scored slightly lower than another boy in the same flight. Apparently 68 words per minute is better, but this boy was not a math wiz. While the other went on to join the illustrious Public Affairs corps, our boy with dreams of journalism was given his second choice: weather.

The boy knew nothing of weather, save what was in a book he was given when he was eight years old. That he passed Earth Science in high school was a miracle. However, it was probably a good thing this boy with the dreams of journalism did not end up getting any of the other jobs that were on that list. He did not believe in the slightest that he was cut out for anything else. At 125 pounds, being a loadmaster[c] would have killed him, the stress of being an Air Traffic Controller was too much, and he feared fire.

As you can probably guess that boy was me.

❧ ℺ ❧

THE WEATHER CAREER field in the U.S. Air Force has undergone quite a bit of changes since my initial entry in 1990. At that time, I was shipped off to the U.S. Air Force's Weather Training Center at Chanute AFB[d] in the windy flatland of central Illinois to attend the observer course.

At the "schoolhouse" as it was known, I would learn the 27 states of

---

[c] A loadmaster is a member of an aircraft's crew responsible for the cargo. As you can imagine, strength is a prerequisite.

[d] Sadly, Chanute AFB fell victim to the Base Closure and Realignment Commission and shut down in 1993. While the location may not have been the best in terms of social interaction, it was great for watching the weather from the observatory of the newly constructed Weather Training Center.

the sky, how to plot a **Skew-T**[e] and **surface chart,** how to use a **sling psy-chometer**[f] without spilling mercury, the proper way to speak to pilots in flight, and how not to screw up on a telewriter.

The latter was a really cool machine for that time: you wrote your observation of the weather in code on a piece of paper and on the other side of the runway, a matching telewriter would auto-magically scrawl out exactly what you wrote...provided you pressed hard enough, didn't scribble, and someone remembered to put paper in the machine. It may have been 1920s or 1930s technology (it was described in a 1910 *Popular Science* article), but it worked.

Figure 2. A telewriter as used in the 1970s.

---

[e] A Skew-T is a snapshot of the atmosphere from the surface to about the 100 millibar level. See https://www.weather.gov/source/zhu/ZHU_Training_Page/convective_parameters/skewt/skewtinfo.html for more information

[f] A sling psychrometer is an older tool (analog) comprised of two mercury thermometers, one of which contained a wick dipped in water. You literally slung it around in a circle to obtain both the ambient air temperature on one thermometer and the wet bulb temperature on the second. From this, a calculation of dew point and humidity can be made. I once got stopped by the U.S. Secret Service for using one of these within a quarter mile of Air Force One while the elder George Bush was visiting Shaw AFB. I guess they thought it was a weapon.

Within the weather stations of the late 1980s and early 1990s, there were several other amazing instruments that were fascinating to play with and broke often. For example, the **FPS-77** radar—the predecessor to the current **WSR-88D Doppler radar** you know of now—was a beast of a machine that used over 200 vacuum tubes. Data came down through an 8-foot parabolic reflector antenna and ended up as a green blob on a screen that would show you—the dutiful observer—where thunderstorms were relative to the airfield.

This assumed something wasn't broken.

It usually was.

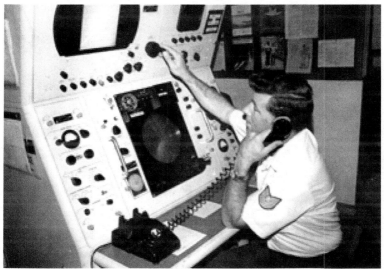

Figure 3. AN/FPS-77 radar operator. This radar was the mainstay of the USAF's bases from 1965 to the early 1990s.[11]

In all honesty, the best feature of the FPS-77 radar display was a plug near the bottom where you could power a vacuum to clean up the sunflower seed mess left by the forecaster on duty. Not that was I ever bitter about those seeds.

From those early days of observing the weather, I learned quite a bit. For the boy who wanted to be a journalist and run around the jungles of Vietnam like Joker in *Full Metal Jacket*—"I wanted to see exotic Vietnam... the crown jewel of Southeast Asia. I wanted to meet interesting and stimulating people of an ancient culture...and kill them"[12]—this was much more fun (and less violent). When the rains fell or the hurricanes approached or the winds blew, my responsibility as a weather observer grew tenfold. I would put on my rain slicker and run outside in a maelstrom to put a cedar measuring stick into a metal bucket on the edge of a runway to record just how wet I was...and I loved it.

No, really. I loved it!

For the next twenty years, I was embedded in all things weather. While I started off as an observer on an airfield in South Carolina and later in a town named after a fish in Alaska (who couldn't love a place called King Salmon?), I also launched weather balloons as a rawinsonde

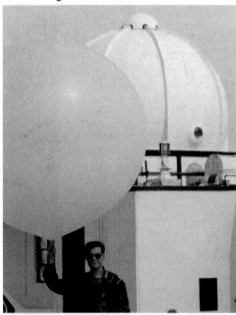

operator, forecasted the weather, managed radar systems (of the newer variety that actually worked), briefed pilots on the hazards in their flight path, determined the correct settings for infrared weapons to pick out a tank in the middle of the desert, and even built climatological web applications. From 2000 to 2003, I returned to that weather schoolhouse (now located on the coast of Mississippi) to teach atmospheric dynamics to kids

Figure 4. Me holding a weather balloon prior to launch...and in need of a haircut

who may have wanted to be journalists, too, but, well, ended up in the weather career field because they listened to their recruiter.

It wasn't all about the weather, though. Even if I wasn't a journalist, I still had the itch to write. I had written my first story when I was eight about a banyan tree in my uncle's yard that didn't want to be chopped down. In high school, the only two classes I really loved were Creative Writing and Anthropology. The teacher of that Creative Writing class, Mr. Troy Hutchings, was a master of drawing out the creative in just about anyone. I loved to write stories in that class, and in fact, the first novel I ever finished[g]—twenty-some odd years later—started off as an assignment.

Poetry? Loved it, and like many maudlin teenagers, I wrote quite a few really depressing poems I still have in binder. (Looking through them recently, they will stay there.)

Essays? Give me more! And because the other class I loved so much was Anthropology, I was in heaven every time Ms. Phyllis Stanford would slap her wooden pointer down on her desk and make us write a paper. (My teachers liked to slap wooden pointers.) That I got a D- in the class had nothing to do with those papers—I loved to write but *hated* homework.

If it could be written, I would write it.

In 1991, I took one of those assignments from the Creative Writing class and started to turn it into a novel. During my first year in the Air Force with a real job, I saved up my pennies and bought a state-of-the-art, top-of-the-line, whiz-bang laptop computer for $1,500. The Toshiba T1000LE had an amazing 80C86 processor and a 20-megabyte hard drive. Can you believe the *size* of that thing? I took the stories I had written before along with all my poems and typed them all into my brand new copy of WordPerfect (purchased for only $499 on ten 5.25-inch floppy disks).

While weather brought in the money, writing was life. I was going to take my laptop (which weighed 6.5 lbs or 3 kgs) and my dot matrix printer (which weighed close to 30 pounds) and write the next Great American novel. I was going to be Stephen King, Clive Barker, Ray Bradbury and Isaac Asimov all in one. I was sure of it.

---

[g] *Difficult Mirrors*. It was originally called *Void*, then *A Difficult Mirror* and finally ended up with its current name. The original story that started the novel was called "The Game" and it was loosely based on a video by Kansas. That story contained my only use of the word vespertilian (bat-like).

Of course, life gets in the way. The military likes to move you around a bit, you get married, have kids, go to college, end up in charge of something and before you know it, those dreams you once had rust away inside a now worthless laptop.

All was not lost, however. As a writer, I was also a reader, and I read everything I could get my hands on—from novels to books of poetry to essays to articles to standard operating procedures. The dream of writing didn't go away. It never did, and when I retired from the military, everything seemed to click into place all at once.

IN HIS INTRODUCTION to the life of Luke Howard, an amateur meteorologist credited with the naming of clouds, Richard Hamblyn writes that "the sky...is the province of words."

> Yet meteorology is not an exact science. It is, rather, a search for narrative order among events governed not by laws alone, but by the shapeless caprices of the atmosphere. Weather writes, erases and rewrites itself upon the sky with the endless fluidity of language; and it is with language that we have sought throughout history to apprehend it...The sky has always been more read than measured.[13]

When I read a book or watch a movie, I'm probably more aware of the weather than most people. It's a symptom of years spent looking at charts, watching patterns, studying green blobs on a screen, and guessing.[h] Not that people aren't observant—they are—but their observations will often take them somewhere else, some place that doesn't have to do with fog or wind or thunderstorms or clouds or precipitation or whatever.

To me (and I believe you, too, as it was you who picked up this book

---

[h] As I often say, "forecasting the weather meant I am 50% right 20% of the time." What other job can you say that about? Surely you wouldn't want your cardiac surgeon to tell you that.

to read) weather in writing creates an atmosphere that can make or break a scene. It not only sets the mood, but it can mirror the stages of plot development, enhance themes or create tension where before there was none. It can drive emotion and possibly even tap into the amygdala of a reader and trigger a trauma response.

To give you an example of this, the following two passages are the same, but different. One with the weather, one without. (This passage comes from *Silence and Fire*, one of my earlier novellas.)

> She looked through tear-filled eyes at the shadows and the patterns the rain drew for her on the canvas of the tent. The noise—pounding, driving, beating, thrashing, drubbing—was barely audible as her mind swirled from past to present to a future she was almost certain would never come.

> She looked through tear-filled eyes at the canvas of the tent. Her mind swirled from past to present to a future she was almost certain would never come.

You can take two things from this:

1) the weather doesn't matter; it doesn't help to set any stage and the second paragraph is less cluttered without expository language; or

2) the weather fits the mood of the character (Claire) by describing how the shadows on the tent wall are being drawn in a world that's noisy but muted by her own thoughts.

To me (and this is really all opinion as both readers and writers view the world through a subjective lens), descriptions of the weather enhance the mood of the setting (i.e., the atmosphere) because, as Twain said, "weather is necessary to a narrative of human experience." Good descriptions are not asides; they are part of the whole. Is it cold? Is it hot? Do the clouds create a shadowed/muted scene? Does the rain/snow/hail relate to a feeling? Is there fear in a character that's increased by a thunderstorm (thereby increasing the fear/nervousness/anxiety of the reader)?

In *Great Expectations* by Charles Dickens, Pip narrates for us and describes how the weather mimics his gloomy feeling.

> ...stormy and wet, stormy and wet; and mud, mud, mud, deep in all the streets. Day after day, a vast heavy veil had been driving over London from the East, and it drove still, as if in the East there were an Eternity of cloud and wind...gloomy accounts had come in from the coast, of shipwreck and death. Violent blasts of rain had accompanied these rages of wind, and the day just closed as I sat down to read had been the worst of all.[14]

Gloomy, indeed. In this short bit, we are told of storms, clouds, winds, rain, and flooding. And we as writers can do this directly: tell the reader what the weather is at any given moment to set a scene. But there's another way to look at weather in narratives.

Think of a thunderstorm on the horizon, far away. Thunderstorms are created by a combination of moisture, instability and some sort of trigger. We can equate that simple description to something like an **exposition**. Once a trigger is reached (such as air forced up a mountainside or intense heating throughout the day), a thunderstorm is born. You could call that the **conflict**, if you will, or the **inciting incident**. As the thunderstorm builds and moves closer, there is **rising action**. Perhaps the first lightning crash and sudden deluge of rain or the tornado that snakes its way down to destroy a farmhouse is like the **climax**, and the dribbling aftermath as the storm moves away can be viewed as **falling action** leading to a satisfactory **dénouement**.

This is very simplistic in its design, and the story could move through each plot element the same if the weather had been removed. However, the reader knows what it feels like to see a storm approach (**anxiety**); they know what it feels like to be in a downpour and hear thunder crash or see a tornado (**fear**); and they know what it feels like as a storm moves on (**relief**).

≈ ↺ ≈

WRITING THE WEATHER (atmosphere) into a setting is not that difficult, but you can also screw it up. Imagine a sad character. Does it help your reader feel her emotion if you describe the sunrise on a clear, perfectly temperate day, or would it set a better mood if there were undulating clouds hanging over the scene like a smothering blanket? Writers in the 18th and 19th centuries really understood this, which is probably one reason why Victorian literature feels so bleak. You can, however, use **contrast** to show the reader sadness even on a clear day with the birds signing and the butterflies making whoopie. We'll touch on that throughout this book.

Poor writing can take you out of a story, though. Perhaps it's a misplaced word, the hideousness of seeing "there" instead of "their" on a tweet, or facts you know are wrong. You cringe, maybe internally or maybe externally. It can be jarring, like skiing down a slope and running over a platypus that got lost. Something doesn't fit.

I recently read a great story where this happened, and it took me out of the author's world for a moment. I won't bring up the author or the book, but there were two glaring errors. In one passage, one of the author's characters said a "front is coming" in reference to an approaching thunderstorm. A front (cold or warm, stationary or occluded) can be thousands of miles long and typically brings with it immense change (e.g., hot to cold, dry to wet). It is a transition between airmasses. A front is not a thunderstorm, although thunderstorms can certainly form *along* a front and outflow boundaries can be considered microscale fronts. A front is not a wall cloud—a large, *localized* and often sudden lowering of cloud that develops beneath the surrounding base of a **cumulonimbus** cloud. This was not what was being described, so...I tripped on that platypus and thought to myself: that's not a front. It took me out of the author's world for a moment.

The second example of incorrect weather came with the naming of a cloud. The author used "nimbus" in place of cumulonimbus, again in reference to a thunderstorm. While "nimbus" can be an archaic reference to a cumulonimbus—and would have been appropriate if the setting was 17th century New England—the story was set in the present. Nimbus clouds are typically mid-level. There is **nimbostratus,** which is a sheet of clouds that might rain, snow or drizzle on you, but that's not what this cloud was doing. As the author described it, the cloud had teeth: lightning, torrential rain, and strong winds. There's a difference in the term and again, I tripped.

There are readers who have studied meteorology for years, and like anything, the genius is in the details. While we weather nerds (that's an official term) have our meteorological knowledge, we are also interested in immersing ourselves in a story. We don't want to hit that platypus on a ski slope. We want to sail right on down to the bottom. Clouds aren't likely to hang in the air like bricks (although that can be a funny phrase if used correctly), and there's no such thing as a Category 7 hurricane...even if that book wasn't all that bad.

JOHN RUSKIN, A 19th century art critic, once railed against artists (writers included) who attributed human emotions to the natural world. In his view, this was a "pathetic fallacy" (which sounds rude, but really means "emotional falseness"). Ruskin argued that skies have never wept, nor has the sun shone mercilessly.

> An inspired writer, in full impetuosity of passion, may speak wisely and truly of 'raging waves of the sea, foaming out their own shame;' but it is only the basest writer who cannot speak of the sea without talking of 'raging waves,' 'remorseless floods,' 'ravenous billows,' etc.; and it is one of the signs of the highest power in a writer to check all such habits of thought, and to keep his eyes fixed firmly on the pure fact, out of which if any feeling comes to him or his reader, he knows it must be a true one.[15]

That's the point of this book: *to state fact but extract feeling.* I remember learning all about anthropomorphism in school, that is assigning human behavior to non-human things: the river that bleeds, the leaves that dance, the engine that growls. And I can see Ruskin's point: 19th century literature is filled with anthropomorphisms.

In this book, however, I won't say that you should avoid those literary endeavors. Tell me how that cloud is galloping across the sky or how the wind is whispering sweet nothings. Maybe your fog rolls in on little cat feet. We can, however, do more as Ruskin suggested. We can "keep [our] eyes fixed firmly on the pure fact, out of which if any feeling comes to [us] or [our] reader, [we] know it must be a true one."

Human emotion can be drawn out or set by using the weather as a tool. By accessing the human experience, we can create atmosphere with atmosphere.

How This Book is Arranged

THE START OF this book is a framework for the rest. In 2022, I ran a highly scientific experiment (sarcasm intended) on social media wherein I asked people to relate twenty-six different pictures of weather to an emotion. Really, it was a survey. Most of the results were what I expected, but some were rather surprising. We'll talk about that first.

After that, this book is broken down in the same way I would have broken down a class I taught in the early 2000s at the weather school-house. We will start with the most basic of weather elements, something you see on just about every day of the year. I am referring to **clouds**.

Next, we'll bring that cloud down the surface to discuss **fog** and mist and how visibility (or the lack thereof) can really get your characters on edge. How many remember the movie *The Fog* with Jamie Lee Curtis or read Stephen King's novella *The Mist*? But does fog always have to be so threatening? Can it be...romantic?

From this, the natural segue would be to talk about **precipitation**: snow, rain, freezing rain, hail, sleet, drizzle, and my favorite, ice crystals. Just as there are differences in the terms, there are different emotions which can be brought up in a reader.

Temperature drives most of our weather, so next we'll look at heat and cold and also discuss a few differences between wet and dry atmospheres. You may know what they are, but do your characters "sweat buckets" in the middle of the Sahara Desert? Probably not as much as you think, since physiology and genetics have something to say about how much sweat is produced.

Weather, as you know, moves. Those clouds you see over there will be over here later. Probably. Unless they aren't. Then they might be somewhere else. **Wind** plays a part in that movement, and it can play a very important part in your settings. Wind goes up, down, around a corner and sneaks up a mountainside before falling back (and warming as it does so). Wind blows fences over. (And as I write this introduction, there is in fact a downed fence in my backyard from a windstorm that occurred yesterday. I'll need to fix that.)

This book will devote an entire chapter to **thunderstorms**. Like the example I gave above, I want to relate the birth and death of a thunderstorm to your plot in ways that may not seem apparent. We'll get into the differences between airmass thunderstorms and supercells and why standing in one place near a storm may not result in the weather you think.

Weather on Earth is guided by the sun, which affects our world in many ways. It's important to look at how **solar weather,** or more accurately **space weather**, causes disruptions in our daily life. Understanding solar weather may help you add just a bit of drama into your narrative, and we'll look at some of the major solar events to hit in the last two hundred years.

Afterwards, we'll get to some nuances of weather that deserve attention: **things to know** about hurricanes, floods, El Niño, weather features unique to the stratosphere, rainbows and climate change. There's more than trivia, however. There are stories buried in weather events that can really set your novel apart from others. What if, instead of *just* a tornado or *just* a thunderstorm, the weather in your book acted like a character?

Finally, I want to touch a little on a subject that's dear to my heart: **alien weather.** I recall working with a National Weather Service forecaster in Alaska. One day, while observing nothing outside for the third day in a row and passing the time watching reruns of *Star Trek*, this gentleman told me his dreams, about the things he wanted to accomplish in life. The most prominent of those was to forecast the weather on Mars...while on Mars. I doubt he will get the chance, but it got me thinking about the weather on other planets.

Some of you who might be weather nerds may notice that I have not included a chapter on **atmospheric pressure**, and therefore this cannot be a complete book. Well, it's not. I included elements of meteorology which could enhance the fictional narrative, either by bringing something unique to the table (e.g., the effects of El Niño) or by using a specific element like rain to paint a picture and create a mood. Twain's comment that "weather is necessary to a narrative of human experience" speaks to this, and while atmospheric pressure *is* weather, it does not quite meet the criteria for inclusion here. Can you imagine using high or low pressure to evoke a feeling in the reader? Other than saying "my knee hurts" when the pressure drops, barometry is just not that helpful.

I hope you find a little in this book that will help you create atmosphere in your stories. Bounce around. Skip the science if you'd like and head straight to the sections on emotions. Use the index to find what you're looking for. Try out the writing exercises I've placed at the end of some chapters. Do what makes you happy in a way that is good for you as a writer.

As I mentioned, this book is not a comprehensive review of all things weather, nor is it intended to be a review of all atmospheric phenomena in literary works since the dawn of the written word. What it is, hopefully, is a seed for you, the writer. Through basic science and relatable examples of the use of meteorology in narrative form, I hope to get that seed to germinate a little and perhaps help your next novel or short story bloom.

Meteorology is a science, and all sciences go through advancement through experimentation. We may learn more about how and why hurricanes behave the way they do, or maybe one day be able to predict exactly when and where a tornado will strike. Who knows? But for now, we can be as true to the weather as possible and allow the atmosphere to set the atmosphere in our stories.

A Note on Notes

THIS BOOK CONTAINS a lot of references, but also notes which attempt to expand on some things presented in the main text. For that reason, I have kept the expanded notes on the bottom of the page rather than move them to the end of the chapter or (worse) pile them all up at the end of the book.

I *highly encourage* you to check out the footnotes in each chapter for additional information (and stories) that are not in the main text. Of course, the bibliographic information is at the end of each chapter, too, if you want to check out the references.

---

[1] Lytton, E.B. (1830).*Paul Clifford*. Cassell Pub. Co.

[2] Petit, Z. (2013, January 18). *Famous first lines reveal how to start a novel.* Writer's Digest. Retrieved May 1, 2022, from https://www.writersdigest.com/whats-new/famous-first-lines-learn-how-to-start-a-novel

[3] L'Engle, Madeleine (1962). *A Wrinkle in Time*. New York: Farrar, Straus and Giroux. OCLC 22421788.

[4] Gaiman, N., & Pratchett, T. (1993). *Good Omens*. Opus Press.

[5] Dumas, A. (1844). *The Three Musketeers*.

[6] *Our Story | The Bulwer-Lytton Fiction Contest*. (n.d.). Bad Writing Contest. https://www.bulwer-lytton.com/about.

[7] *Home | The Bulwer Lytton Fiction Contest*. (n.d.). Bad Writing Contest. https://www.bulwer-lytton.com/

[8] Gambino, M. (2017, March 14). *One Writer Used Statistics to Reveal the Secrets of What Makes Great Writing*. Smithsonian Magazine. https://www.smithsonianmag.com/arts-culture/one-writer-used-statistics-reveal-secrets-what-makes-great-writing-180962515/

[9] Twain, M. (1892). *The American Claimant*. Charles L. Webster.

[10] Woolf, V. (1941). *Between the Acts*. Hogarth Press.

[11] *File:FPS-77 operator.png - Wikimedia Commons*. (2012, May 12). https://commons.wikimedia.org/wiki/File:FPS-77_operator.png.

[12] Kubrick, S. (Director). (1987). *Full Metal Jacket* [Film]. Warner Bros. Pictures.

[13] Hamblyn, R. (2001). *The Inventions of Clouds*. Farrar, Straus and Giroux.

[14] Dickens, C. (1861). *Great Expectations*. Chapman & Hall.

[15] Ruskin, J. (1856). *Modern Painters* (Vol. III). Smith, Elder and Co.

FIRST, A LITTLE EXPERIMENT

YOU KNOW AND I KNOW THAT READERS KNOW THAT WEATHER can elicit an emotion in a reader. It can also do so on screen, and often extreme weather is used in ways that are, well, extreme— maybe to lash out at a certain character, to punish a town, or even tip a boat over. Yet exactly what emotion comes up is subjective, is it not? I may look at a tornado and find awe, while you may laugh at the way it dances around like a drunk near closing time. Others may cower in fear anticipating sure death.

Curious if there was a pattern, however, I did a little digging. Last year, I set up a small (and non-university-supported) study. As with all great studies of the current era (there's that sarcasm again), my methodology involved going to the one place where people are happy to help and, of course, offer their opinion. I'm talking about social media.

Methodology

I BUILT A survey with twenty-six pictures of various weather phenomena, from wind to clouds, to storms to heat, rain, etc. From there, I asked the survey participants (the subjects or respondents) to pick a word that described the emotion they associated with the image. I didn't use any word, however. I needed to define some parameters, so I turned to my psychology education to find classifications of emotion that would work for what I wanted to do.

There are a lot of classifications, apparently.

After a bit of research, I settled on Robert Plutchik's Wheel of Emotions, which he developed in the 1980s. Plutchik attempted to classify human emotional response and grouped them into eight core or primary emotions which are bipolar in their presentation. These are: **surprise** versus **anticipation**; **joy** versus **sadness**; **trust** versus **disgust**; and **anger** versus **fear**.[16]

These primary emotions can be expressed at different intensities along a vector or spectrum, if you will. You can also mix one with another to form different emotions, just like a color wheel. For example, **pensiveness** and **distraction** can mix to form **disapproval**, just like **interest** and **annoyance** can mix to form **aggressiveness**.[a]

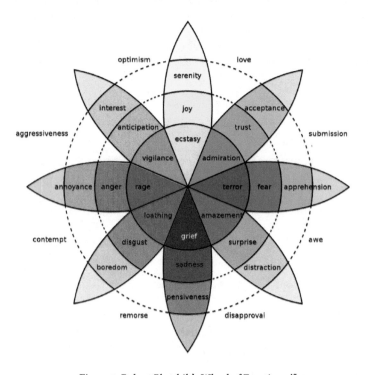

Figure 5. Robert Plutchik's Wheel of Emotions.[17]

---

[a] An aside: when I presented this concept at a writers conference, I used the latter combination as a joke saying I hope the audience wasn't both interested and annoyed with me and would therefore turn aggressive. The joke fell flat.

There are many models of emotion out there, and because this isn't a psychology book, I won't go into them. But Plutchik's was useful for my little survey on weather and emotion. Specifically, I wanted to know if there was a correlation to what one might see (or experience) and a core or primary emotion.

My sample size was over 700, and after removing duplicates and bad data, I ended up with nearly 600 useful answers (n=580 for those who really want to know). These were then plotted on top of Plutchik's Wheel of Emotions.

The results were somewhat expected, or you could say several of my hypotheses were correct. Here's a sample question (with the photograph to go with it):

What emotion pops up in your mind when you look at the picture below?

Figure 6. An image of a dust cloud.

The subjects were then presented with a randomized list of thirty-two emotions, again all based on Plutchik's work.

The choices were:

ecstasy	joy	serenity	optimism
vigilance	anticipation	interest	aggressiveness
rage	anger	annoyance	contempt
loathing	disgust	boredom	remorse
grief	sadness	pensiveness	disapproval
amazement	surprise	distraction	awe
terror	fear	apprehension	submission
admiration	trust	acceptance	love

Results

SO, WHAT DID I learn? Well, as expected, the emotions most associated with happy-ish clouds and snow were along the spectrum of joy. With extreme weather, the emotions fell on the fear spectrum but also showed a leaning towards both the anticipation and rage spectrums.

Heat was interesting. When shown pictures of hot days, respondents typically categorized their emotions either toward fear or more commonly toward sadness. This may have been because the pictures presented could have been interpreted as climate change, but without additional data on that, I can't be sure.

Rain was all over the place. The only emotion that wasn't really associated with rain was trust. In fact, no element really leaned toward trust.

I guess no one trusts the weather.[b]

---

[b] This was another joke that fell flat at the writers conference with the exception of two distinct chuckles I heard in the back of the room. They could have been coughs, though.

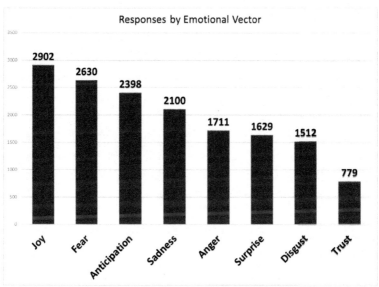

Figure 7. Responses by Emotional Vector

Below is a radar graph of the data. In each chapter, I will present a closer view of an element along with the distribution (since you probably can't read this one very well).

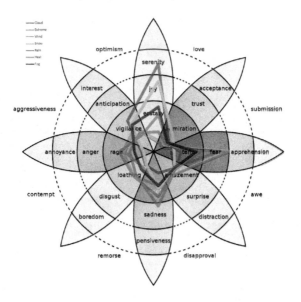

Figure 8. Weather elements mapped to Plutchik's Wheel of Emotions.

The real result was this: to help you, as a writer, convey a specific emotion in your reader, you can select the weather element that best corresponds with it. Looking for love? Snow and idyllic cloud scenes work great. Looking to ramp up tension? Try heat or an extreme weather event like a tornado, thunderstorm, or hurricane. You might even try snow. More on that secret later.

On the following pages, I have broken down each of Plutchik's eight core emotions and the frequency with which certain types of weather were associated with them. You can use this as a reference, and we will get a little more specific in the coming chapters.

NOTE: For the following charts, percentages are relative to that weather element, not to each other. Using the below chart as an example, 14% of all extreme weather pictures fell into the anger spectrum.

Winter Scene on a Frozen Canal by Hendrick Avercamp (1620)

Anger

Along the spectrum of anger, subjects might have selected rage, annoyance, aggressiveness, and contempt.

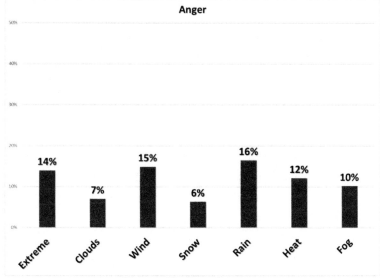

Figure 9. The Anger Spectrum.

The frequency isn't as wide as you might think. Extreme weather, wind, and rain are roughly represented by the same amount. Readers may equate these elements with anger, rage, annoyance, aggressiveness, or contempt but it's not a given. When you see something like this, it might be helpful to combine those three weather elements into one event such as a thunderstorm with strong winds and pounding rain.

Because these main emotional vectors contain four other types of emotions, you won't want to always connect a specific weather element to just anger. For example, imagine your protagonist (or antagonist) is stuck at an airport in a plane, waiting to take off. They are anxious to get to their destination, and that **anxiety** creates **annoyance** that the reason their flight hasn't taken off is due to an approaching thunderstorm. Maybe your character believes the pilot should just go around the storm and they're delaying for no good reason. Maybe your character has narcissistic personality traits and they're convinced the pilot is working against them. They are, in a word, **annoyed**. You can increase that annoyance by describing the approaching storm and the resulting behavior of the other passengers or the crew. Maybe there's a crying baby in the seat in front of them, or the steward won't let anyone deplane. The bathrooms are full, and your protagonist has just downed their third cup of coffee.

Now, put *yourself* in a stuffy metal tube with two hundred other grumpy or irritated people, a full bladder, and a seemingly heartless airline steward. Would your annoyance get worse as the storm approaches knowing it will only delay you further? Lightning flashes on the runway, more babies cry, and more people grumble about the delay. Do you see how far you can take this? It's no slip of the imagination to see your character's **annoyance** turning to **aggressiveness**. Suddenly, someone is punching the steward and demanding to get off the plane. Of course, any situation where the character is forced to wait because of weather can lead to annoyance or even go so far as rage.

The weather can also be an allegory to a character's passion. In *Moby Dick*, Ahab is described as prone to fits of rage, comparable to a storm. As the carpenter puts it in the chapter called "The Deck," "He goes aft. That was sudden, now; but squalls come sudden in hot latitudes...In a straitjacket, he swung to the mad rockings of the gales."[18] Here, Ahab's anger is analogous with "squalls" and "gales" both associated with thunderstorms, especially at sea.

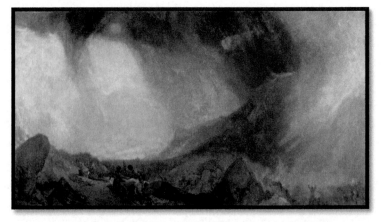

Snow Storm: Hannibal and his Army Crossing the Alps by
J.M.W. Turner (1812)

Fear

With fear comes emotions such as terror, apprehension, awe, and submission.

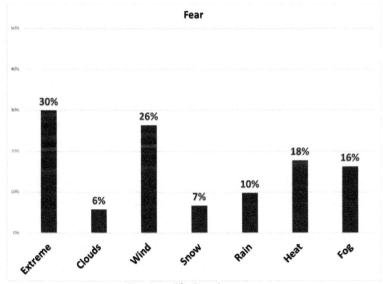

Figure 10. The Fear Spectrum.

The frequencies here are clearer, as you might expect. Extreme weather accounted for 30% of the responses while wind was a close second at 26%. So, if you're trying to set an atmosphere of **fear** in your story, you might do well to describe an extreme weather event (e.g., a tornado, hurricane, massive hail) or strong winds.

We'll talk more about why wind can drum up fear, terror, apprehension, awe, or submission in the chapter titled SOWING THE WIND. Personally, I find it one of the most powerful meteorological literary devices out there.

In *Wuthering Heights* by Emily Brontë, a storm rages the night Heathcliff runs away. As Nelly narrates:

> About midnight, while we still sat up, the **storm** came
> rattling over the Heights in full fury. There was a **vio-
> lent wind**, as well as **thunder**, and either one or the
> other split a tree off at the corner of the building: a

> huge bough fell across the roof, and knocked down a
> portion of the east chimney-stack, sending a clatter of
> stones and soot into the kitchen-fire.[19]

It's hard not to see the fear, terror, apprehension, awe, and even sub-mission in that example. Now go back to your character on a plane. A thunderstorm can become an extreme weather event quickly depending on location and atmospheric dynamics. Put that plane in the air and see just how quickly the previous emotion of annoyance or aggressiveness can turn into fear as passengers are jostled about in extreme turbulence.

When leaving for a vacation one summer, my wife and I were in a similar situation. For those who've had to wait on a runway before, you know the air feels stuffy after a while. That heat, coupled with the annoy-ance of waiting for the plane to take off—there was a connecting flight we were sure to miss—led to **annoyance**. But that annoyance quickly turned to **fear** as soon as the plane took off. The pilot had to circle around the airport for twenty minutes while waiting for a break in the line of thunderstorms that stood between us and the destination. Turbulence on the edges of the storm caused a great deal of fear in the passengers (in-cluding me, by the way). The result was the plane returning to the depart-ing airport and our annoyance returning.

As a writer you might opt to gloss over the weather and simply get your character to the next airport rushing to make their next flight. You might say "the plane was delayed by a thunderstorm," but you have an opportunity here to show the dynamic between two characters on a plane that is enhanced by the storm outside. Describing that storm while inter-spersing dialogue can really put your reader into the mindset of your character.

Many people have been in the same situation, after all. Maybe you, too.

Sadness

The spectrum of sadness includes grief, pensiveness, remorse, and disapproval.

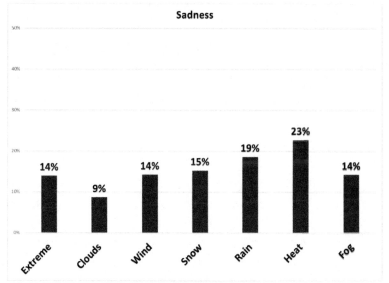

Figure 11. The Sadness Spectrum.

One might expect that rain or fog would be most associated with sadness, but in this case, my study revealed it was heat. As I mentioned before, this could be a "climate change" phenomena as it is devilishly hard to find a picture of heat (or cold, for that matter). Still, it's worth noting that sadness, grief, pensiveness, remorse, or disapproval can be elicited from your reader if you drop in some heat (23%) or rain (19%).

Looking back on Pip's narration of the weather in *Great Expectations*, we can see that Dickens was fond of using rain as a mirror of sadness and grief with phrases such as "...stormy and **wet**, stormy and **wet**...", "a vast heavy **veil** had been driving over London..." and "Violent blasts of **rain**..."[20]

Recently, I came across the following passage in *Twenty-Eight*, a collection of short stories by Raymond Beaman, an Indie horror writer.

I knew of all the self-defeating thoughts that had
swirled before, I knew of the **storm** which would **rage**
within but I also knew of the silence, the **tranquility**
that would follow in the path of the revelation that had
settled once the **wind** and **rain** had **subsided.**[21]

I highlighted what I think are key words in the above paragraph. For a moment, think about the aftermath of a thunderstorm. We'll get into the cycle in a later chapter, but quickly when the storm is over, it moves into a dissipating stage. You've probably experienced this before: the torrential rain and booming thunder wanes and you're left with a light downpour. Now, equate that with emotions: once our **rage** subsides, we're often left with a **sadness** that weighs heavier than normal. All that adrenaline we felt from the **anger** has left us drained. This is precisely what Beaman is showing us in this passage above, "the tranquility" that follows the storm. Rain here becomes a mirror of **sadness.**

Thunder God (detail) by Suzuki Kiitsu (19th Century)

Disgust

Along the spectrum of disgust, we find loathing, boredom, contempt, and remorse.

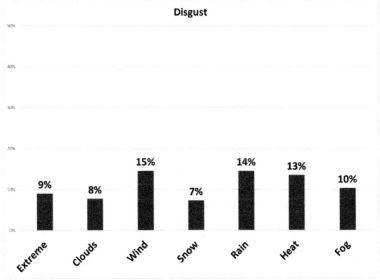

Figure 12. The Disgust Spectrum.

The pitter-patter of constant rain on the roof of a house can certainly bring about feelings of boredom or even thoughts of remorse. This is not true of deluges—rain that falls in buckets, to use the cliché. While rain (14%) is second here to wind (15%), it is important to note that **rain** is often used in situations when you want to **slow the action down**. Having your character step inside and out of the rain to drink tea while looking out a window, can bring up other emotions, too, like **pensiveness** or **anticipation.**

Referring to the passage I wrote in the introduction, this pensiveness and remorse is what I was shooting for by describing the rain on the fabric of a tent.

> She looked through **tear-filled eyes** at the shadows and
> the patterns the **rain** drew for her on the canvas of the
> tent. The noise—pounding, driving, beating, thrash-
> ing, drubbing—was almost muted as her mind swirled

from past to present to a future she was almost certain **would never come.**

You can also bring in that feeling of **boredom** easily. You don't want to bore the reader, of course, but not all characters have to live with the powerful emotions of anger or ecstasy all the time. Sometimes our characters get bored, and it is in these moments when we can use the rain to slow the action down and really get into the head of our protagonist. I wrote a poem about this once. It was all about the patterns of rain on the window and it wasn't very good (it was high school, after all). But it was specifically designed to show my boredom and reflective mood.

Thunderstorm by Józef Chełmoński (1896)

Surprise

With surprise, emotional responses may include amazement, distraction, disapproval, and awe.

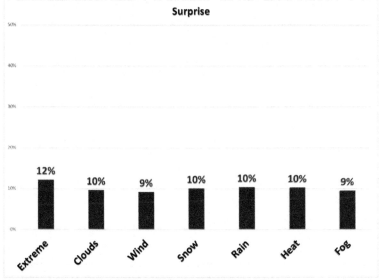

Figure 13. The Surprise Spectrum.

The average of all elements here is right about 10%. That means that about 10% of each group of photos brought up feelings of surprise, amazement, distraction, disapproval, or awe. Nothing really stuck out. Extreme weather is the highest here, likely because of some of the images. They were, after all, *extreme* and **awe** was selected quite frequently. Awe, though, can be linked in Plutchik's Wheel of Emotions with the spectrum of fear, so there could be some muddied waters.

That doesn't mean you can't use any of these elements to establish surprise, amazement, distraction, or disapproval. A massive dust cloud a thousand feet high can not only bring fear, it can also be surprising and awe-inspiring in its own right. Like fog, dust can obscure things and that's where surprise can come in. It can distract, too.

Fog, or the emergence of something out of the fog (usually unpleasant), can also have a surprising effect when added to a narrative. In *Something of Myself*, Rudyard Kipling writes:

...the months of amazement which followed my return to England—I was so ignorant, I never guessed when the great fogs fell that trains could take me to light and sunshine a few miles outside London. Once I faced the reflection of my own face in the jet-black mirror of the window-panes for five days. When the fog thinned, I looked out and saw a man standing opposite the pub where the barmaid lived. Of a sudden his breast turned dull red like a robin's, and he crumpled, having cut his throat. In a few minutes—seconds it seemed— a hand-ambulance arrived and took up the body. A pot-boy with a bucket of steaming water sluiced the blood off into the gutter, and what little crowd had collected went its way.[22]

Waterloo Bridge by Claude Monet (1904)

Anticipation

The spectrum of anticipation includes vigilance, interest, optimism, and aggressiveness.

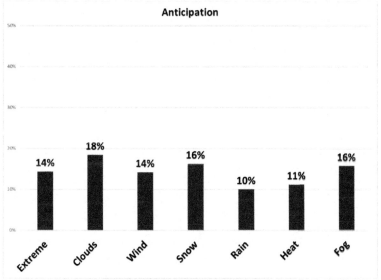

Figure 14. The Anticipation Spectrum.

Pictures of clouds, fog, and snow came out on top in this chart. While fog makes some sense—it is often used as a device in movies to generate **anticipation** in the audience—snow and clouds are interesting. Why would these two weather elements bring up feelings of anticipation, vigilance, interest, optimism, or aggressiveness?

With clouds, I suppose it has to do with the idea of an approaching storm. Depending on how the cloud looks (how you as a writer describe it), you can increase the anticipation in your character.

In *The Wonderful Wizard of Oz* by L. Frank Baum, we see this buildup of anticipation.

> Today, however, they were not playing. Uncle Henry
> sat upon the doorstep and looked anxiously at the sky,
> which was even grayer than usual. Dorothy stood in
> the door with Toto in her arms, and looked at the sky
> too. Aunt Em was washing the dishes.[23]

(Personally, if I had been Baum writing this story, I might have spent a little more time on the approaching storm to further the tension. But I suppose it was not Baum's attempt to traumatize the children for whom the book was written.)

In the above passage, we can feel the anticipation of Dorothy and even Uncle Henry as they look up at the sky. While the word "anxiously" was applied directly to Uncle Henry, it was not to our protagonist. Dorothy simply "stood in the door with Toto." Yet because of Uncle Henry's own anticipation of the coming storm (as he inspected the gray clouds), we now know what Dorothy must have felt.

I will say also that there is an interesting note on Aunt Em. A few paragraphs prior to the above passage, Aunt Em is introduced.

> When Aunt Em came there to live she was a young,
> pretty wife. The sun and wind had changed her, too.
> They had taken the sparkle from her eyes and left
> them a sober **gray**; they had taken the red from her
> cheeks and lips, and they were **gray** also.[23]

Note that in the first passage, Aunt Em "was washing the dishes." She's already as gray as the clouds of the approaching storm, and as a result, there is no anticipation in her at all. Ho hum, another storm. Contrast that with Dorothy watching the sky in the other paragraph, and perhaps Dorothy's own anticipation is increased not only by Uncle Henry's concern but also by Aunt Em's apparent nonchalance.

Waterspout at New Galloway from the *Illustrated London News* (1850)

Trust

Along the spectrum of trust, we find admiration, acceptance, submission, and love.

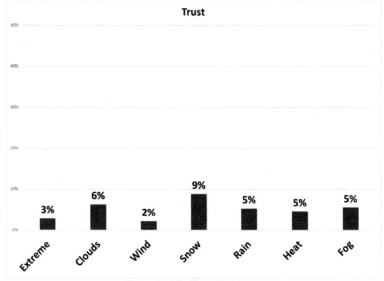

Figure 15. The Trust Spectrum.

This was difficult. I said no one trusts the weather, and that seems to be true here. While respondents could choose any of the four—admiration, trust, acceptance, submission—or a combination of trust and joy leading to love, the consensus was that no particular weather element really led to one of these emotions unless it was combined with joy.

Where there any outliers? The following picture generated responses of trust 19 times (the most). It is the sun as seen through a veil of cirrostratus creating a halo.

Figure 16. A halo as seen through cirrostratus.

I'm not sure of how trust can be pulled from this picture. **Serenity**, maybe, but that falls along the spectrum of joy (below). The runner-up to the above picture was a picture of someone walking through snow. Trust would not be my choice.

Figure 17. Picture of a person walking through a snowstorm.

I'm cold just looking at this picture.

Joy

Finally, the spectrum of joy includes ecstasy, serenity, optimism, and love.

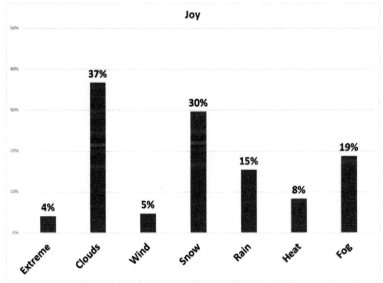

Figure 18. The Joy Spectrum.

First, a side note. Since my methodology was so sound (ahem), I had to go back and remove all those survey entries that listed "ecstasy" for *every single* picture. I mean, I know the weather is exciting, but not every picture should bring up that emotion. There are passages in 18th and 19th century literature which use clouds as erotic symbolism. *Clouds*, mind you, not *every weather element* out there. Just *clouds*.

Joy, to include ecstasy, serenity, optimism, and love, is most associated with clouds, specifically happy-ish looking clouds. You can't *not* have joy when listening to Bob Ross describe painting a happy cloud, after all. Second to clouds (37%) is snow. Nearly 30% of all pictures of snow were linked to some emotion along the spectrum of joy.

That said, you can see where a reader's emotional response is likely to go when you throw in a description of those happy clouds (which I talk about in the next chapter) or throw in an idyllic scene with freshly fallen snow. In the survey, 96 people chose the emotion of **joy** for the below picture, while a whopping 166 people chose **serenity**. And if you're curious, 70 people chose **ecstasy** which fits with how clouds can be used as erotic symbolism (especially in poetry).

Figure 19. Cumulus clouds.

Joy, however, is in the heart of the character and may not be as joyful to anyone else. It is subjective. In a passage from *Frankenstein; or, the Modern Prometheus*, Mary Shelley describes Frankenstein's **joy** at seeing a thunderstorm replete with "flashes of lightning [which] **dazzled** my eyes, illuminating the lake, making it appear like a vast sheet of fire....While I watched the tempest, so **beautiful** yet terrific, I wandered on with a hasty step. This noble war in the sky **elevated my spirits**...."[24]

Pick What Works

AS YOU MIGHT have noticed, the secret to eliciting an emotion in the reader when using weather as a literary device is not straightforward. Since many of these emotions can be equated with different weather elements, it becomes less about *what* you choose and more about *how* you write it.

If snow, for example, is associated most often with the spectrums of joy (ecstasy, serenity, optimism, love) or trust (admiration, acceptance, submission, love), how can you use descriptions of a snowy day to drive anxiety or anticipation?

Here is a passage from *The Life and Adventures of Nicholas Nickleby* by Charles Dickens. You tell me what emotion is intended here.

> The night and the snow came on together, and dismal enough they were. There was no sound to be heard but the howling of the wind; for the noise of the wheels, and the tread of the horses' feet, were rendered inaudible by the thick coating of snow which covered the ground, and was fast increasing every moment.[25]

If you chose **anticipation** or **vigilance**, you might be on to something. Dickens uses the image of increasing snow to amplify the dread of the reader in an event which leads to an accident on the road. Never once did he need to say the protagonist felt anticipation. It's all about the *show* and not the *tell*: the weather explained it well enough. The author did not, in the words of Twain, "stop every few pages to fuss-up the weather."[26]

If you're using weather to enhance a character's emotion, my suggestion is to pick what works for you (as a human who has experienced weather) and might also work for your reader (as another human who probably also experienced weather). As with both Baum and Dickens, you won't need to tell about the emotion if you can show it by using the weather.

In the following chapters, we will get into each weather element (the ones most often seen in literature) and attempt to make that emotional connection. It may not be obvious at first, but a few exercises will (hopefully) get you in the right frame of mind to create atmosphere with atmosphere.

EXERCISE: Journal Your Feelings

Weather can be a powerful tool in creative writing, whether it's to create a mood, set a scene, or convey a character's emotions. By observing and reflecting on the weather around us, we can gain a deeper understanding of how it affects our moods and behaviors. Keeping a weather journal is a simple and effective way to harness the power of weather as a literary device.

In this exercise, you'll learn how to keep a weather journal and use it to inspire your writing. You'll record your observations and emotions related to the weather each day for a set period of time, and then reflect specifically on how the weather affected *your* mood. Since writers often incorporate their own psychological reactions to events, you can infer how your moods might also be the moods of your characters.

Instructions:

Set up your weather journal: Find a notebook or a document on your computer to record your weather observations. Create a table with columns for the date, time, temperature, weather conditions. Add a final column for mood (as in, *your* mood).

Record your observations: Each day, record your observations of the weather. Fill in the columns of the table with the date, time, temperature, and weather conditions (such as sunny, cloudy, rainy, or snowy). For clouds, be specific as discussed in the next chapter.

In the last column, write down any thoughts, emotions, or physical sensations which come to mind as you experience the weather. Focus on how the weather affects your mood and productivity. Try to use the emotions from the following list.

ecstasy	joy	serenity	optimism
vigilance	anticipation	interest	aggressiveness
rage	anger	annoyance	contempt
loathing	disgust	boredom	remorse
grief	sadness	pensiveness	disapproval
amazement	surprise	distraction	awe
terror	fear	apprehension	submission
admiration	trust	acceptance	love

Be consistent: Try to record your observations at the same time each day, such as in the morning or before going to bed. Make sure you record your observations every day for the set period of time you've chosen.

Be specific: When recording your observations, be as specific as possible. For example, instead of just writing "happy clouds," you could write "bright sunshine, cumulus all over, gentle breeze from the north." This level of detail will help you recall your observations later, find related information in this book, and use them in your writing.

Reflect on your observations: After a week or a month of recording your observations, take some time to reflect on what you've written. Consider how the weather affected your mood and productivity. Did you notice any patterns or trends in your observations? Did any particular weather conditions stand out to you?

Use your observations in your writing: Finally, use your weather observations as inspiration for your writing. You could write a short story, a poem, or a character sketch that incorporates the weather in a meaningful way. Or you could use your observations to create a vivid and realistic setting for a story.

Example:

Date	Time	Temp	Weather	Feelings
2/16	8:00 am	45°F	nimbostratus, light rain	sadness, boredom
2/16	2:00 pm	36°F	stratocumulus, cold wind from west	joy but with some vigilance

EXERCISE: Being Mindful

You will want to approach this exercise with a sense of curiosity and openness, without any pressure to "get it right." This is an opportunity for you to connect with your environment and your own internal experiences in a deeper way.

1. Find a quiet and comfortable outdoor location where you can sit or stand for a few minutes. This could be a park, a garden, or simply a quiet spot in your yard or even at work or school.
2. Take a few deep breaths and bring your attention to the present moment. Notice the sensations of the ground beneath your feet, the air on your skin, and any sounds or smells in the environment.
3. Take a few moments to observe the current weather conditions. Is it sunny, cloudy, rainy, or windy? Take note of the temperature, the quality of the light, and any other sensory details.
4. Tune into your body and notice any **physical sensations** that arise in response to the weather. Are you feeling warm or cool? Is the wind causing you to shiver or making your hair stand on end? Pay attention to any tension or relaxation in your muscles.
5. Now, you'll want to tune into any **emotions** or moods that arise. Do you feel energized by the sunshine or lethargic on a cloudy day? Does the rain make you feel calm or anxious? Are you feeling more introspective or social depending on the weather?

6. Allow yourself to fully experience these sensations and emotions without judgment or criticism. Simply observe them as they arise and pass away.

7. When you are ready, take a few more deep breaths and return your attention to the present moment. Take time to reflect on how the weather affects your state of mind and attempt to categorize what you felt using the 32 emotions from this chapter.

---

[16] Plutchik, R. (1982). A Psychoevolutionary Theory of Emotions. *Social Science Information, 21*(4–5), 529–553. https://doi.org/10.1177/053901882021004003

[17] *File:Plutchik-wheel.svg. - Wikimedia Commons.* (2011, February 12). https://commons.wikimedia.org/wiki/File:Plutchik-wheel.svg

[18] Melville, H. (1851) *Moby Dick; or, The Whale.* New York, Harper & Brothers.

[19] Brontë, E. (1847). *Wuthering Heights.* London: TC Newby.

[20] Dickens, C. (1861). *Great Expectations.* Chapman & Hall.

[21] Beaman, R. (2022). *Twenty-eight.* http://www.awritestruggle.com/

[22] Kipling, R. (1937). *Something of Myself.* Macmillan of London.

[23] Baum, L. F. & Denslow, W. W. (1900) *The Wonderful Wizard of Oz.* George M. Hill Company.

[24] Shelly, M.W. (1818). *Frankenstein; or, the Modern Prometheus.* Lackington, Hughes, Harding, Mavor & Jones.

[25] Dickens, C. (1839). *The Life and Adventures of Nicholas Nickleby.* Chapman and Hall.

[26] Twain, M. (1892). *The American Claimant.* Charles L. Webster.

THAT ONE LOOKS LIKE A LLAMA RIDING A BICYCLE CHASING

A PLATYPUS ON A SKATEBOARD

> HAMLET: Do you see yonder cloud that's
> almost in shape of a camel?
> POLONIUS: By th'mass, and 'tis like a
> camel indeed.
> HAMLET: Methinks it is like a weasel.
> POLONIUS: It is backed like a weasel.
> HAMLET: Or like a whale?
> POLONIUS: Very like a whale.
> —*Hamlet*, 3.2.338-344[27]

CLOUDS AND EMOTION GO TOGETHER WHEN YOU THINK ABOUT IT. We have been trained since birth to recognize signs in the sky, whether we did so deliberately or not. For example, when you were a child playing on the soccer field with your child buddies and saw a cloud in the distance that was spitting lightning, you may have notified the coach (who should have been paying attention) and let them know there was a looming danger. That's **anxiety**.

When that same cloud moves over your soccer field and all of you are safe inside the park's communal restroom (where it stinks), that lightning carries with it booming thunder that crashes all around you and makes it impossible to talk to one another. Then the rain falls, usually in buckets, and the noise on the tin roof of the restroom drowns out even the thunder. Here you might be **excited**.

Then, far off in the distance, you hear the warble of a tornado warning. Suddenly the torrential rainfall that's above you is not nearly so exciting. You are now **frightened**, hoping that a tornado doesn't fall from the sky and take out the restroom in which you and your buddies thought you were safe.

When the rains let up and the thunderstorm moves on, you step outside. Here you may be **relaxed**, but at the same time **jittery**. You may think another storm is coming, and that's probably right. Your heart may be racing, your palms sweaty and even though you joke with those around you, in reality, you all are **thankful** you are still alive. The coach's car has been flipped over, however, and that both **surprises** you and fills you with a sense of **awe** at the raw power contained in a single storm.

Since we could all probably tell a similar story about weather and the impact on our emotions as part of the human experience, it makes sense that a writer would want to use weather to set the mood within a story. Maybe a darkening sky enveloped by thickening stratus to create a sense of dread, or happy clouds floating in a cerulean blue sky above an Aegean beach might be called upon to make the reader feel the same relaxing, romantic feeling the characters share.

As Martin Heusser notes, "cloud imagery refers to positive or negative areas of meaning: on the one hand negative symbolism such as notions of absence and threat and on the other hand positive symbolism such as presence and fertility."[28] If you do it wrong (e.g., using clouds in the wrong context, incorrectly describing a meteorological feature, using the wrong name), you can ruin the mood (emotion) you wish to draw out of the reader.

The mystery of clouds, or more specifically, their constitution, is something that has elicited theories from a variety of ancient civilizations going back centuries. Each had their own take on what clouds were, from the resulting push-pull of yin and yang to the wrathful vengeance of deities to more rational explanations such as the rise of meltwater into the atmosphere. From Aristotle to Seneca and later on to René Descartes and

Johann Wolfgang von Goethe, scientists and philosophers alike had their take on **nephrology**, or the study of clouds. Prior to the 1800s, in fact, one of the prevailing theories on the formation of clouds held that acid in the air corroded water into shapes and kept them suspended. Oliver Goldsmith discounted that idea and claimed—with no real confidence—that clouds were balls of vapor thrown into the air by the heat of the sun and broken up by wind. And the most widely held belief was that clouds were bubbles of rarified air that rose like balloons.[29]

The names of the clouds were also in debate. Robert Hooke, one of the foremost scientists of the 17th century attempted to solidify a classification of clouds according to their appearance (the "faces of the Sky" as he called it) rather than their structure or composition. Given that clouds are constantly changing in shape and size, you can imagine just how unlikely this might be. Nevertheless, it stuck for a while.

For the faces of the Sky they are soe many that many of them want proper names, & therefore it will be convenient to agree upon some Determinate ones by which the most usuall May be in breif exprest.

As let *Cleer Blew*, signify a very cleer sky without any cloudes or Exhalations.

Checkerd blew, a cleer Sky with many great white round clouds such as are very usuall in Summer.

Hazy, a Sky that looks whitish by reason of the thickness of the higher parts of the air by some exhalations not formd into Cloudes.

Thick, a Sky more whitned by a greater company of Vapours. these doe usually make the Luminarys looke bearded or hairy & are oftentimes the cause of the appearance of Rings & haloes about the Sun as well as the moon.

Overcast, when the Vapours soe whiten and thicken the air that the sun cannot break throw. and of this there are very many degrees which may be exprest by, *a little, much, more, very much overcast.* &c.

Let *Hairy*, Signify a Sky that has many small thin & high Exhalations which resemble locks of hair or flakes of hemp or flax. whose varietys may be exprest by, *Straight* or *Curld* &c according to the resemblance they beare.

Let *Waterd*, signify a Sky that has many high thin & small clouds looking almost like waterd tabby, calld in some places a maccarell sky from the Resemblance it has to the spots on the Backs of those fishes.

Let a sky be calld *Waved* when those cloudes appear much bigger & lower but much after the same manner.

Cloudy, when the Sky has many thick Dark cloudes.

Lowring, when the sky is not only *very Much overcast* but has also underneath many thick dark clouds which threaten raine.

The Significations of Gloomy, foggy, misty, sleeting, driving, rainy, snowy, reaches or racks, variable &c are well known they being very commonly used. there may be also severall faces of the Sky compounded of

two or more of these, which may be intelligibly
enough exprest by two or more of those names.[30]

It wasn't until December 1802 when clouds were first classified as we
know them today by a young industrial chemist named Luke Howard
who used a Latin classification system to describe clouds: **cirrus** (hair),
cumulus (pile), and **stratus** (layer). **Nimbus** (cloud) was a rainy combination of all three types. Simple enough for a start, but Howard wasn't
done. By using a combination of these terms (e.g., cirrus and cumulus
combined as cirrocumulus) Howard could classify the clouds at varying
levels of the atmosphere and in transition states.[31]

Cloud Atlas

THERE WAS A book I had in school, and it was called a *Cloud Atlas*. Not
that book by David Mitchell, but the *International Cloud Atlas* published
by the World Meteorological Organization (WMO) with a bunch of a
pretty pictures. This is what I learned: 1) don't lose the book—the
schoolhouse only has a few copies; and 2) there are 27 states of the sky.
Not that there are 27 specific cloud *types*, but in the world of meteorology,
there are 27 *ways* in which the sky can present itself.

(Before I go any further, if you are a meteorologist, weather nerd, or
took a class in atmospheric dynamics once as an elective because Psychology of the Common House Cat 101 was full, I know there are **many
more cloud types** than I have listed in this book. I hear you. I feel your
pain as you find your favorite cloud type is not listed. But this is a **creative
writing book**, not a comprehensive meteorological encyclopedia. That
might bore people.)

Clouds are what we really see when it comes to weather. They make
up most of it. You do not have a thunderstorm without clouds, nor does
it snow without them (although ice crystals do form/fall in clear skies).
Clouds can portend an idyllic scene, or they can undulate in threatening
ways. Nearly half of all references to "cloud" in *Wuthering Heights*, for
example, are symbols for the emotional state of a particular character.[32]

Clouds can be grouped into three main levels based on the *bottom* of the cloud, not the top. These levels, or **étages** (because French words make things sound fancier), are:

- Low (with bases between the surface and 6,500 feet[a])
- Mid (between 6,500 and 23,000 feet)
- High (above 16,500 feet)

Within the low étage (see? it sounds *so* fancy), there are several forms:

- cumulus
- towering and moderate cumulus
- cumulonimbus
- stratus
- stratocumulus
- stratus fractus
- cumulus fractus
- mammatus

When you look up at the sky and you say, "there's a rabbit in that one," you are likely looking at a **cumulus** cloud. If the rabbit is incredibly skinny and very tall but does not look like it's urinating on the ground, it's likely **towering cumulus**. If the rabbit is dark and huge and looks like fire is coming out of it while it yells and you and spits buckets of water or balls of ice, then you can safely assume that to be **cumulonimbus**.

In the mid étage, there are four main cloud forms:

- altocumulus
- altostratus
- nimbostratus
- altocumulus standing lenticular

In the case of the latter, if you're looking at what might be a UFO over a mountain or maybe an almond hanging in the sky, then you're probably looking at **altocumulus standing lenticular**. PRO TIP: do not fly into these clouds. Bad things happen.

Finally, in the high étage, there are three main forms:

---

[a] Heights for cloud bases are given above ground level or AGL versus atmospheric pressure which is presented in reference to mean sea level or MSL.

- cirrus
- cirrocumulus
- cirrostratus

Cirrus appears much like those airbrushed wisps made by Bob Ross way up there. (Incidentally, the "happy cloud" is probably cumulus). **Cirrocumulus** looks like tiny speckled dots in the sky. Essentially, cirrocumulus is cumulus in the high étage, so what you're seeing are happy clouds far above you. **Cirrostratus** is, well, boring. If you paint the sky white with only a few shades differing between west and east or north and south, you're probably being covered by cirrostratus. However, cirrostratus can be a very good foreshadower, which we'll discuss later.

There are other cloud types—over 100 combinations listed in the most current version of the *International Cloud Atlas*—but we're not going to get into them here. The point of the above is to show you that describing a "puffy cloud" to a weather nerd is going to make them imagine a happy cloud with no animosity toward the people below. If your "puffy cloud" spits lightning bolts, the weather nerd might say "that's not possible because it's not happy and therefore cumulonimbus."

Before I go on, there is a state of the sky called "**chaotic.**" This is an observational term meaning "there's so much up there at every level and I don't know what it is, so I'll call it chaos." Officially, the WMO says that this type of sky "exhibits a diversity of clouds belonging to the low and high levels."[33] It's usually altocumulus at many different levels, but it's more fun to call it chaotic.

On the Nature of Clouds

LET'S TAKE THAT list and break it down a little more. While we do this, we're also going to assign those clouds an emotion or two and try to get in touch with our feelings.

Low Clouds

Cumulus

This is the puffy, happy-go-lucky, cotton ball cloud that often forms on a nice sunny day when the birds are singing, and the bees are doing their bee thing. The clouds are spaced apart, no larger than your fist at arm's length, and they do not precipitate. They are more or less white, although the larger the cloud becomes, the darker the base of it will be. If it grows really large or fat and gets rather dark but has not yet precipitated, you may want to call it *cumulus mediocris* or **moderate cumulus**. Moderate cumulus is the next step to being a mean cumulonimbus cloud, which will get to later.

Cumulus clouds form because parcels of air rise until the moisture condenses (called the convective condensation level). The more humid the air, the lower the base of the cloud will be. In dry climates like the deserts of the Southwest, should these clouds form, they will have very high bases. In more humid places like the swamps of Louisiana where the gumbo is tasty, the clouds will form very low, typically only a few hundred feet above the ground. They will also grow faster.

Should the air have a strong vertical lift (that is, a parcel of air is more buoyant than the air around it), the cumulus cloud may stretch in the vertical. This is what we call **towering cumulus** and is a step before a thunderstorm, in much the same way as moderate cumulus. The faster the rise, the taller the cloud, the quicker the thunderstorm will eventually form.

Emotionally, cumulus conveys a **happy** feeling. If you think of Bob Ross painting happy clouds, you are thinking of cumulus. Or think of it this way: the technical term for those happy clouds is *cumulus humilis*, which in the Latin means "low heap" or "humble pile." So your happy clouds are humble. When you write a scene in which you wish to convey that same feeling, you can use cumulus clouds to set the stage.

Cumulonimbus

We've already covered towering cumulus above, so let me skip over that and talk a little bit about cumulonimbus. This will not be as long a section because there's a whole chapter on it later in the book.

Cumulonimbus means "heaped rainstorm" in Latin. Another term we could safely use is, you guessed it, thunderstorm. Some other words you might write to describe a cumulonimbus in your novel are thundercloud or thunderhead. Don't. Personally, I eschew those two words, but

I don't know why. Stick to thunderstorm.

For ways to describe cumulonimbus, refer to the chapter LIGHT-NING COMING OUT OF THAT ONE later in this book. There, I will also discuss the emotional impact of thunderstorms that can be weaved into narration to strengthen your story.

There's an entire chapter devoted to cumulonimbus (and mammatus), so we'll move on.

Stratus

Stratus, from the Latin, um, *stratus*, literally means "strewn about." That's pretty much what you can expect of any type of stratus cloud, to include stratocumulus and stratus fractus (below). Stratus proper forms in a typically stable atmosphere. Soft breezes raise cool and wet air over colder land or water.

Warm over cold is considered a stable atmosphere, while cold over warm is unstable. Recall from ninth-grade Earth Science class that cold air is more dense and therefore sinks. Warm air rises. If warm air rises into sinking cold air, instability is created. But if cold air sinks below warmer air (which is already rising), the weather normalizes. This is why we say stratus forms in a stable atmosphere.

Stratus can be rather boring to look at, but it has its uses in literature. When I lived in Alaska, stratus was often found hanging about the little town of Naknek on the Kvichak Bay. The grayness of the world created by those layers of stratus was enough to make it feel colder than it was. It was also downright gloomy.

Sometimes, the layer of stratus is thick enough that it seems opaque, letting little sun to pass through. This gloom may last for several days, too, and depending on the psychological makeup of your character, they may get depressed. While stratus can be thick, the tops of the clouds are usually not that high, so even if it looks like there's a ceiling above a pilot, they shouldn't be in the clouds for very long. A short jaunt up and they're above it all. If the layer is thick enough, you might find drizzle falling from the bases of stratus, or what some have described as a fine mist falling from the sky.

Like I said, stratus can be boring. It's also found more in maritime environments than in, say, deserts. In *Moby Dick* by Herman Melville, our narrator Ishmael lets us know just how **bored yet self-reflective** the crew of the *Pequod* is by mentioning the clouds (likely stratus) and the drab color of the environment.

> It was a **cloudy, sultry** afternoon; the seamen were la-
> zily lounging about the decks, or vacantly gazing over
> into the **lead-coloured** waters. Queequeg and I were
> mildly employed weaving what is called a sword-mat,
> for an additional lashing to our boat. So **still and sub-**
> **dued** and yet somehow preluding was all the scene,
> and such an incantation of reverie lurked in the air,
> that each silent sailor seemed resolved into his own in-
> visible self.[34]

Yawn.

Stratocumulus

If stratus means "strewn about" and cumulus means "heap", then stratocumulus must be strewn about heaps, right? That's essentially what these clouds are, but there are several ways in which they form and four main categories.

- Stratocumulus stratiformis—These are clouds with flat bases and spaced rather tightly; they are the most common.
- Stratocumulus cumulogenitus—When cumulus clouds rise into a temperature inversion (air that warms above a colder layer), they may spread outward and cluster together.
- Stratocumulus castellanus—These clouds can produce a bit of drizzle and often look like castles in the sky. The tops (turrets) of the castles are made when convection starts within a stable atmosphere. As the convection increases and the atmosphere destabilizes, stratocumulus castellanus may form into moderate cumulus or maybe even cumulonimbus.
- Stratocumulus lenticularis—Usually found in hilly locations and caused by atmospheric waves (think of a stream moving

over and around rocks), these "lentil beans in the sky" are similar to, but different from, the UFO-clouds (otherwise known as altocumulus lenticularis).

Stratocumulus forms from either the breaking up of stratus as the atmosphere changes, or the breaking down of cumulus as upward vertical motion is lessened. These types of clouds are the most common on Earth and can occur just about anywhere. It doesn't matter if the atmosphere is stable or less stable. And while rain may occur with stratocumulus, it is rarely the cloud that is the culprit. Precipitation typically results from the presence of other clouds in the area (e.g., moderate cumulus, a thunderstorm that's hasn't quite dissipated, a thicker layer of stratus).

Even if stratocumulus clouds are the most common on Earth, they are rarely described in literature except for that which comes at the end of a storm. I couldn't tell you what kind of emotion is drummed up by a narrative that describes, in excruciating detail, a stretched-out heap of fluffy stuff.

Stratus fractus

Fractus means "broken." When you see "scud" in the lower part of the atmosphere, typically after the sun has broken apart a layer of stratus, then you may be looking at stratus fractus. Often stratus fractus will appear to speed rapidly by, really an optical effect than anything else due their small size. When you see this scud, it's more a sign of things **changing** as Ishmael tells us in *Moby Dick*:

> But high above the **flying scud** and dark-rolling
> clouds, there floated a little isle of sunlight, from
> which beamed forth an angel's face; and this bright
> face shed a distinct spot of radiance upon the ship's
> tossed deck, something like that silver plate now in-
> serted into the Victory's plank where Nelson fell. 'Ah,
> noble ship,' the angel seemed to say, 'beat on, beat on,
> thou noble ship, and bear a hardy helm; for lo! **the sun
> is breaking through; the clouds are rolling off**—se-
> renest azure is at hand.'[34]

Cumulus fractus

Like its counterpart, stratus fractus, cumulus fractus is broken off pieces of other clouds, this time larger cumulus. Also called "scud," these torn fluff balls have an ill-defined base (if one is present at all) and rapidly change in shape and size. They may form into larger clouds as convection works its magic or they may simply disappear.

In storms, you might find cumulus fractus in the vicinity of the area where the wind is being "sucked up" (called the updraft) or where the air has been cooled off by precipitation and is sinking rapidly (the downdraft).

Scud can be an indicator of development. If the cumulus fractus clouds move toward the updraft, then the thunderstorm is still developing. You will also find cumulus fractus along the outflow of a thunderstorm, or the leading edge of the downdraft. In addition, these clouds are found near **shelf clouds**, which we will talk about later in the chapter devoted to thunderstorms.

Mammatus

I love the look of mammatus, especially in the evening when the sun is low on the horizon. These clouds, which are typically associated with large cumulonimbus, have unusual formations that may look like bulges or pouches. The formation of these clouds begins with turbulence inside the parent cumulonimbus, normally on the underside of the anvil.

As mammatus is associated with thunderstorms, we'll take a deeper dive in the chapter titled LIGHTNING COMING OUT OF THAT ONE. In the meantime, recall my survey on weather and emotions. Photos of mammatus clouds that were indicative of extreme weather often brought up emotions along the spectrum of **fear** (terror, apprehension, awe, and submission). Inserting a description of a thunderstorm with mammatus can have a powerful effect on the emotions of the reader (assuming fear or apprehension is what you're aiming for).

Figure 20. Mammatus, taken at sunset in Colorado.

Mid Clouds

Mid clouds, those whose bases are typically between 6,500 feet and 20,000 feet, are rarely used in writing with a few exceptions. They are the middle child, the ones that can portend coming storms and yet, at the same time, unable to extract much awe. The exception to this rule is **altocumulus standing lenticular**, which has been associated with UFOs for many years.

I won't go into much detail here (except for the aforementioned UFO cloud), since I don't believe you'll get as much out of describing a mid-level cloud as you would a cloud in the low étage. The same holds true for high clouds, those with bases at 20,000 feet or more. While they have their uses visually in cinema, it's not often that you be able to pull emotion out of a reader by describing these in narration.

I could be wrong. I challenge you, dear writer, to try.

Altocumulus

Just as cumulus clouds are "heaps" so, too, are altocumulus clouds. The difference is the height and size of the individual cloud elements (called "cloudlets"). I learned a trick in my schooling long ago: if you hold your hand out at arm's length and the cloud disappeared behind three fingers, then it was likely altocumulus. If it disappeared behind one finger, it was **cirrocumulus** (see below). Whether this holds true is debatable. I asked my instructor if this "rule" would apply to someone with fatter fingers or someone who had lost four of them to a woodshop accident. I never got an answer.

Altocumulus clouds are usually a mix of both ice and water (they are higher in the atmosphere, so the air is colder). This gives them a little more ethereal look than their cumulus cousins. There are four main types:

- Altocumulus stratiformis - tightly packed altocumulus usually covering the whole sky that might be separated by "rivers" of air
- Altocumulus castellanus - altocumulus with a definite vertical extent, much like towering cumulus in the low étage; castellanus can appear like turrets in the sky (queue a Jimi Hendrix song) and indicate atmospheric instability which may lead to thunderstorm formation later in the day
- Altocumulus floccus - floccus (Latin: flock) are usually found around altocumulus castellanus; more ragged, there could be virga hanging below the cloud (more on virga later in this chapter)
- Altocumulus lenticularis (also known as altocumulus standing lenticular) - lentil beans that hang in the sky and don't move much; these clouds may be almond-shaped or appear like UFOs over hilly or mountainous terrain

Figure 21. An image of altocumulus standing lenticular.[35]

When shown a picture of altocumulus standing lenticular (ACSL), respondents were more grouped together than with other clouds. Twenty-six percent chose an emotion along the spectrum of **anticipation** (vigilance, interest, optimism, aggressiveness). Of those choices, **interest** was chosen 101 times. As you can see from the picture above, it is rather interesting.

Typically, in the winter or spring, stable, super-quick air may be forced perpendicularly up a mountain or hill (some sort of barrier). When that happens, gravity waves develop downwind. That sounds all scientific but think of what happens when you drop a rock in a lake: waves form. If there is moisture (remember that clouds need moisture), ACSL will form near or just downwind of the crest of the mountain or hill. They are constantly forming and dissipating, too, and while they look stationary, the winds within the cloud are often fast.

Here's a plot thought for you: when aircraft run into mountain waves, they experience severe turbulence. And while the most obvious sign of this wave is a nice UFO-shaped ACSL hanging about, if the air is *too* dry, the wave may still exist *without* the presence of the cloud. Remember our two passengers on the plane delayed by a thunderstorm? Now, put that plane in the air approaching an invisible mountain wave and tell me what emotions might be conjured.

Altostratus

Altostratus clouds are even more boring than stratus. These clouds, which are a mixture of ice crystals and water droplets, are typically gray or bluish gray and cover the entire sky. If there isn't a layer of clouds above, the sun or moon may shine through and look fuzzy.

As the old saying goes, "If a circle forms 'round the moon, 'Twill rain soon." Might 'twill snow, too. This applies equally to cirrostratus (below). However, if rain (or snow) hits the ground, then the cloud has thickened and lowered, becoming **nimbostratus**. You will normally find altostratus ahead of a warm front.

Emotionally, there's nothing here. Sorry. I can't find any emotion in me when I'm staring at a layer of altostratus, unless it's abject boredom and a hope for something more.

Nimbostratus

Nimbostratus clouds are an extension of altostratus. As the altostratus thickens and lowers ahead of a warm or occluded front, the cloud gets darker and a continuous precipitation falls. Nimbostratus clouds are the only ones in the mid étage that can exist within the low étage.

To me, these clouds are not as boring as altostratus because they are dark, gray, and featureless. The fact that precipitation is falling and the world looks that much bleaker is like stepping into gothic novel. In the passage from *Great Expectations* earlier in this book, Dickens describes what I would only assume to be nimbostratus: "Day after day, a **vast heavy veil** had been driving over London from the East, and it drove still, as if in the East there were an **Eternity of cloud** and wind."[36]

Notice, though, that Dickens doesn't call out the cloud by name. The scene is set for us by the description, and it is through that description that we, as a reader, feel what Pip feels.

High Clouds

Cirrus

Cirrus is a Latin term for "lock or tuft of hair," which is precisely what this cloud looks like. They are high étage wispy clouds and may appear whiter than any other cloud in the sky. Cirrus is responsible for amazing sunsets in the desert. I remember them well.

Formed through deposition (a chemical process wherein gas is turned into a solid without the transition to liquid), cirrus is all ice crystals. These clouds can also form through contrails (although as we all know contrails are really a way to disperse chemicals that will cause sterilization and mind control so that we are beholden to the alien lizard overlords).

When shown the below picture of cirrus, respondents to the weather and emotion survey overwhelmingly associated the emotion of **serenity** to the cloud, followed distantly by **pensiveness** and then **boredom**.

Cirrus is more often described in literature than other clouds, althhough rarely by name. I personally like to describe cirrus in narrative form, simply because it creates an atmosphere of serenity. It also serves as a striking contrast to more extreme weather events—like the calm before a storm or relief as higher pressure and blue skies set in.

Figure 22. Cirrus clouds.

As I look through my old manuscripts, I note that I do use the word cirrus often. In *Difficult Mirrors*, I painted a sunset to open a chapter. The point was to transition from the beauty of the desert to a murder scene as well as call attention to the changes the protagonist had been going through. While I started with cirrus, I ended with a thunderstorm that was sure to make any investigation of the body found difficult. In tandem, throughout the chapter we learn that the protagonist has been feeling as if his own life had been going through a similar transition—from serenity to a chaotic mess.

> The sun dropped from the sky at a snail's pace, creep-
> ing past a few wispy **cirrus** clouds, past a small hill, a
> saguaro cactus arm and on and on. In time, the sky
> changed from a brilliant blue to a deep, blood red with
> spats of yellow and orange. The day's heat remained,
> as it typically did in the rainy season. It wasn't quite

official yet, but the seasonal shift of wind was only a few short weeks off and the humidity had already shown its ugly face. Off in the distance, a thunderstorm grew taller, its anvil transforming from bright white to orange to red as the sun finally disappeared without fanfare. Lightning flashed in chaotic patterns, stabbed at the desolate landscape, and illuminated a torrential rainfall that flooded the land below.

Of all the clouds in the high étage, I recommend cirrus. You don't have to use the proper name for the cloud, of course, but painting serenity before or after a tumultuous climax is a good way to manipulate the emotions of your readers.

Cirrocumulus

Imagine that happy cloud, the cumulus, then toss it up into the air above 20,000 feet. That would be cirrocumulus, for the most part. If you hold your hand out at arms-length and one finger covers a cloudlet, then you're probably looking at cirrocumulus. While cumulus is composed of water droplets, however, cirrocumulus is made up of ice crystals and supercooled water droplets (water which exists in a liquid state below 0°C or 32°F).

As with altocumulus (and stratocumulus), there are subcategories of cirrocumulus called **stratiformis** (spread out), **lenticularis** (UFO-shaped but elongated), **floccus** (grouped together), and **castellanus** (tiny castles in the sky).

You may have heard the term "mackerel sky" or "buttermilk sky" especially if you're into old timey sayings. This refers to either altocumulus or cirrocumulus, sometimes a combination of both. The French call this *ciel moutonné* (fleecy sky), the Germans *Schäfchenwolken* (sheep clouds), the Spanish *cielo empedrado* (cobbled sky), and to the Italians it is *pecorelle* (like little sheep). This is about as literary as it gets (and I don't know what's up with the sheep reference).

In *Anne's House of Dreams* by L. M. Montgomery, the mackerel sky (cirrocumulus) helps paint the picture of the reflective day before Anne's marriage to Gilbert as she visits her guardian's grave. The reference to mackerel sky may be a specific nod to the maritime saying "Mackerel sky, mackerel sky, Never long wet, never long dry." Basically, a change is coming.

> She left on his grave the flowers she had brought and walked slowly down the long hill. It was a **gracious** evening, full of **delectable** lights and shadows. In the west was a sky of **mackerel clouds**—crimson and amber-tinted, with long strips of apple-green sky between. Beyond was the **glimmering radiance** of a sunset sea, and the ceaseless voice of many waters came up from the tawny shore. All around her, lying in the **fine, beautiful** country silence, were the hills and fields and woods she had known and **loved** so long.[37]

Cirrostratus

When you look up at the sky and see hazy blue with maybe the slightest hint of white, you are likely looking at a veil of cirrostratus, thin clouds formed of ice crystals which can cover large areas of the sky. When the sun or moon shines through, halos often appear, which is why sailors say, "If a circle forms 'round the moon, 'Twill rain soon." Cirrostratus may occur long before a front arrives.

Even more boring than altostratus and especially stratus, cirrostratus will rarely (if ever) be called out in literary circles, unless the story happens to be about a sailor at sea who's calling out an approaching storm.

The Oddball Clouds

Kelvin-Helmholtz

A Kelvin–Helmholtz instability occurs when there is a velocity difference across the interface between two fluids. The atmosphere being a fluid, this instability can be viewed in dramatic clouds like the one pictured below.

Figure 23. Kelvin-Helmholtz clouds[38]

I highly doubt you will ever read (or write) "look at that there Kelvin-Helmholtz cloud, boss," but it is not outside the realm of possibility that you might describe them in order to tease out **awe** or **surprise** in your characters.

Wall Clouds & Shelf Clouds

A **wall cloud** is a dramatic lowering of a cloud below the base of a cumulonimbus, often with visible rotation and upward vertical motion. Tornadoes often form in these clouds. A **shelf cloud** forms on the leading edge of a system of storms (like a line of chaos marching toward you). They can be miles long and have non-rotating clouds that reach toward the ground. Small tornadoes may form with shelf clouds, but not big monsters.

If you're curious about what to call a cloud that you're staring at while standing in the middle of the Kansas prairie because your car broke down, consider where the winds are. If they are at your back (being sucked *toward* the dark feature in front of you), you're likely looking at a wall cloud. If the winds are coming at you, it is probably a shelf cloud.

Since both the wall cloud and shelf cloud are part of a thunderstorm, most of the discussion on these features will be found in the chapter LIGHTNING COMING OUT OF THAT ONE later in this book. When asked to relate an emotion to the following picture of a wall clouds, respondents to the weather and emotions survey overwhelmingly picked **terror** and **fear** with **vigilance** a close third.

Figure 24. A wall cloud.[39]

In *The Wonderful Wizard of Oz*, Uncle Henry figures that a tornado (which he mistakenly calls a "cyclone") is coming based on the direction of the grass in the wind. "...Uncle Henry and Dorothy could see where the long grass bowed in waves before the coming storm."[40] One can picture the wind here bowing *towards* the storm, meaning an inflow of air *into* a wall cloud. Had the grass bowed away from the storm, they might have been looking more at a shelf cloud and Dorothy may have never visited Oz.

Asperitas

Translating from the Latin, asperitas means "roughness," although if you look at pictures of the cloud, they look anything but rough. In fact, they look fluid and probably the coolest cloud type out there that's not related to a UFO or thunderstorm. That's just my opinion though.

Asperitas is the most recent cloud added to the International Cloud Atlas, published by the WMO. Interestingly, it took eight years of lobbying by the Cloud Appreciation Society (CAS) to get the WMO to recognize it.[41] This is how the WMO defines it (note my highlight and the nearly poetic way in which this cloud can be described):

> Well-defined, wave-like structures in the underside of the cloud; more chaotic and with less horizontal organization than the variety undulatus. Asperitas is characterized by localized waves in the cloud base, either smooth or dappled with smaller features, sometimes descending into sharp points, **as if viewing a roughened sea surface from below**. Varying levels of illumination and thickness of the cloud can lead to dramatic visual effects. Occurs mostly with Stratocumulus and Altocumulus.[42]

I had intended to use a picture of asperitas to see what emotions might be related, but in the end I had to cut the number of questions to something people would be willing to take without getting survey fatigue. Below is the picture I would have used, and I'll ask you the same question I asked on the survey: "*What emotion pops up in your mind when you look at the picture below?*"

Figure 25. Asperitas, the newest addition to the International Cloud Atlas.

Virga

Virga is *not* a cloud. From the Latin meaning rod, branch, or sprig, virga is precipitation *from* a cloud that has not reached the ground usually because of evaporation or sublimation. If you've ever been in the desert, you've likely seen virga under high-based thunderstorms. Often, clouds with virga under them will resemble jellyfish in the sky.

The Emotional Connection

IN *DRACULA* BY Bram Stoker, Jonathan Harker gives us his observation of the weather through letters.[43] On May 5th, he relates that "There were dark, rolling clouds overhead, and in the air the heavy, oppressive sense of thunder. It seemed as though the mountain range had separated two atmospheres, and that now we had got into the thunderous one."[44] This is a good example of setting the atmosphere in a story (**apprehension,** perhaps?) not by telling us of his or his fellow passenger's nervous disposition, but by *showing* us the oppressiveness and darkness into which they were traveling that weighed heavy on them.

The emotional impact of clouds in creative writing may best be seen in lower cloud types, those that impact our lives more than the others. Comparing clouds to physical objects is as natural as our human experience. We cannot look at clouds and not see something or feel something inside of us. To view a canvas of blue and see chaos invites our minds to create order. What does that cloud look like? See how that cloud morphs from a rabbit to an elephant?

In psychology, this is called **apophenia,** or the human tendency to find patterns and meaning in random information. This could be auditory, tactile, or visual. Related to this and more specific to the visual is **pareidolia,** the tendency for us to perceive meaning in the chaos. A good example of this from modern times is the "face on Mars" or the myriad "ducks" and "aliens" we've seen in pictures taken by rovers coming from the red planet. And then there are clouds.

Our first step in writing clouds into our scenes is to determine which emotion we want to elicit in the reader. One way to do that is to use the concept of pareidolia. What does your scared character see in the clouds?

Is it a clown with a knife or a rabbit with fangs? Perhaps the feeling called for in your narrative is one of love or serenity. What do your characters see in the clouds at that time? Are they attempting to ascribe a meaning to the chaos above them by seeing "castles in the sky" as opposed to alto-cumulus castellanus? Is that a rose floating through a cerulean sky?

As we can compare clouds, we can also contrast them with our emotions. As I mentioned near the beginning of this chapter, using clouds in the wrong context or incorrectly describing a meteorological feature can ruin the mood (emotion) you wish to draw out of the reader. But you can also do wrong...on purpose. A feeling of unbridled rage while staring at a cloud that looks like a baby duck is dramatic because it does not fit our cognitive biases. The baby duck *should not* be there because we are angry. An ominously dark sky portending rain, hail, and possibly a tornado *should not* be the place for two lovers to kiss. To have an argument under happy clouds makes the darkness of the moment stand out more in the innocence of the scene.

In *Wuthering Heights*, Catherine tells Ellen of such a quarrel between her and Linton, contrasting Linton's cloudless sky with her own of "bright white clouds flitting rapidly above." (Contrasted here also is the breezeless hot July day versus the west wind blowing as well as being in the middle of the moors versus having the moors at a great distance.)

> We were near quarrelling. He said the pleasantest
> manner of spending a hot July day was lying from
> morning till evening on a bank of heath in the middle
> of the moors, with the bees humming dreamily about
> among the bloom, and the larks singing high up over-
> head, and the blue sky and bright sun shining steadily
> and **cloudlessly**. That was his most perfect idea of
> heaven's happiness: mine was rocking in a rustling
> green tree, with a west wind blowing, and **bright white
> clouds flitting rapidly above**; and not only larks, but
> throstles, and blackbirds, and linnets, and cuckoos
> pouring out music on every side, and the moors seen

at a distance, broken into cool dusky dells; but close by
great swells of long grass undulating in waves to the
breeze; and woods and sounding water, and the whole
world awake and wild with joy. He wanted all to lie in
an ecstasy of peace; I wanted all to sparkle and dance
in a glorious jubilee. I said his heaven would be only
half alive; and he said mine would be drunk: I said I
should fall asleep in his; and he said he could not
breathe in mine, and began to grow very snappish. At
last, we agreed to try both, as soon as the right weather
came; and then we kissed each other and were
friends.[45]

Unless your character is a pilot, it will be rare to ever need to describe the sky above the low étage. Perhaps your character is a Hurricane Hunter. In this case, clouds like altostratus or cirrostratus may show up in your narrative, but what emotional connection could you make with the reader?

Another problem I see in using mid- or high-level cloud types in narrative is the lack of what I would call "creative naming." If you noticed, almost all clouds names are formed from Latin. If I saw *altocumulus floccus* in a novel, I might expect it to be over a field of *ovis aries* (sheep) surrounded by *bellis perennis* (daisies). None of that rolls off the tongue in a way that would make the fiction palatable.

That's not to say you can't or won't use mid- or high-level clouds to set an atmosphere in your story. I have provided a few examples above. There are also cloud "forecasts" sailors used which rely on these types to portend certain weather. These same sayings have been used by campers, farmers, and others, too. Here's a few of them:

- **"If a circle forms 'round the moon, 'Twill rain soon."** Halos are the circles that form around the sun or moon and are caused by the light refracting as it passes through ice crystals in higher clouds (e.g., cirrus or cirrostratus). As mentioned above, neither of these two clouds will produce any precipitation, but they often come in advance of a low-pressure system. Not mentioned in the proverb above, the halo will disappear when the clouds thicken and lower or altostratus takes over. That's when you know a storm is getting closer.

- **"Trace in the sky the painter's brush, The winds around you soon will rush."** Bob Ross painted wispy cirrus at times, using the tip of a fan brush (his favorite) and a flick of the wrist. Those happy paintings were moments in time, but as you know, weather moves. Those wispy cirrus are ice clouds that may show up in advance of an approaching system. This isn't always true, however. In drier atmospheres like the desert Southwest, feathery cirrus may show up because the sky is bored of being so blue all the time.

- **"Mares' tails and mackerel scales Make lofty ships carry low sails."** Mares' tails is a 15th century term referring to an aquatic plant (horseweed) or cirrus which resembles the flowing tail of a horse in the wind. The term "mackerel scales" is a derivative of "mackerel sky" and refers to altocumulus or cirrocumulus clouds, especially when arranged in a wave pattern with a bit of blue sky peeking through. The combination of mares' tails and mackerel scales was not only for rhyme, but indicative of an approaching front.

- **"Red sky in morning, sailors give warning. Red sky at night, sailors delight."** This is probably the most well-known mariner "forecast." Weather in Northern Hemisphere moves from west to east. The rising sun will shine on clouds approaching from the west, supposedly turning the sky red. The opposite appears at sunset when those clouds have moved over you and exited stage east. I challenged this one day and said that the sun setting precisely in the west only occurred twice per year; at all other times, it was either west northwest or west southwest. I was told, in so many terms, to be quiet.

- **"The higher the clouds, the better the weather."** This one is straightforward: higher clouds are indicative of dry air and higher pressure—a hallmark of fair weather. You might ask "well, how high?" and you would probably not be surprised to know that I asked the same question and was, once again, told to be quiet.

With all the nifty sayings of old timers, it would not be out of the realm of fiction to have, say, a wagon master leading a cast of pioneers across the Kansas prairie remarking that the halo they saw in the "white silky sheet of clouds" has now disappeared. The cook, looking up from making calf slobbers (meringue) might ask, "What of it, hoss?" The wagon master scratches his whiskers. "Rain's a-coming."

That would make for bad Western, come to think of it, but the point is that unless you're using low-level clouds, you may struggle with making an emotional connection with the reader.

My suggestion here (and in later chapters) is to first identify the specific emotion you want to convey to the reader. What is the atmosphere? Is it melancholy? Tumultuous? Romantic? From there, look back at those lower clouds and see which one of them might match. Then, as you set the scene, you can pepper in something that clues the reader in to what's about to happen or what's presently going on—either through contrast or comparison. Readers, being humans who have likely been outside and have seen a cloud before, will connect the dots.

In my novel *Castles*, the weather takes a complementary position alongside the protagonist, Maggie. For those who are wondering why (there *must* be someone), I started the novel based on a short story I had written for a writers' group prompt that said, "Write a story about the weather." Being a weather nerd, I said sure. Anyway, the clouds that Maggie sees and mentions throughout the novel grow in size and shape. Her reflections on the weather were intended to set the stage for her eventual outburst at the climax. In one passage, after years of trauma, she is contemplating something that would lead to a major change in her life.

I looked out at the horizon past the Bus. A few small clouds had formed in the distance, tinted red. The storms were still out of season, but just the hint of instability led me to believe a change was coming. I lifted my lips in a faint smile. "Have you ever stood inside a dust storm?"

Later, much closer to the climax of the novel...

I still felt the fire inside me, Mama's flame she wasn't strong enough to feed. But I was so tired. I looked out the window toward the distance and saw the billow of clouds. It would be a few hours, I thought. Just enough time.

This change was not sudden, and each mention of the weather was intentional. If you can start a story with a small puffy white cloud (cumulus) and grow it through the novel until it becomes a monster cumulonimbus, you've essentially mimicked the old plot curve we learned long ago in school. I'll show you what I mean in the chapter titled LIGHTNING COMING OUT OF THAT ONE.

I'LL LEAVE YOU with this poem by Theodore H. Rand from 1897.

THE CUMULUS CLOUD

Mountains of heaven, in stainless white ye shine,
    Islanded in calm of pearl- and sapphire-blue!
    The pillared heights are lifted into view
    In spectral power reposeful as divine.
A timeless peace abides in every line
    Soft moulded from the quarries of the dew,
    Yet fateful fire the inmost heart throbs through,
    And thunder slumbers in the brows benign.

Paling before the massive whiteness there,
  The faltering moon comes up the waiting night;
  The faithful stars, like folded lilies, sleep
Till Love's wide wonder of the lullëd air
  Melts with its rose-tipt crests in azure deep,
  And sets the skyey plains abloom with light.[46]

Cirrocumulus, cloud study by Luke Howard (1803)

Cirrus clouds depiction, engraving by Luke Howard (1803)

A Nifty Table of Emotions and Clouds

Emotion	Cloud Type
acceptance	clear skies, cumulus, altocumulus, altostratus (thin with halo), cirrus, cirrocumulus, cirrostratus
admiration	clear skies, cumulus, altocumulus, altostratus (thin with halo), cirrus, cirrocumulus, cirrostratus
aggressiveness	cumulonimbus (with or without mammatus, wall cloud, or shelf cloud), stratus, nimbostratus, altostratus (thick with no halo)
amazement	cumulonimbus (with mammatus, wall cloud, or shelf cloud), asperitas, altocumulus standing lenticular,
anger	cumulonimbus (with or without mammatus, wall cloud, or shelf cloud), stratus, nimbostratus, altostratus (thick with no halo)
annoyance	cumulonimbus (with mammatus, wall cloud, or shelf cloud)
anticipation	cumulonimbus (with or without mammatus, wall cloud, or shelf cloud)
apprehension	cumulonimbus (with mammatus, wall cloud, or shelf cloud)
awe	cumulonimbus (with or without mammatus, wall cloud, or shelf cloud), asperitas, altocumulus standing lenticular
boredom	altostratus (thick with no halo), cirrostratus, cirrocumulus
contempt	cumulonimbus (with or without mammatus, wall cloud, or shelf cloud), stratus, nimbostratus, altostratus (thick with no halo)

Emotion	Cloud Type
disapproval	stratus, nimbostratus, altostratus (thick with no halo)
disgust	cumulonimbus(with or without mammatus, wall cloud, or shelf cloud), stratus, nimbostratus, altostratus (thick with no halo)
distraction	cumulonimbus(with or without mammatus, wall cloud, or shelf cloud)
ecstasy	clear skies, cumulus, altocumulus, altostratus (with halo), cirrus, cirrocumulus, cirrostratus
fear	cumulonimbus (with mammatus, wall cloud, or shelf cloud)
grief	stratus, nimbostratus, altostratus (thick with no halo)
interest	cumulus (in the shape of something), asperitas, altocumulus standing lenticular
joy	clear skies, cumulus, altocumulus, altostratus (thin with halo), cirrus, cirrocumulus, cirrostratus
loathing	cumulonimbus(with or without mammatus, wall cloud, or shelf cloud), stratus, nimbostratus, altostratus (thick with no halo)
love	clear skies, cumulus, altocumulus, altostratus (thin with halo), cirrus, cirrocumulus, cirrostratus
optimism	clear skies, cumulus, altocumulus, altostratus (thin with halo), cirrus, cirrocumulus, cirrostratus
pensiveness	altostratus (with or without halo), asperitas, cirrostratus, cirrocumulus

Emotion	Cloud Type
rage	cumulonimbus (with mammatus, wall cloud, or shelf cloud)
remorse	stratus, nimbostratus, altostratus (thick with no halo)
sadness	stratus, nimbostratus, altostratus (thick with no halo)
serenity	clear skies, cumulus, altocumulus, altostratus (thin with halo), cirrus, cirrocumulus, cirrostratus
submission	cumulonimbus(with or without mammatus, wall cloud, or shelf cloud), stratus, nimbostratus, altostratus (thick with no halo)
surprise	cumulonimbus (with mammatus, wall cloud, or shelf cloud)
terror	cumulonimbus (with mammatus, wall cloud, or shelf cloud)
trust	clear skies, cumulus, altocumulus, altostratus (thin with halo), cirrus, cirrocumulus, cirrostratus
vigilance	moderate or towering cumulus, cumulonimbus (with or without mammatus, wall cloud, or shelf cloud)

EXERCISE: Describing Clouds

How would you describe a cloud? The first consideration, of course, would be to decide what type of cloud it is. What does it portend? A coming storm? A grey morning? A picnic in the park?

For this first exercise, we will start with a box. In that box, draw yourself a cloud. Any cloud. Whatever you want and as big as you want. (Or just pull out a piece of blank paper and do the same.) [b]

---

[b] If you need help, step outside with a notebook on a day that presents itself with the cloud or clouds you chose. Alternatively, a simple Internet search will net you thousands of pictures.

Now that you've let loose your inner Michelangelo and you have a cloud, what type is it? _____

For each of the words below, write one complete sentence using the stated descriptor. Describe your cloud with...
...a shape

_____
_____
_____

...a color

_____
_____
_____

...a sound

_____
_____
_____

...a tactile feel

_____
_____
_____

...a smell

_____
_____
_____

...an action verb

_____
_____
_____

Take what you've written above and see if you can put it into a paragraph. Try to keep the name of the type of cloud out of your writing. You want your description to be enough to inform the reader what's hanging over your characters.

_____

_____

_____

_____

_____

_____

_____

_____

_____

_____

Next, ask yourself what emotion you want to convey in your reader. Find that cloud you've just described in the table above. What emotions are normally associated with it (there may be more than one)?

_____

_____

Does your description match the emotion? For example, if you said the clouds are "happy" but chose one that matches with the emotion of "boredom," then you might want to rethink how you described the clouds. Be as poetic as you want but keep your description to the sky itself.

Next, place your character(s) in the scene. Don't let your characters re-mark about the weather (unless, of course, they are meteorologists). And show your emotion (i.e., don't tell the reader what it is).

_____

_____

_____

_____

_____

_____

_____

In the final, step, **remove the weather** and let someone else read it. Ask them what emotion is present. What do they, as a reader, feel? Then, with the weather put back in, ask your reader if anything has changed.

If there is an incongruency, your description of the weather worked. If there is not and your reader chose a different emotion from the one you intended, you might want to rework the description of the weather.

[27] Shakespeare, W. (1992). *Hamlet, Prince of Denmark*. C. Watts & K. Carabine (Eds.). Wordsworth Editions. (Original work published 1599).

[28] Heusser, M. (2004). Camel, Weasel or Whale: Cloud Symbolism in English Literary Texts. *Variations: Literaturzeitschrift der Universität Zürich, 12*, 225-241.

[29] Hamblyn, R. (2001). *The Inventions of Clouds*. Farrar, Straus and Giroux.

[30] Hooke,R. (1667). "A Method for Making a History of the Weather," in Thomas Sprat, *The History of the Royal-Society of London, for the Improving of Natural Knowledge*.

[31] Howard, L. (1832). *Essay on the Modifications of Clouds*. John Churchill & Sons.

[32] Brontë, E. (1847). *Wuthering Heights*. London: TC Newby.

[33] *International Cloud Atlas*. (2017). https://cloudatlas.wmo.int/en/cm-9.html

[34] Melville, H. (1851) *Moby Dick; or, The Whale*. New York, Harper & Brothers.

[35] Richards, Jeremy. (Photographer). *Lenticular clouds over the mountains of Torres del Paine National Park in Patagonia, Chile* [digital image]. Retrieved from https://www.shutterstock.com/

[36] Dickens, C. (1861). *Great Expectations*. Chapman & Hall.

[37] Montgomery, L.M. (1917). *Anne's House of Dreams*. McClelland, Goodchild and Stewart.

[38] Red Buffalo Studios. (Photographer). *Kelvin Helmholtz cloud formation* [digital image]. Retrieved from https://www.shutterstock.com/

[39] KEYC Weather (Photographer). *Well defined wall cloud on storm near Canadian, TX May 27, 2015*. Retrieved from https://www.keyc.com/

[40] Baum, L. F. & Denslow, W. W. (1900) *The Wonderful Wizard of Oz*. George M. Hill Company.

[41] ABC News. (2017, March 22). *Asperitas among newly-classified clouds to join World Meteorological Organisation's atlas*. https://www.abc.net.au/news/2017-03-22/asperitas-cloud-formation-classified-meteorological-organisation/8376340

[42] *Asperitas*. (2017). International Cloud Atlas. Retrieved from https://cloudatlas.wmo.int/en/clouds-supplementary-features-asperitas.html

[43] Mary Reed notes in an article in *Weatherwise* that "it was apparent to me that more than one character in Dracula would have made a fine meteorologist. They recorded everything, in diaries, letters—even on a phonograph, and had a habit of looking out their windows." See Reed, M. (1990). Beastly weather. *Weatherwise, 43*(5), 274.

[44] Stoker, B. (1897). *Dracula*. Grosset & Dunlap.

[45] Brontë, E. (1847). *Wuthering Heights*. London: TC Newby.

[46] Rand, T.H. (1897). *At Minas Basin and Other Poems*. William Briggs.

LITTLE CAT FEET

The fog comes
on little cat feet.

It sits looking
over harbor and city
on silent haunches
and then moves on.
—Carl Sandburg, "Fog" (1916)[47]

I WAS IN 4TH GRADE WHEN I READ THE ABOVE POEM "FOG" BY CARL Sandburg. This was my first exposure to how much weather can impact literature. Mind you, in fourth grade I was not thinking about using weather as a literary device but instead what I was going to do at recess. I want to say it probably rained the day I read the poem in class, but as I was in Phoenix at the time, that's doubtful. It was probably blisteringly hot unless it was winter. Then it was only mildly warm.

What images come to mind when you read Sandburg's poem? For me, who lived with a cat, I connected with the first line in ways that were intended: my cat would frequently come into my bedroom on his little cat feet. One moment I would be alone, the next looking at a cat. Like that cat (named Friday, by the way), fog does not announce itself very well. It's stealthy, serene at times, and so often shows its face early in the morning when the coffee still hasn't brewed.

Merriam-Webster defines this weather phenomenon as a "vapor condensed to fine particles of water suspended in the lower atmosphere that differs from cloud only in being near the ground."[48] Second to that would be "a state of confusion or bewilderment." There are other definitions (e.g., "long grass, second growth of grass after mowing", "long grass in a moist hollow"[49]), but I'll stick with these two for the purposes of this chapter.

The Dynamics of Fog

FIRST OFF, FOG is essentially a cloud near the ground. When the temperature and the dew point of the air come within 5°F (2.8°C) of each other, fog may form. This happens because the atmosphere either cools or enough moisture is added to raise the dew point.[50] Any fog made up of ice crystals is called **ice fog** (and is, by far, the prettiest to look at).

When meteorologists look at fog, they decide whether it is one of six types:

- Advection fog
- Radiation fog
- Upslope fog
- Steam fog
- Frontal fog
- Ice fog

Advection fog forms due to moist air moving (advecting) over a colder surface. If the air near the surface cools enough to approach the dew point, you get fog. It should be noted that for the air to advect, it needs to be moved and therefore requires a light wind. Too much wind (say greater than 10 knots or 12-ish mph) will be too much. If this advection occurs over water, you'd call it **steam fog**, which might look like wisps of vapor rising from the surface of the water. It can be both creepy and beautiful. In fact, the picture of this type of fog below resulted in the most alike responses (174) of all emotions: **serenity**. But put that picture at night, and the response may be different.

Figure 26. Fog over a mountain lake.

Radiation fog, also known as ground or valley fog, is created by the cooling of the atmosphere when the sun goes down. The ground radiates its heat, cooling the air around it. When the heat rises, it is replaced by cooler air and an inversion sets up (the air above is warmer than the air below). This traps the moisture near the ground. Depending on how much moisture is trapped, the dew point may rise nearing the temperature and create fog.

If the terrain lifts the air because air is pushed up against it by wind, it will cool. This is called adiabatic cooling (the temperature decreases with height). If it reaches the dew point of the surrounding air, **upslope fog** may form. This type of fog (colloquially known as Cheyenne fog) may form at higher elevations and appear to "sink" down into the valleys. If the wind is too high, though, you might find stratus instead of fog.

Frontal fog may form concurrently with a front. There are three types: that associated with a warm front, that associated with a cold front, and that occurring after a front has passed. When rain falls into cold air, the dew point is increased bringing it near or at the ambient temperature. If the air is forced up a frontal slope, fog can form much the same as it does with upslope fog.

The final type is **ice fog**. Always made up of ice crystals, ice fog may be formed in extremely cold arctic air. Interestingly, ice fog is often created when hydrocarbon fuels add water vapor to the air, either through car or jet engines or steam vents. When I was in Alaska, I recall many times when the temperature was extraordinarily cold and a jet would take off. The exhaust from the engine condensed the air behind it and ice fog formed, shutting the runway down as visibility dropped to less than a quarter mile. At the base where I was assigned, two F-15 jets were on constant alert to prevent airspace incursions from Russian bombers. During extremely cold days, both jets would need to take off at almost the exact same time lest the other be left in a sudden fog bank.

Without getting into too much detail (there is plenty available on the Internet and this is a creative writing book), fog can disappear as quietly as it appeared. All you need to do is increase the distance between the temperature and dew point by removing moisture. You can also raise the temperature, strengthen your winds, or switch the upslope to downslope.

Mist

Fog is not **mist**, nor is it haze. While all these reduce visibility and obscure things, there are differences. Mist contains water droplets at a lower density than fog and reduces visibility to *greater than or equal to* 5/8 of a mile (1 kilometer). Fog reduces visibility to *less than* 5/8 of a mile. Both are made of water droplets, but which is more sinister? Surely not being able to see the creature standing a few hundred feet away is more frightening than it being hidden but over a kilometer away. The movie *The Fog* with Adrienne Barbeau and Jamie Lee Curtis probably would not have had the same impact if it had been called *The Mist*, and its depiction was accurate. Stephen King's novella *The Mist*, however, might not have been the same had it been called *The Fog*. Regardless, they are different. Arguably, the reduction in visibility apparent in *The Mist* should have been called a fog, but if I were Stephen King, I'd name it whatever I wanted.

Haze and Other Lithometeors

To be in a haze is the same as being in a fog (clouded thought). Yet **haze** is officially defined as the "suspension in the air of extremely small, dry particles invisible to the naked eye and sufficiently numerous to give the air an opalescent appearance."[51] The chief difference is the type of particles suspended in the air: fog and mist are created by **hydrometeors** (microscopic water droplets) while haze is formed from **lithometeors** (microscopic dry particles).

Haze is used less as a sinister obscuration than as a way to paint slight muted scenes that may be soft around the edges. From "a soft blur of golden haze"[52] to a "milk-white haze"[53], "a fine haze"[54], "a blue haze"[55], or a "misty tropic haze"[56] you normally won't read about a haze in a way that purposefully drives tension. Perhaps this is because the visibility is not reduced as much or because the colors haze produces are quieter. There is less of a gloom.

Dust haze is different from haze. Created from a dust storm or sandstorm, dust haze produces a vivid display of orange and red in the air. The storm that raised the dust does not have to be nearby to produce this effect. Every so often, strong low- to midlevel winds in the atmosphere over central Africa advects dust across the Atlantic producing vivid sunsets in America.

Figure 27. Visible satellite imagery of Saharan dust over the North Atlantic Ocean.[57]

The same effect can be produced by **smoke** or **volcanic ash** in the atmosphere. In May 1980, in one of those childhood memories that seem to stick with me even if I want to erase them, I recall seeing a plume of smoke in the air while standing atop a waterslide at a community pool. Foolishly, I exclaimed to all those around me that what we were witnessing was ash from the explosion of Mt. St. Helens which had dominated the news cycle.

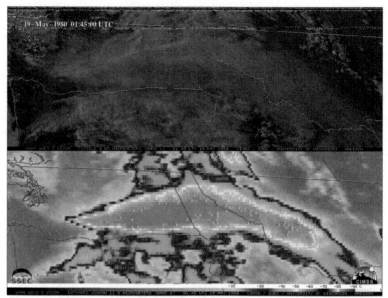

Figure 28. GOES-3 visible (top) and infrared (bottom) image of the ash plume from Mt. St. Helens in 1980.[58]

While it was true that the ash plume from the volcano was forecasted to go over my little part of the world (central Alabama), that's not what I was looking at. Since no one disputed my false observation, all those other kids thought I was smart.

I was 8, and so I'll excuse myself.

Smog

Although one could be excused for thinking smog is the name of a dragon (it's spelled "Smaug"), the simple reality is that this visibility re-ducer is a combination of fog or haze and smoke or pollution. Smoke fog, or smog, was coined in 1905 by a member of the Coal Smoke Abatement Society in London. That's really it.

Great Fogs of History

There have been some notable events in history related to fog. As you can imagine, if you've ever been driving in a thick fog, you know that accidents can happen. But fog can also provide cover. Below are a few events I've culled over time. Some have been made into movies, some have found their way into novels as a backdrop for the plot, and some are just interesting.

Empress of Ireland

In 1914, the Canadian steamship *Empress of Ireland* carrying 1,477 passengers left port at Pointe-au-Père, Quebec in clear weather. Soon, however, a thick fog enveloped the St. Lawrence Seaway thanks to warm spring air over the cold water which led to a collision between the *Empress* and the Norwegian steamer *Storstad*. As Captain Henry Kendell of the *Empress* recounts in his testimony:

> After passing Rock Point Gas Buoy I sighted the steamer *Storstad*; it then being clear. At that time I saw a slight fog bank coming gradually from the land and knew it was going to pass between the *Storstad* and myself...Then the fog came and the *Storstad's* lights disappeared...I looked over the side into the water and saw that my ship was stopped...It was very foggy. About two minutes afterward I saw his red and green lights...Almost at the same time he came right in and cut me down in a line between the funnels."[59]

The *Storstad's* bow went "between the liner's steel ribs as smoothly as an assassin's knife."[60] As a result, the *Empress* sank in fourteen minutes, and only 465 of those passengers survived.

Dunkirk

In May 1940, Allied forces were stranded on the northern French coast near the town of Dunkirk. An advancing German army forced approximately 338,000 British, Belgian, and French troops to retreat. Cloud cover and fog obscured the beaches and prevented the Luftwaffe from bombing, allowing the troops to retreat across the English Channel. According to the UPI in an article written on May 31, 1940:

Thick fog covered the English Channel and Flanders coast today, the official news agency reported, protecting evacuating Allied troops from German air attacks.

The agency indicated that, because of weather conditions, the Germans air fleet had been forced to discontinue for the time being the terrific rain of bombs and machine gun fire with which it harassed the Allied retirement.[61]

Great Smog of London

Fog is not a stranger to London, nor is smog for that matter. In 1661, John Evelyn wrote to King Charles II about "the inconveniencie of the aer and smoak of London."[62] And in many novels written from the 18th to early 20th century, the fog of London is a thing which must be mentioned as a part of daily life. It is typically described as yellow, a color derived from its sulphur content. That sulphur content "hurts your eyes, and takes away your breath; it keeps one in doors."[63]

In December 1952, high pressure settled over London creating a temperature inversion (cool, stagnant air under a layer of warmer air). Coupled with the day-to-day pollution of the city, the worst smog in London's history took over for five days. Daylight never arrived and the yellow smog dropped the visibility so much that some pedestrians could not see their own feet.[64] The particulates in the air, mostly tar and sulphur dioxide gas from coal fires, had about the same pH as a car battery. Four thousand people died from the acid in the air as it irritated lungs and choked people to death. And the Great Smog of London is *still* affecting some people's health more than 60 years later. Exposure to the smog caused a 20 percent increase in incidents of childhood asthma and a 9.5 percent increase in incidents of adult asthma.[65]

The Emotional Connection

WITHOUT FOG IN our stories, you'd lose a lot of 19th century literature from Sir Arthur Conan Doyle to Dickens. Fog was so ubiquitous in London at the time, that any novel set there would be incomplete and horribly inaccurate had there been no mention. Dickens used fog almost as a character to really hammer home the bleakness of the city. In the aptly titled *Bleak House*, Dickens writes:

> Fog everywhere. Fog up the river, where it flows
> among green aits and meadows; fog down the river,
> where it rolls defiled among the tiers of shipping and
> the waterside pollutions of a great (and dirty) city. Fog
> on the Essex marshes, fog on the Kentish heights. Fog
> creeping into the cabooses of collier-brigs; fog lying
> out on the yards and hovering in the rigging of great
> ships; fog drooping on the gunwales of barges and
> small boats. Fog in the eyes and throats of ancient
> Greenwich pensioners, wheezing by the firesides of
> their wards; fog in the stem and bowl of the afternoon
> pipe of the wrathful skipper, down in his close cabin;
> fog cruelly pinching the toes and fingers of his shiver-
> ing little 'prentice boy on deck. Chance people on the
> bridges peeping over the parapets into a nether sky of
> fog, with fog all round them, as if they were up in a
> balloon, and hanging in the misty clouds.[66]

In *The Sign of the Four*, Sherlock Holmes lets Dr. Watson know of how awful it is to have no investigations of late. It's boring. Note that in this case, fog was also used as a metaphor for the clouding of mental faculties from a lack of use.

> I cannot live without brain-work. What else is there to
> live for? Stand at the window here. Was ever such a

> **dreary, dismal, unprofitable** world? See how the yel-
> low **fog** swirls down the street and drifts across the
> **dun-coloured** houses. What could be more **hopelessly**
> **prosaic and material?**[67]

Fog can hide the mysterious and invoke feelings of **apprehension** and **fear**. While Captain Robert Walton was sailing the arctic ice in the begin-ning of *Frankenstein; or, the Modern Prometheus*, he writes to his sister about their ship being "compassed round by a very thick fog" just prior to the appearance of first a "man...apparently of gigantic stature" (the Monster) on a sled followed hours later by another "dreadfully emaci-ated" man (Victor Frankenstein) in pursuit.[68] While the mention of the fog could have been left out, in this case the reference to the weather sets our minds back to a time when we, as a reader, might have wondered if something was hidden out there. We have probably all been there.

Often with fog comes mystery, and with mystery comes **anticipation**. In *The Strange Case of Dr. Jekyll and Mr. Hyde* by Robert Louis Stevenson, the pervasiveness of the fog in the city implies that it's something you just have to deal with, "a great chocolate-coloured pall" that becomes ines-capable.

Fog lowers visibility and therefore hides things from view. Steven-son's placement of the fog in the story is not unintentional; it mirrors the hidden monster within Dr. Jekyll. Note that "even in the houses" could be read as "even within a man."

> The fire burned in the grate; a lamp was set lighted on
> the chimney shelf, for even in the houses the fog began
> to lie thickly; and there, close up to the warmth, sat
> Dr. Jekyll, looking deathly sick.[69]

For the purposes of contrast, take out the fog from that sentence and you would need to remove the fire, the lamp and the warmth. Without the imagery of fog, you would then have "There sat Dr. Jekyll, looking deathly sick." It doesn't have the same imagery or evoke the same emotion as it does with the fog. In addition, the metaphor is missing.

Must it always be gloom and doom? Can descriptions of fog give rise to more positive emotional responses? Claude Monet believed the fog gave London "magnificent breadth."[a] Recalling my survey on weather and emotions, clouds typically conjure up feelings of serenity or joy, provided they are high in the sky and not angry (stormy). The below radar graph superimposed on Robert Plutchik's Wheel of Emotions, shows this.

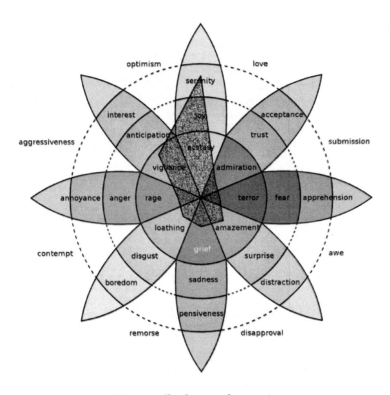

Figure 29. Clouds mapped to emotions.

When on the ground, however, those feelings are morphed a little. It's still a cloud, but the emotions are definitely more diverse.

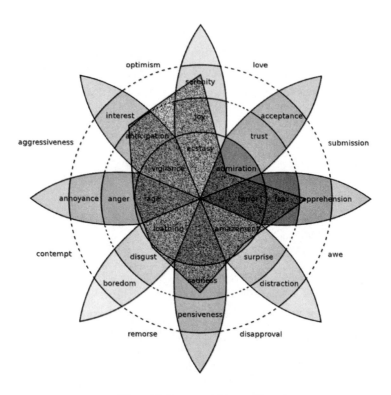

Figure 30. Fog mapped to emotions.

While respondents still selected emotions along the spectrum of **joy** (ecstasy, serenity, optimism and love), there is an equal push toward both the spectrums of **anticipation** (vigilance, interest, aggressiveness and optimism) as well as **fear** (terror, apprehension, submission and awe). So while it's not all happy clouds on the ground for many people—just look at Victorian London—times have changed and there appears to be a push toward the other side of the emotional spectrum. Fog may hide things from us, but we can be *hidden* in fog, as well. We can disappear into the ether.

While fog obscures things and hides them away from the world, what happens when the fog lifts or dissipates? What was hidden becomes visible again. Look at the following image and tell me what you feel?

Figure 31. Photo of fog.

For me, I see this as an idyllic scene, one wet yet mysterious, open to the possibilities of whatever is out there just over those hills. Respondents overwhelmingly chose **serenity** (77) versus the next closest emotion **annoyance** (44). For you, this may conjure emotions that are vastly different. Stick a colorful flower right there in the middle of that first hill and what comes up? Hope, maybe. Optimism.

I ran across something like this years ago. In 1990, a fire destroyed a good portion of a forest on the edge of the Mogollon Rim in central Arizona. About a month after the fire, I went camping, never intending to go into the burn scar, but winding up at the edge, nonetheless. During the monsoon season in Arizona, that portion of the Rim gets a lot of rain. In the mornings, it's not uncommon for radiation fog to form, plummeting the forest into what might be considered creepy to some people.

Figure 32. Fog in a burn scar in central Arizona.

I didn't really think it was creepy at all. The farther I hiked into the forest on that camping trip, the more amazed I was at the surreal world in which I was now a part. From that camping trip, came a short story I wrote which incorporated the fog in a more ethereal way. The main character, Troy, similarly walked through the fog-shrouded forest, attempting to recall his memories (assisted by a ghost, of course).

> Even through the fog, memories of what lay in the sky above persisted. There was Orion the Hunter, Gemini the Twins, and if you looked just above that tree, you could see Mars. In the briefest of seconds, Troy felt like he was there again, the night cold but electric, the wind soft and inviting, the Milky Way painted across the sky in fine brush strokes by a master painter.

> Ian's ghost materialized next to Troy. "What are you looking at?"

> "Can't you see it?"

"I see lifeless trees and death. Fog everywhere."

"In the middle of the clearing, Ian. Look." Troy
pointed a shaking hand. "There's a beginning."

Twenty feet away, two small ferns grew from the
ashes, the green a sharp contrast to the surrounding
palette of gray fog and despair.

In truth, those ferns *were* there, and in the fog I was in at the time, it
really did look like only two. However, when the fog lifted later in the day,
I snapped a picture and found more.

Figure 33. Ferns growing in the middle of a burn scar.

That's the beauty of using weather as a literary device. While there is
diversity in the feelings that may come up when describing a certain
weather event in your stories, there is a pattern to what the reader will
feel. Very few of my nearly 600 respondents said that fog conjured emotions along the spectrum of trust, rage, or amazement. It was mostly **joy**,
anticipation, or **fear**.

IF YOU'RE LOOKING to guide the reader toward a particular emotion in your scene setting, you can use fog in a few different ways. We've seen this in movies, and we've felt this reading certain books. It can be the blurring line between illusion/dreams and reality, or it can portend uncertainty and mystery. Like Merriam-Webster's second definition, it can also be synonymous with confusion, like a wandering loner in your story stumbling through the fog unsure of who or where she is. That same loner might be depressed, but there is data that says it's not all gloom. While sadness is certainly indicated as a response to images of fog, it is not primary.

When we say "out of the fog," is this a reference to freeing ourselves or our characters from something that was holding us or them back? Phrases such as "a great fog was lifted from her eyes" or "the man stepped out of the fog and into the light" come to mind. Fog in this case can be analogous to psychological barriers on the path to healing. FOG—or Fear, Obligation, and Guilt—is a term coined by Susan Forward and Donna Frazier denoting the emotional blackmail that can occur between those who manipulate (typically someone with a personality disorder such as narcissism) and those who are manipulated (the victim).[70] In close relationships, the manipulator uses the known **fears** of another to force them into an **obligation**. The **guilt** felt by the victim is triggered by acting on the obligation (against their desires) or by not acting on it. It is a tense situation and can provide an ideal conflict for many stories.

THERE ARE MANY ways to use fog in stories, and the more you look at it, the more things you can see. Try this on a foggy day: stand outside and look. Don't say anything, don't let anyone talk to you. Put your phone away. Just be one with the ether and melt into the moment. Ask yourself: is something hiding in the fog or are *you* hiding in the fog from something else? After a minute, ask yourself how you feel. If you're tense, perhaps it is because you cannot see that monster just over there. If you're calm, feeling more serene, it may be because you feel protected by the air around you.

Fog may come in on little cat feet, but in doing so, it can play with your state of mind like a ball of yarn. Because it can do that, the same can be said for your reader. Put *them* in the fog and let them be one with the ether. Turn off their phone and let no one speak. The reader is either faced with that which is hidden or hiding themselves.

Procession in the Fog by Ernst Ferdinand Oehme (1828)

EXERCISE: Describing Fog

How do you describe fog? For each of the words below, write one complete sentence using that type of descriptor. For example, if the descriptor is "shape" you might write "An amorphous grey hung over the field." Try not to use the word "fog." If you're having a little trouble, look up "fog" in a thesaurus.

Describe fog with...
...a shape

_____

_____

_____

...a color

_____

_____

_____

...a sound

_____

_____

_____

...a tactile feel

_____

_____

_____

...a smell

_____

_____

_____

...an action verb

_____

_____

_____

Now, take what you've written above and see if you can put it into a paragraph. Again, keep the word "fog" out of your writing. Your description should be enough to inform the reader what weather is there.

_____

_____

_____

_____

_____

_____

_____

_____

_____

_____

EXERCISE: Hidden Things

What emotion do you want to convey in your reader? Describe a foggy day, but first, decide on a **setting**. Is it a forest, a city, a farm? Is it day or night? Don't limit yourself by what you won't be able to see if fog were present, but what you *can* see without it.

_____

_____

_____

_____

_____

_____

Next, roll in the fog. What features disappear? Are they trees, a building, the man standing on the street corner looking at you with what might be an umbrella or knife in his hand? Rewrite the same scene above, but as your character might view it with the fog in place. Is there anything left that you *can* see?

_____

_____

_____

_____

_____

_____

Now, place your character(s) in the scene. Don't let your characters remark about the weather. Show your emotion (i.e., don't tell the reader what it is). How would your characters behave? What would they say to each other?

_____

_____

_____

_____

_____

_____

In the final, step, **remove the weather** and let someone else read it. Ask them what emotion is present. What do they, as a reader, feel? Then, with the weather put back in, ask your reader if anything has changed.

If there is an incongruency, your description of the weather worked. If there is not and your reader chose a different emotion from the one you intended, you might want to rework the description of the weather.

---

[47] Sandburg, C. (2016). *Chicago Poems*. Palala Press.

[48] *fog*. (n.d.). In The Merriam-Webster.com Dictionary. https://www.merriam-webster.com/dictionary/fog

[49] *Origin and meaning of fog*. (n.d.). Etymonline. https://www.etymonline.com/word/fog

[50] *Fog Guide*. (n.d.). National Weather Service. https://www.weather.gov/media/zhu/ZHU_Training_Page/fog_stuff/fog_guide/fog.pdf

[51] *Haze*. (n.d.). International Cloud Atlas. https://cloudatlas.wmo.int/en/haze.html

[52] Graham, M.C. (1905). *The Wizard's Daughter and Other Stories*. Houghton, Mifflin & Company.

[53] Bewsher, P. (1917). *The Dawn Patrol*. Erskine MacDonald, Ltd.

[54] Snell, R.J. (1928). *Witches Cove*. The Reilly & Lee Co.

[55] Reed, M.V. (1919). *Futurist Stories*. Mitchell Kennerley.

[56] Becke, L. (1901). *The Tapu of Banderah*. C. Arthur Pearson Ltd.

[57] Jenner, L. (2020, June 19). *NASA Observes Large Saharan Dust Plume Over Atlantic Ocean*. NASA. https://www.nasa.gov/feature/goddard/2020/nasa-observes-large-saharan-dust-plume-over-atlantic-ocean/

[58] *40th anniversary of the Mount St. Helens eruption — CIMSS Satellite Blog, CIMSS*. (2020, May 18). https://cimss.ssec.wisc.edu/satellite-blog/archives/36701

[59] Marshall, L. (1914). *The Tragic Story of the Empress of Ireland*. L.T. Myers.

[60] *PBS Online - Lost Liners - Empress of Ireland*. (n.d.). https://www.pbs.org/lostliners/empress.html

[61] Grigg, Jr., J. W. (1940, May 31). *Germans say fog let British escape from Dunkirk*. UPI. https://www.upi.com/Archives/1940/05/31/Germans-say-fog-let-British-escape-from-Dunkirk/6502251818433/

[62] Darley, G. (2014). *John Evelyn: Living for Ingenuity* (Illustrated). Yale University Press.

[63] Schlesinger, M. (1853) *Saunterings In and About London*. J. Wertheimer and Co.

[64] Martinez, J. (2021, November 28). *Great Smog of London. Encyclopedia Britannica*. https://www.britannica.com/event/Great-Smog-of-London

[65] Bharadwaj, P., Zivin, J. G., Mullins, J. T., & Neidell, M. (2016). Early-Life Exposure to the Great Smog of 1952 and the Development of Asthma. *American Journal of Respiratory and Critical Care Medicine, 194*(12), 1475–1482. https://doi.org/10.1164/rccm.201603-0451oc

[66] Dickens, C. (1853). *Bleak House*. Bradbury & Evans.

[67] Doyle, C. A. (2022). The Sign of the Four. In *The Complete Sherlock Holmes Collection*. Welbeck Publishing.

[68] Shelly, M.W. (1818). *Frankenstein; or, the Modern Prometheus*. Lackington, Hughes, Harding, Mavor & Jones.

[69] Stevenson, R. L. (1886). *The Strange Case of Dr. Jekyll and Mr. Hyde.* Longmans, Green & Co.

[70] Forward, S. & Frazier, D. (1998). *Emotional Blackmail When the People in Your Life Use Fear, Obligation, and Guilt to Manipulate You.* New York: Harper Collins.

IT'S RAINING MEN, IT'S SNOWING FLAKES

The day is cold, and dark, and dreary;
It rains, and the wind is never weary;
The vine still clings to the mouldering wall,
But at every gust the dead leaves fall,
And the day is dark and dreary.

My life is cold, and dark, and dreary;
It rains, and the wind is never weary;
My thoughts still cling to the mouldering Past,
But the hopes of youth fall thick in the blast,
And the days are dark and dreary.

Be still, sad heart! and cease repining;
Behind the clouds is the sun still shining;
Thy fate is the common fate of all,
Into each life some rain must fall,
Some days must be dark and dreary.
> —Henry Wadsworth Longfellow, "The Rainy Day"
> (1842)[71]

WHAT GOES UP, MUST COME DOWN. PRECIPITATION IS NOT THE most writerly word in terms of weather. Rain, snow, sleet, hail, ice crystals—these are more likely to show up in your writing. To be annoyingly specific, precipitation in the world of meteorology is any sort of water particle, frozen or liquid that falls and reaches the ground. It is much more common to see the word "precipitation" used for "haste" in literature as demonstrated in Washington Irving's *Rip Van Winkle*. "The moment Wolf entered the house, his crest fell, his tail drooped to the ground...and at the least flourish of a broomstick or ladle, he would fly to the door with yelping precipitation."[72] Shakespeare used an even earlier definition of the word to describe the act of hurling or casting down.[a]

I have personally witnessed the many forms of precipitation listed in this chapter, as you most likely have as well. So have your characters (if they have been around for any length of time and don't exclusively live in a tropic paradise or rainless desert). There are feelings associated with precipitation. Just imagine a child staring out a window when it's raining outside and they want to play. Or imagine a messenger prompting his horse along as he frantically tries to get to another town in the middle of a snowstorm. What about floods? Floods are common throughout literature and except for those caused by tsunamis or evil masterminds destroying dams, are mostly caused by rain or the runoff of snow as it melts.

Types of Precipitation

IN THIS SECTION, I'll briefly define the basic types of precipitation without a whole lot of scientific explanation. Frankly, it's more fun to talk about the extremes of weather rather than the minutia of atmospheric dynamics. It is the extremes that allow us to craft vivid stories.

Rain

Precipitation that falls from a cloud and reaches the ground as a liquid is called **rain**. We've all been in rainstorms before, so we're aware that rain can be warm or cold, heavy or light, continuous or more showery. There is acid rain (rain which has absorbed pollution) and supercooled

---

[a] The specific usage is in reference to a Roman method of execution wherein a person was thrown from a cliff. It's *Coriolanus*, Act III, Scene 3, if you're curious.

or **freezing rain** (where the water remains in liquid form below 32°F (0°C) and freezes upon contact with a surface). Rain provides fresh water and is an important part of the ecology of Earth.

Not all rain is the same, and there are categories to be considered. A rain is considered light (and not drizzle) when it falls at less than 2.5 mm or 0.098 inches per hour. It is moderate at between 2.5 mm and 10 mm (0.39 inches) and heavy if it is greater than 10 mm. It is unlikely you will go outside and measure this to determine intensity, although that used to be part of a weather observer's job before automated systems took over.

Have you been caught in a deluge before, a rain that "falls in sheets?" When I was stationed in South Carolina, afternoon thunderstorms could produce heavy rains that would flood the runway and make travel difficult. On one such day, with an atmosphere influenced by a tropical system off the coast, I recall going out to measure the rainfall with the highly technical stick and bucket.[b] It was in the middle of the night, but in the airfield's lights I saw that the taxiway was under what had to be two inches of water. There was a pond near the golf course that had flooded, and the runoff had flowed down a hill past Base Operations. It was there that I witnessed a large carp hopping across the runway, looking for someplace to take off, probably dreaming of becoming a flying fish.

Rain droplets are created through coalescence in the atmosphere and fall based on gravity. At the smallest size, which is 0.5 mm, droplets strike Earth at roughly 4.5 mph (7.2 km/h). The larger the droplet, the faster the terminal velocity. A 5 mm droplet will hit the ground at around 20 mph (32.2 km/h). When that rain is cold, it feels like it's hitting you harder, though.

I'm a person who loves extremes. As a kid, I bought the *Guinness Book of World Records* annually with my allowance. Roaming a Waldenbooks or B. Dalton (in a place called the "mall"), I would frequent the reference section after getting my fill of fantasy and science fiction. Yes, I was *that* kid. Anyway, I learned that places like Mt. Wai'ale'ale on the island of

---

[b] The ML-17 was a can with a cedar stick used to measure precipitation that fell. I can't tell you the number of times I was told to never break the stick. In an age when toilet seats could cost the government $600, how much do you think this stick cost?

Kaua'i gets about 375 inches of rain per year[73] while Mawsynram, India gets about 464 inches.[74] On the opposite extreme, the Atacama Desert in Chile receives an average of 0.1 mm per year, and during a 14-year period between 1903 and 1918, no rainfall was ever recorded there.[75]

It's not just water that falls. Depending on the source (from the Library of Congress to *Britannica* to some book I once found on idioms), the phrase "raining cats and dogs" has different origins. It could have been Scandinavian or in reference to dogs and cats hanging around in thatched roofs to escape the rain and then crashing through.[76] Around 1630, Richard Brome wrote in a comedy called *City Witt* that "The world shall flow with dunces; Regnabitque, and it shall raine Dogmata Polla Sophon, Dogs and Polecats, and so forth."[77]

I don't ever recall reading an article about cats and/or dogs falling from the sky, but it has rained frogs, lizards, and salamanders. Julia Lawton reports that "amphibious rain seems to be picking up in frequency."[78] I find this more an example of our information age, but from the Bible to more recently in Odzaci, Serbia[79], frog deposition by meteorological phenomena is not unheard of. Essentially, some cyclonic rotating thing—a water or land spout—picks up frogs and deposits them elsewhere. Lawton goes on to say this is apparently more a British thing, although in all honesty, it's not that uncommon worldwide.

Drizzle

Rain less than 0.5 mm (0.02 in) diameter qualifies as **drizzle**, not that you (or your characters) would catch a drop and measure it. Drizzle, for the most part, is light precipitation that is less than rain but more than mist. It still falls. When the droplets are supercooled and freeze on contact with a surface, we call that **freezing drizzle** and swear we will never drive in it again.

Drizzle is not as fun as rain in literature (it doesn't drizzle frogs)[c], but it can make a scene that much more depressing. The opening of *Pawned* by

---

[c] However, Twain wrote in *A Yankee in King Arthur's Court* that "we stood under a steady drizzle of microscopic fragments of knights and hardware and horse-flesh." Not exactly a meteorological phenomenon.

Frank L. Packard starts us off with a rather dismal scene replete with drizzle.

> A hansom cab, somewhat woebegone in appearance,
> threaded its way in a curiously dejected manner
> through the heart of New York's East Side. A fine driz-
> zle fell, through which the street lamps showed as
> through a mist; and, with the pavements slippery, the
> emaciated looking horse, the shafts jerking and lifting
> up at intervals around its ears, appeared hard put to it
> to preserve its footing.[80]

In looking through literature that mentions drizzle, I find that it is most associated with words of woe: "frosty drizzle," "a steady, remorseless drizzle," "a quiet drizzle...desolation," "the sullen November drizzle," "a gray drizzle that fell...ceaselessly." It's rare to see drizzle in literature come out as something pleasant to look at.

Hail

Hail forms when a water droplet inside a thunderstorm is lifted above the freezing level. Additional moisture freezes once it comes in contact with the frozen droplet, causing a hailstone to grow. Since hail is ubiquitous with thunderstorms, there is more (including the emotional impact of hail) in the chapter titled LIGHTNING COMING OUT OF THAT ONE. However, it can be said here that in *Meteorologica*, Aristotle figured out *some* of the dynamics of hail production despite it being the most confounding weather element to him. (How, he wondered, could ice fall from warm skies?) It should also be noted that most of the meteorology in *Meteorologica* is **so wrong** that its only purpose now is antiquarian interest. I highlighted the specific sentence, and although technically he's wrong here, too, it's much closer than some of his other conclusions about weather.

> It is also odd that water should freeze in the upper re-
> gion; for it cannot freeze before it becomes water, and

yet having become water it cannot remain suspended in the air for any length of time. Nor can we maintain that just as drops of water ride aloft because of the minuteness and rest on the air, like minute particles of earth or gold that often float on water, so here the water floats on the air till a number of the small drops coalesce to form the large drops that fall. This cannot take place in the case of hail, because frozen drops cannot coalesce like liquid ones. Clearly then **drops of water of the requisite size must have been suspended in the air**: otherwise their size when frozen could not have been so large.[81]

Ice Pellets

Somewhat related to hail, **ice pellets** are translucent drops of frozen precipitation less than 0.5 mm, essentially drizzle hail (although this is not an official term). Ice pellets start off as either rain or snow which falls from altostratus or nimbostratus clouds. As they fall through a warmer layer, the snow melts. If the melted snow then falls into a cold layer (below 32°F or 0°C), the droplets refreeze and appear as ice pellets. If the snow didn't entirely melt before it refroze, the pellets may be partly opaque. One difference between ice pellets and snow grains (below) is that ice pellets are not easy to crush between your fingers. They also bounce, which is kind of neat to look at. From my review of literature, however, I found that *if* ice pellets are used, it is almost always in reference to small hail.

Snow

When minute ice crystals in clouds come together for a party, the result is **snow**. If enough of those crystals join in the festivities, their mass will become heavy enough to fall to the ground. The warmer the air, the bigger the flake (the more "epic the party"). Powdery snow falls through cold, drier air, usually as single flakes (not stuck together). While we associate snow with temperatures below freezing, the biggest snows usually happen one or two degrees above freezing (32°F or 0°C).

Like rain, snow falls in intensities. Unlike rain, however, the intensity is determined by the reduction in visibility rather than rate. A light snow will not drop the visibility any less than 1 km. If the visibility is reduced between 1/2 and 1 km, we'd have moderate snow. Any snow that reduces the visibility to less than 1/2 km will be called heavy. To have a **blizzard**, strong winds must accompany the snow and the visibility needs to be reduced even further to 400 meters or less (a quarter mile).

Snow can be created by a variety of methods. For example, **lake-effect snow** happens when cold air flows over warmer water. There are regions of the United States that are primed for this type of snow, especially those that border any of the Great Lakes to the east (e.g., New York, Michigan, Ohio, Pennsylvania) or the Great Salt Lake in Utah. In November 2022, upwards of 77 inches of snow fell on Orchard Park, NY in one storm.[82] Other places in the world include the west coasts of northern Japan, the Caspian and Black Seas, the North Sea, and the Baltic and Adriatic. Lake-effect snows happen in bands and are highly localized. It is not uncommon for heavy snows to fall in a 20- to 30-mile band while clear skies persist on either side.

My favorite winter weather is called **thundersnow**, not because it is more intense but because the sound of thunder is different than that which comes out of a warmer thunderstorm. The snow acts to dampen the sound of thunder, such that it is only heard within a few miles of the lightning strike that caused it.

When I was younger, I recall having a snow day. This would not be unusual for most of the world, but in Phoenix, it was nearly unheard of. In 1985, a "blizzard" left about 1/2 inch of snow on the roads and the school busses were asked to stay home. Without transportation, the schools essentially shut down (although in reality it was one of those situations where absences were excused). No, it wasn't a true blizzard, but I think any snow in Phoenix would be called that. In fact, I used to have a shirt that proclaimed, "I Survived the Blizzard of '85."[d]

---

[d] I also had a shirt that said I survived 122°F in June 1990. Apparently, I liked weather-related shirts as a teenager. These went well with my Bruce Springsteen muscle-shirts and U2 concert tees.

As for massive snow storms in history, there is a plethora of events from which to choose. In 1888, a storm left 30- to 40-foot drifts of snow in a blizzard that killed 400 people from Virginia through Maine. New York City received 55 inches of snow while New Haven, Connecticut received 45 inches. *The New Haven Evening Register* gave the storm a bit of a victorious feel, however.

> Winter saved its best trump for the last. It threw it today and won the pot. A bewildering, belligerent, blinding blizzard...If there was ever anything like it before in this part of North America, no one remembers it and if they did their testimony against the reputation of this blizzard as the prize storm wouldn't be received.[83]

It should also be noted that "some students were arrested yesterday for throwing snowballs on Chapel St." This from the *Yale Daily News*.[84] How dare they!

Not to be confused with the Stephen King novel of the same name, the "Storm of the Century" in 1993 battered a wider area than any other storm in recorded history stretching from eastern Canada to southern Alabama. Daytona Beach, Florida recorded a low of 31°F (-0.5°C) and places that had likely never seen snow in hundreds of years found themselves looking out at white stuff falling from the sky. Snow amounts ranged from a trace of snow which fell in Jacksonville, Florida to upwards of 60 inches which fell on Mt. LeConte, Tennessee.[85] The death toll was over 250, with 44 of them occurring in Florida, and estimated damages were in excess of $5.5 billion ($11.3 billion in 2022).[86]

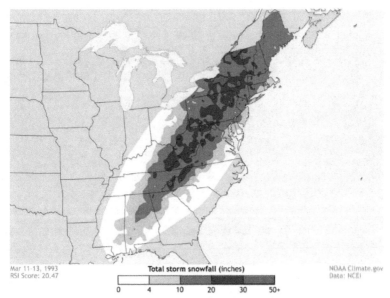

Mar 11-13, 1993
RSI Score: 20.47

Total storm snowfall (inches)

0   4   10   20   30   50+

NOAA Climate.gov
Data: NCEI

Figure 34. Total storm snowfall from March 11-13, 1993.[87]

For the single largest snowfall in a 24-hour period, you can look to Silver Lake, Colorado where 76 inches fell in 1921. The French Alps attempted this feat by producing almost 68 inches in 1959, but the snow stopped after only 19 hours. Rate wise, that's over 3.5 inches per hour. If you were to place a character in that type of snow, what emotion do you think they would feel? Would they be in awe at how much was falling or would they be scared?

Snow Grains & Snow Pellets

If drizzle is to rain, then **snow grains** are to snow. Sometimes referred to as "baby snow," snow grains are flat and very small—less than 1 mm—and they don't bounce. Unless your character is in the mountains, they will not see any accumulation. Unlike ice pellets, snow grains are almost always the offspring of stratus clouds, not cumulus.

Figure 35. Grains of snow.[e]

What *does* fall from cumuliform clouds are **snow pellets**. These are larger opaque round balls of frozen precipitation that may be as large as 5 mm. When they fall, they bounce and break. Occasionally, your character may observe snow falling with the snow pellets or single ice crystals that have not formed around a nucleus. If snow grains are "baby snow," snow pellets are like "Styrofoam snow."

Ice Crystals or Diamond Dust

By far my favorite frozen item that falls from the sky are **ice crystals**— also called ice needles or diamond dust. These are usually seen in polar regions or where the temperature is less than 14°F (-10°C) on clear, calm days. Well-developed plates of ice crystals may appear suspended in the air and create halos around the sun or moon.

In my review of literature, I noted that if "diamond dust" was used in reference to the weather, it was often to describe the appearance of dew (e.g., "the dew-drenched green slopes above and below them shimmering like diamond-dust in the early sunshine."[88])

---

[e] This is one of the few pictures I took with my macro lens that actually came out the way my brain intended.

Figure 36. Ice crystal halo in diamond dust.[89]

The Emotional Connection

Typically, writers (me included) stick to rain and/or snow in their fictional tomes. They are the most prevalent and well-known of the precipitation types, but both can conjure different emotions. When I ran the survey described in an earlier chapter, I discovered there was no one clear winner when it came to rain. In fact, the only emotion that wasn't associated with rain was trust.

Here are two charts where rain showed up more prominently.

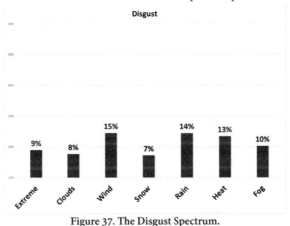

Figure 37. The Disgust Spectrum.

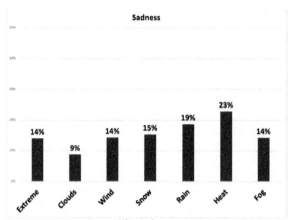

Figure 38. The Sadness Spectrum.

Rain came in second to heat under the emotional spectrum of **sadness**. It also came in second to wind along the emotional spectrum of **disgust**.

In this passage from *Les Misérables* by Victor Hugo, Favourite describes her mood aptly, starting with an observation of the weather which infects the reader right away.

> I am **sad**, you see, Dahlia. It has done nothing but **rain** all summer; the **wind** irritates me; the **wind** does not abate. Blachevelle is very **stingy**; there are hardly any green peas in the market; one does not know what to eat. I have the spleen, as the English say, butter is so dear! and then you see it is horrible, here we are dining in a room with a bed in it, and that **disgusts** me with life.[90]

When I created a radar graph of rain (see below), you can see clearly see the wide distribution among most emotional spectrums. It was more obvious, however, that feelings associated with rain were heavily weighted toward what I would call negative emotions (anger, disgust, sadness) rather than more positive (or at least neutral) emotions (joy, trust, anticipation/interest).

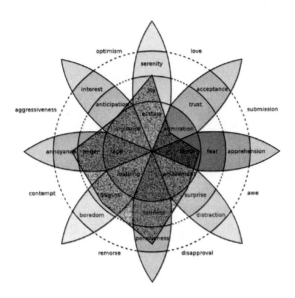

Figure 39. Rain mapped to emotions.

Compare the above to snow in the radar chart below. Note the difference in the distribution. Snow—which is just frozen rain, right?—aligns more prominently with **joy** than anything else.

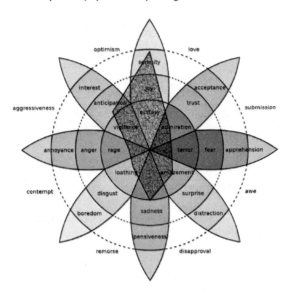

Figure 40. Snow mapped to emotions.

Why is that? Humans (at least as far as my survey shows) appear to feel more **serenity** when looking at images of snow. To me, that made some sense. After all, the image of fresh snow covering the ground and trees on a Christmas morning is pleasant. I also feel that same serenity when looking out the window at newly fallen snow on my deck as my dogs decide whether or not they want to get their feet cold to pee.

Put me in a car, however, and I won't feel that same serenity or joy. I grew up in Phoenix, so driving in snow is not something that comes naturally to me. It might to many others, but in my case, seeing snow fall through the windshield of a car is enough to spark **anticipation** and **vigilance** in me. The emotion your characters might feel (and therefore the emotions you want to tease out of your readers) are more environmental—that is, your character's history (backstory) matters.

As we have seen, using something like rain can also be used to have the opposite effect of what is expected, thus highlighting or exaggerating the emotion intended. Rain can be used to wash away the sins of others or represent rebirth. Without rain, after all, plants won't grow, reservoirs won't be refilled, and silt won't be washed downstream. The same could be said for using rain in romantic or happy scenes. If you've seen *Singin' in the Rain*, you know what I'm talking about. The MsMojo YouTube channel helpfully identified twenty rainy kisses in film. Translate the below list to the written narrative, and you've effectively juxtaposed the expected emotion that comes up with images of rain (based on the weather and emotions survey) with its opposite.

Spiderman (2002)
Breakfast at Tiffany's (1961)
Singin' in the Rain (1952)
Four Weddings and a Funeral (1994)
The Notebook (2004)
A Cinderella Story (2004)
Chasing Amy (1997)
Enchanted (2007)
Garden State (2004)

Pirates of the Caribbean: At World's End (2007)
Daredevil (2003)[91]

ॐ ℗ ॐ

WHILE RAIN AND snow are mentioned above, it's important to look at some of the other precipitation types and how they relate to emotions. So what of them? While I did not specifically call them out in my study, I do have a few thoughts. Mind you, these thoughts are in some ways inferred from experience, the weather and emotions survey, and my reading. They may not be *your* thoughts, and that's great. Our characters are written from our own experience and if that experience was the same, our characters would probably be the same. That would be boring.

Drizzle (droplets of precipitation less than 0.5 mm in diameter) lowers the visibility. As I mentioned in the previous chapter on fog, lowered visibility conjures up feelings of **joy** (ecstasy, serenity, optimism and love), **anticipation** (vigilance, interest, aggressiveness and optimism), and **fear** (terror, apprehension, submission and awe). It all depends on how you set the scene.

You can also use a light drizzle to "dampen the mood" or create a simply dismal atmosphere. To show that the image of drizzle in literature can cause eventual madness, look at this passage from a short story by Swedish novelist Hjalmar Söderberg. God has a dilemma. While He promised He would not again flood the world to purge sinners as He did with Noah, the new world had become just as wicked. What was He to do?

> But the good God said to himself: "Hereafter it shall always **drizzle**. The clouds shall never clear; the mist never lift, the sun never shine more. It shall be **dark** and **gray** to the end of time."

> The umbrella makers and the overshoes manufacturers were happy at the start, but it was not long before the smile froze upon even their lips. People do not know what importance fair weather has for them until they are for once compelled to do without it. The gay

became **melancholy**. The melancholy became **mad**
and hanged themselves in long rows or assembled to
hold prayer-meetings. Soon no one worked any more,
and the need became great. Crime increased in a diz-
zying scale; the prisons were overcrowded, the mad-
houses afforded room for only the clever. The number
of the living decreased, and their dwellings stood de-
serted. They instituted capital punishment for suicide;
nothing did any good.

Mankind, who for so many generations had dreamed
and poetized about an eternal spring, now went to
meet their last days through an eternal autumn.[92]

Talk about dismal. The above passage is obscure, but you can see how
drizzle might drive people mad.

Ice pellets are interesting. When I was in school for all things meteorology, I was told to never call ice pellets **sleet**. Sleet is not a real thing (as
far as my instructor was concerned). But it is to most people, and most
people feel chilled, anxious, or annoyed when there is sleet outside. Think
about driving in it and the anxiety it may cause.

James Oliver Curwood opens *Philip Steele of the Royal Northwest
Mounted Police* with a description of sleet that at once set my nerves on end.

The wind is blowing a furious gale outside. From off
the lake come volleys of sleet, like shot from guns, and
all the wild demons of this black night in the wilderness seem bent on tearing apart the huge end-locked
logs that form my cabin home. In truth, it is a terrible
night to be afar from human companionship, with
naught but this roaring desolation about and the air
above filled with screeching terrors. Even through
thick log walls I can hear the surf roaring among the
rocks and beating the white driftwood like a thousand

> battering-rams, almost at my door. It is a night to
> make one shiver, and in the lulls of the storm the tall
> pines above me whistle and wail mournfully as they
> straighten their twisted heads after the blasts.[93]

Written in 1911, it's not about the sleet on the windshield, but a storm outside a cabin that may or may not be able to take the onslaught of foul weather. For an opening, the passage sets the tone for how the whole book is laid out.

Snow grains are essentially frozen drizzle, but as rain does not bring up the same emotional response as snow, snow grains are unlikely going to bring up the same emotions as drizzle. Frankly, I have only read one story where snow grains were incorporated, and the effect on the character was one of **whimsy** (which was not a choice among my list of emotions). Here's the passage from D.H. Lawrence's *The Prussian Officer*.

> We came directly on a large gleam that shaped itself
> up among flying grains of snow.
>
> "Ah!" she cried, and she stood amazed.
>
> Then I thought we had gone through the bounds into
> faery realm, and I was no more a man. How did I
> know what eyes were gleaming at me between the
> snow, what cunning spirits in the draughts of air? So I
> waited for what would happen, and I forgot her, that
> she was there. Only I could feel the spirits whirling
> and blowing about me.[94]

In my experiment, I did in fact have some images of **hail**. Since hail is associated with thunderstorms, however, the responses to those images fell along the same spectrum as extreme weather, that is **fear** with a slight lean toward **anticipation** and **rage**. Rage makes sense if you imagine hail beating crops to death or breaking car windows.

The emotional impact of **ice crystals** or diamond dust is more **awe** than anything else. I love ice crystals and first saw them when I was living in Alaska. Ice crystals can come in the forms of columns, needles, plates or dendrites. They are so small that they seem to be suspended in the air and occur at very low temperatures in a stable atmosphere.

Figure 41. Ice crystals. Image taken in Russia, date and exact location unknown.

As I mentioned before, it is rare to see diamond dust in literature unless it is being used to describe the glitter of ice on a surface or dew on grass. Ice crystals might show up as **hoar frost** (ice produced by the freezing of water vapor in the surrounding air). Yet this particular meteorological phenomenon has a grace to it that is unequaled, regardless of what you call it. George Marsh in *The Whelps of the Wolf* uses "snow crystals" to evoke feelings of forlorn remembrance. Here the implication that they are actually ice crystals is apparent by the use of the phrases "danced in the air" and "sun-dogs" and "shimmering sea."

> Marcel was walking on the high river shore above the
> post with Julie Breton and Fleur. Like a floor below
> them the surface of the Great Whale moved without
> ripple in the still June afternoon. Out over the Bay the
> sun hung in a veil of haze. Back at the post, even the
> huskies were quiet, lured into sleep by the softness of

> the air. It was such a day as Jean Marcel had dreamed
> of more than a year before, in January, back in the bar-
> rens, when powdery **snow crystals danced in the air** as
> the lifting **sun-dogs** turned white wastes of rolling tun-
> dra into **a shimmering sea.** He was again with Julie on
> the cliffs, but there was no joy in his heart.[95]

Okay, I might be a bit overdramatic here, but I think the addition of ice crystals proper in literature is an opportunity to really create an atmosphere of awe, serenity, and love all at once. You can also juxtapose those feelings with the opposite side of the emotional circle in a way that can be jarring to the reader (in a good way) as Laura Lee Davidson does in the passage below from *A Winter of Content.* The author uses the happiness of being surrounded by ice crystals (identified by the "sky so blue" and "snow crystals so brilliant") to jar us quickly to the fear of an approaching "imbecile."

> I was walking briskly along on the ice, singing at the
> top of my lungs, because just to be alive on a day when
> the air was so cold and clean, the **sky so blue** and the
> **snow crystals so brilliant**, was happiness, when I came
> full on a figure that robbed the morning of its joy.[96]

ॐ Ⓖ ॐ

FLOODS, WHICH ARE covered in more detail in a later chapter, destroy lives and property, but rain can be refreshing. Snow falls gently like cotton on a breeze, but enough of it covers the world in a frozen blanket. While the tendency for authors is to use rain or snow in their narrative because they are known, we can use other types of precipitation to set an atmosphere. There is quite a lot that falls from the sky, some cold, some warm. Turn a raindrop into a snowflake and your scene will change. Drop the temperature enough to allow ice crystals to dance on the air like suspended diamond dust, and your romantic scene will go to a new level of awesomeness. Let your lovers kiss in a downpour of ice pellets and see if that passion lasts.

EXERCISE: Describing Precipitation

How do you describe rain? Snow? Ice crystals? For each of the words below, write one complete sentence using that type of descriptor. For example, if the descriptor is "shape" you might write "Prisms of ice clung together like little balls of cotton." Try not to use the type of precipitation, though (e.g, rain, snow, sleet).

First, pick a temperature: is it above freezing or below?

Describe [your chosen precipitation type] with...
...a shape

_____

_____

_____

...a color

_____

_____

_____

...a sound

_____

_____

_____

...a tactile feel

_____

_____

_____

...a smell

_____

_____

_____

...an action verb

_____

_____

_____

Now, take what you've written above and see if you can put it into a paragraph. Again, try not to use the type of precipitation in your writing. That's the trick to this exercise: if you can describe it well enough by tapping into the senses, you won't need to tell the reader. The reader will know.

_____

_____

_____

_____

_____

_____

_____

_____

_____

_____

_____

EXERCISE: Precipitating Emotions

What emotion do you want to convey in your reader? Describe a day with any specific type of precipitation (e.g., rain, snow, ice pellets, ice crystals). Describe the *effect* of the precipitation on the setting, avoiding any character description or reaction.

_____

_____

_____

_____

_____

_____

Next, place your character directly in the precipitation (don't let them run inside for protection). Have your character do something or say something that isn't related to the weather. The weather in this case should be a background to a conversation between two or more characters or the internal dialogue of a single character.

_____

_____

_____

_____

_____

_____

In the final, step, **remove the weather** and let someone else read it. Ask them what emotion is present. What do they, as a reader, feel? Then, with the weather put back in, ask your reader if anything has changed.

If there is an incongruency, your description of the weather worked. If there is not and your reader chose a different emotion from the one you intended, you might want to rework the description of the weather.

[71] Longfellow, H. W. (2021). *Ballads and Other Poems*. HardPress Limited.

[72] Irving, W. (1887). *Rip Van Winkle*. Blackie & Son.

[73] *Mt Waialeale 1047, Hawaii - Climate Summary*. (n.d.). https://wrcc.dri.edu/cgi-bin/cli-MAIN.pl?hi6565

[74] Abraham, B. (2022, June 18). *Mawsynram And Cherrapunji, The World's Wettest Places See Record Rainfalls In Past 24 Hours*. IndiaTimes. https://www.indiatimes.com/news/india/mawsynram-and-cherrapunji-the-worlds-wettest-places-see-record-rainfalls-in-past-24-hours-572546.html

[75] *World Meteorological Organization's World Weather & Climate Extremes Archive*. (n.d.). https://wmo.asu.edu/content/world-longest-recorded-dry-period

[76] *What is the origin of the phrase "it's raining cats and dogs?"* (2019, November 19). The Library of Congress. https://www.loc.gov/everyday-mysteries/meteorology-climatology/item/what-is-the-origin-of-the-phrase-its-raining-cats-and-dogs/

[77] Tréguer, P. (2022, June 20). *The authentic origin of 'to rain cats and dogs.'* Word Histories. https://wordhistories.net/2016/06/23/to-rain-cats-and-dogs/

[78] Layton, J. (2022, August 24). *Can it really rain frogs?* HowStuffWorks. https://science.howstuffworks.com/nature/climate-weather/storms/rain-frog.htm

[79] *It's raining frogs in Serbia*. (2005, June 7). News24. https://www.news24.com/News24/Its-raining-frogs-in-Serbia-20050607

[80] Packard, F. L. (1921). *Pawned*. The Copp, Clark Co., Limited.

[81] Goold, G. P. (Ed.). (1952). *Aristotle: Meteorologica (Loeb Classical Library No. 397)* (H. D. P. Lee, Trans.; Illustrated). Harvard University Press.

[82] NWS Internet Services Team. (2022, November 19). *NWSChat - NOAA's National Weather Service*. https://nwschat.weather.gov/p.php?pid=202211191624-KBUF-NOUS41-PNSBUF

[83] A Howling Blizzard. (1888, March 12). *The New Haven Evening Register*. https://www.newhavenindependent.org/archives/upload/2013/02/ra_11B327FF69252848_1_4.pdf

[84] Yale Log. (1888, March 15). *Yale Daily News*.

[85] National Weather Service. (n.d.). *Superstorm of 1993 "Storm of the Century."* https://www.weather.gov/ilm/Superstorm93

[86] *NOAA 200th Top Tens: Historical Events: Forecasting the "Storm of the Century."* (n.d.). https://celebrating200years.noaa.gov/events/storm/welcome.html

[87] *On This Day: The 1993 Storm of the Century*. (2017, March 13). National Centers for Environmental Information. https://www.ncei.noaa.gov/news/1993-snow-storm-of-the-century

[88] Oxenham, J. (1916). *1914*. Methuen & Co. Ltd.

[89] andrmoel. (Photographer). *Ice crystal halo in diamond dust* [digital image]. Retrieved from https://www.shutterstock.com/

[90] Hugo, V. (1887). *Les Misérables*. New York, Thomas Y. Crowell & Co.

[91] Not all 20 are listed. See: MsMojo. (2020, November 10). *Top 20 Kissing in the Rain Scenes in Movies* [Video]. YouTube. https://www.youtube.com/watch?v=ryf1JLpAG2o

[92] Söderberg, H. (1923). "The Drizzle" in Stork, C. W. (Ed.) *Modern Swedish Masterpieces, Short Stories*. New York, E. P. Dutton & Company.

[93] Curwood, J.O. (1911). *Philip Steele of the Royal Northwest Mounted Police*. McLeod & Allen.

[94] Lawrence, D.H. (1914). *The Prussian Officer*. Duckworth.

[95] Marsh, G. (1922). *The Whelps of the Wolf*. The Penn Publishing Company.

[96] Davidson, L. L. (1922). *A Winter of Content*. The Abingdon Press.

HOT AND COLD, WET AND DRY

> Summer afternoon—summer afternoon; to me those
> have always been the two most beautiful words in the
> English language.
>
> —Henry James as quoted by Edith Wharton[97]

ON JUNE 22, 1990, WHEN I LIVED IN PHOENIX AND SHORTLY before I joined the military, I mowed the lawn. It wasn't anything special. I went outside, plugged in the 1970s orange lawnmower my dad wouldn't replace, and went to town on the 0.076 acres that made up the little patch of grass in the backyard. When I was done, I put the lawnmower away, poured myself a glass of sun tea (unsweetened, like a heathen) and then proceeded to do whatever it was an 18-year-old boy with nothing but time on his hands would do when he was between jobs.

Nothing of importance.

I didn't think there was anything special about that day, until I was plopped in front of my parents' massive 23-inch television set later that evening. Apparently, the temperature at Sky Harbor International Airport had reached 122°F (50°C) and set a new all-time record (it has since been broken). That's pretty hot when you think about it. Most people would equate that heat to "sticking your head in the oven" hot. As I write this, it's 41°F (5°C) outside, and if my math is correct (I was never good at it), that summer day when I mowed the lawn was 81°F (45°C) hotter than it is right now.

Did I flinch? No. Was I uncomfortable? Maybe, but that's what shorts and Bruce Springsteen muscle shirts are for. Did I think there was anything different about the day? Nope, especially when the days before had been between 115°F (46°C) and 120°F (49°C). What's a few degrees more?

Conversely, when I was stationed in Alaska in 1992 observing the weather in a town named after a fish, I went outside to smoke a cigarette (shame on me). When the air gets really cold, I've noticed a few things: 1) nose hairs can ice over; 2) a deep breath in at a sickeningly low temperature can produce a cough as moisture in the mouth freezes; and 3) cigarettes smoked through a rabbit fur lined parka can ironically prevent any of the other two things from happening while slowly killing you. They can also catch that rabbit fur on fire, but I digress.

The temperature that day had dropped to -34°F (-36.7°C). That was the coldest temperature I had ever been in, but it was nowhere near the coldest recorded temperature on Earth. That happens to be -128.6°F (-89.2°C), which occurred on July 7, 1983 in Vostok, Antarctica. If I do my math correctly again, that would be 250.6°F (139.2°C) colder than the day I mowed the lawn in Phoenix.

Temperature (how we perceive it) is relative. You might be comfortable at 68°F (20°C) and I might shiver a bit as was the case was while living in Hawaii. Anytime the temperature dropped below 70°F (21.1°C), I would grab a light jacket, especially if there was even the slightest of breezes. This perspective will hold true for your characters, as well. Acclimation to our environment helps us survive.

The feel of temperature is also a function of the humidity in the air or the strength of the wind. We know this as the **heat index** and the **wind chill**. Maybe your character grew up in the desert and is perfectly fine when the temperature is above 100°F (37.8°C) but miserable if they move to a more humid climate like Louisiana where that same temperature might feel like 123°F (50.6°C) thanks to the moisture in the air. Or if that -34°F (-36.7°C) I felt in Alaska was accompanied by a 15 knot (17 mph) wind, it would have felt like -64.7°F (-53.7°C). Now that's cold...to most people. I'm sure there's someone out there who would enjoy it.

The Briefest Discussion of Thermodynamics

THERMODYNAMICS IS A cousin of meteorology. Specifically, it plays around with the movement of air and the changes in water because of atmospheric changes in temperature and dew point (the temperature below which dew can form, dependent on pressure). As humans who have experienced weather, we can perceive both the temperature and humidity of the air. You might be aware that on a summer day when the level of humidity is high (i.e., you perceive it as humid), thunderstorms might form. Your body can also predict that on a cold and wet day, ice might form on your car's windshield. Our physiology is a good thermometer and hygrometer.

Visibly, you may have noticed a cumulus cloud grow in the vertical, perhaps becoming a towering or moderate cumulus before your eyes. What you're witnessing is heat rising (convection) and the condensation of moist air into bigger and bigger clouds.

Here are some basic truths: warm air rises and cool air sinks. When warm air rises, it also cools slightly. When it reaches the dew point, the air condenses. There are several factors we won't get into here that can help this convection of air happen more efficiently.[a]

The dew point can have a great impact on the height of the base of clouds. For example, in the desert, air needs to rise higher for it to reach that dew point temperature. As a result, convective clouds (e.g., cumulus, cumulonimbus) have higher bases in desert regions than they do in more humid areas of the world.

Here's another tidbit of information: when warmer air exists over a layer of colder air, the atmosphere is more stable. That is, convective activity—thunderstorms—are not likely to occur. However, if the reverse

---

[a] The Skew-T (a profile of the atmosphere created by a weather balloon) holds vast amounts of information which can be derived from the data. For example, the convective condensation level (CCL) is the level at which condensation occurs if afternoon heating raises a parcel of air to saturation. See
https://www.weather.gov/source/zhu/ZHU_Training_Page/convective_parameters/skewt/skewtinfo.html for more information or if you want to learn a little about Skew-Ts.

is true—cold air over warm air—then the atmosphere is unstable and thunderstorm development is possible. You can look at it this way: WOC is good (like Fozzie Bear saying "Wocka wocka wocka!" while COW is bad (because the atmosphere is "having a cow").

As I mentioned, when air rises, it cools. However, there are times when the atmosphere can be inverted, especially when it's more stable. The air might *warm* as it rises until it reaches a point wherein it begins to cool. This is called a **temperature inversion**, a common occurrence that is often the cause of gloomy days, radio interference, or UFOs.

In July 1952, UFOs were reported over Washington, D.C. These UFOs would disappear when jets attempted to intercept them, and most people described what they witnessed as orange balls of fire, clusters, or white lights. After President Eisenhower took an interest, the U.S. Air Force investigated and explained at a press conference that the sightings were caused by temperature inversions, nothing extraterrestrial and certainly no threat to America. Inversions can reflect distant lights in ways that make it appear like UFOs, and that's what happened. Case closed.

Naturally, this explanation wouldn't stop the public from demanding "the truth." Even the people involved in investigating UFO sightings weren't convinced. The chief of Project Blue Book at the time, Edward J. Ruppelt, wrote in *The Report on Unidentified Flying Objects*:

> On each night that there was a sighting there was a
> temperature inversion but it was **never strong enough**
> to affect the radar the way inversions normally do. On
> each occasion I checked the strength of the inversion
> according to the methods used by the Air Defense
> Command Weather Forecast Center...hardly a night
> passed in June, July, and August in 1952 that there
> wasn't an inversion in Washington, yet the slow mov-
> ing, "solid" radar targets appeared on only a few
> nights... So the Washington National Airport Sight-
> ings are still unknowns.[98]

Naturally, the alien lizard overlords got away. So how do you use this information in your stories? Is there a way to connect the temperature a character feels with their mood? There are probably days when you've been outside, felt the heat, and became aggravated. Perhaps you've even felt sad, unsure of why but you're cold. Are these related?

The Emotional Connection

AS I MENTIONED in the chapter detailing my survey on weather and emotions, there was a possible error. I tried to include pictures of temperature. What picture shows cold (and *not* ice or snow)? What picture shows hot (without people)? Temperature, unlike clouds or precipitation or fog, is not visible yet we feel its presence.

The picture I picked for heat may have unintentionally led people to respond in the wrong way.

Figure 42. A parched desert, dry lake, or just a hot day?

When shown pictures of hot days, such as the one above, respondents typically categorized their emotions either toward **fear** or more commonly toward **sadness**. If this was true, my hypothesis was ruined as I had predicted that images of heat would stir up emotions of anger, rage, or even annoyance. I mean, when I think of heat, I get annoyed these days.

Typically in writing, authors don't add temperature into the story other than to say "it was hot" or "it was cold." They may throw in snow or rain or thunderstorms or tornadoes, but describing a hot day is not as effective for eliciting a response in a reader as, say, describing the drum of hail on the roof of a moving car.

Shakespeare used weather frequently to set the atmosphere of a play. Some have called *A Midsummer Night's Dream* a "wet play" with rather miserable conditions. During the lead up to and any production of *A Midsummer Night's Dream*, England had been entrenched in a Little Ice Age; temperatures were significantly colder in the 1590s and did not begin to warm until the early 1800s.[99] *As You Like It* could be described as a "frosty play" (read: cold).[100] In *Romeo and Juliet*, it can be argued that when Mercutio is killed in the summer, the heat captures both the rhetoric of the Capulets and Montagues as well as the passion between the two lovers.[101]

You can **show** the temperature is cold, of course. Or hot, for that matter. Describing a white field and the crunch of a horse's hooves as it plods through deep snow tells the reader that it's cold. So, too, would describing the profuse perspiration of a man walking down the street, scant clouds in the sky and an overhead sun. On that note: if your character is in a desert, it is rare for them to sweat "profusely." In dry climates, sweat evaporates from the surface of the skin, thus naturally cooling it. In wet climates, however, the air is already saturated with moisture so sweat just stays where it's not wanted. Sweat is our natural air conditioning, so you might feel more comfortable in a desert than a swamp.

Contrast helps. The heat of Verona in summer in *Romeo and Juliet* is contrasted with images of snow. For example, Romeo tells Juliet, "So shows a snowy dove trooping with crows." Later in the play, Juliet parrots those words with "Whiter than new snow upon a raven's back."[102] In *The Adventure of the Cardboard Box* by Sir Arthur Conan Doyle, Watson shows his **annoyance** to the reader near the opening by both contrasting it with the days of winter and saying how he used to be fine with hot weather. As Sherlock Holmes rifles through the paper looking for a case, Watson narrates:

It was a blazing hot day in August. Baker Street was
like an oven, and the glare of the sunlight upon the
yellow brickwork of the house across the road was
painful to the eye. It was hard to believe that these
were the same walls which loomed so gloomily
through the fogs of winter...For myself, my term of
service in India had trained me to stand heat better
than cold, and a thermometer at ninety was no hard-
ship. But the morning paper was uninteresting.[103]

Embedded in the above is what I would call a sort of "lazy hot,"
wherein the day is so hot you just want to lounge around in the shade or
go inside to nap. This is exemplified in *Reginald Cruden*, a young adult
novel written by Talbot Baines Reed and serialized in 1885.

It was so hot that even Squires, after having expressed
the opinion on the weather above mentioned, with-
drew himself into the coolest recess of his snug lodge
and slept sweetly, leaving the young gentlemen, had
they been so minded, to take any liberty they liked
with "his" garden.

The young gentlemen, however, were not so minded.

They had been doing their best to play lawn tennis in
the blazing sun with two of their friends, but it was too
hot to run, too hot to hit, and far too hot to score, so
the attempt had died away, and three of them now re-
clined on the sloping bank under the laurel hedge, di-
viding their time between lazily gazing up at the dark-
blue sky and watching the proceedings of the fourth of
their party, who still remained in the courts.[104]

❧ ❦ ❧

WHAT IS THE connection between temperature and emotion that we can use in our writing? I believe—and this is all conjecture because my survey was flawed when it came to this area—the emotions drummed up by your characters would also be the emotions that *you* feel when you are in that situation. While humans have certain physiological reactions to temperature (e.g., shivering when it's cold, sweating when it's hot), there are also psychological reactions which cannot be discounted.

In an experiment conducted recently, researchers evaluated associations between temperature and emotions both explicitly and implicitly. The study showed that colder temperatures were associated with more negative emotions while warmer temperatures were associated with more positive, arousing emotions. While the emotional spectrum used was slightly different from Plutchik's Wheel of Emotions, the results are somewhat consistent with what you might expect.

> The highest mean values for 0°C were observed with *Blue/Uninspired*, and for 10°C, the highest values occurred with *Passive/Quiet* and *Blue/Uninspired*. For 20°C, the highest mean values were with *Secure/at ease, Relaxed/Calm*, and *Happy/Satisfied*. For 30°C the highest mean values occurred with *Energetic/Excited*, and for 40°C, the highest values occurred with *Energetic/Excited* and with *Tense/Bothered*.[105]

However, the results are based on means. It depends on the individual and their background. For example, I was perfectly calm in Phoenix back on that day in June 1990, more annoyed that I had to mow the lawn than at the heat. But now, if I were to write a story where my characters were placed in such an environment, I would probably do so to show annoyance or anger. Conversely, when the temperature drops below the freezing point, I experience more sadness. So, too, would my characters.

Humidity appears to have an effect on mood as well. This was another area the survey on weather and emotions did not cover, but we can find data on the impact by looking at the research. In a study conducted in Australia on the occurrence of mental health issues correlated with humidity, researchers found that "humidity compounds the negative association between hot weather and mental health."[106] And in a related study looking at emergency department visits in New York state across a fifteen-month window, "hot and humid weather, especially the joint effect of high sun radiation, temperature and relative humidity showed the highest risk of [mental disorders]."[107]

More recently, cli-fi (or climate fiction) has taken root as a subgenre of science fiction. The premise of the genre is to examine the potential effects on the human experience in a world impacted by either natural or anthropogenic climate change. It is typically set in the near future and may contain either utopian or dystopian elements depending on how the writer imagines the human response. In the future world, temperatures are often higher, which brings with it a myriad of other problems (e.g., rising sea levels, increased storm intensities, droughts).

In a recent book by Indie author S.Z. Attwell, the impact of climate change (and the sun's relentless baking of Earth) is shown in striking detail from the beginning. Recall from the survey on weather and emotions that heat often conjures up feelings of **sadness** and **fear** with a little **rage** and **loathing** thrown in. And in the study referenced above, temperatures of 40°C (104°F) were most associated with energetic/exited and tense/bothered.[108] The overall tension (heat) of the characters in Attwell's world is clear throughout, and it is the beginning that sets the tone by describing this so well.

> Even at midnight it was hot, like the slow glowing of an oven that has been left open to cool. The last was punctuated by rock spires and deep canyons that Tark said the Onlar used to hide during the daytime.
>
> Above her rose a massive arc of stardust and shining distant regions, seeming to twist its way across the July sky. She reached out her hand as if to touch it.

Father used to jokingly say that the atmosphere hadn't exactly turned to Venusian fumes after the years of extreme heat began. (She didn't know what Venusian meant, but it sounded bad.) Instead, it seemed to have expanded in the heat, an enormous bubble wobbling and making the stars appear to shimmer and dance, glittering orange and pale shades of pink, melting into the horizon.[109]

YOU, THE WRITER, can use temperature in your stories however you want, of course. To help set a mood or create tension with the reader, it might be wise to look back at the evidence which supports that mood/emotion with that temperature. There is a correlation between emotion and heat (or cold), and while my survey may not have been designed well enough to pull out what that was, other researchers interested in the psychological response to temperature have done so.[110] In addition, we have our own experiences on which to fall, and we can use that experience to craft the reactions of our characters on a hot, cold, or humid day.

Indian Summer by Józef Chełmoński (1875)

Some Helpful Charts

THERE ARE SOME tools you can use both for yourself and for your writing. These are simple charts, but they can give you a sense of "how hot" or "how cold" the scene in your story might be.

Heat Index (from the National Weather Service)

NWS Heat Index — Temperature (°F)

Relative Humidity (%)	80	82	84	86	88	90	92	94	96	98	100	102	104	106	108	110
40	80	81	83	85	88	91	94	97	101	105	109	114	119	124	130	136
45	80	82	84	87	89	93	96	100	104	109	114	119	124	130	137	
50	81	83	85	88	91	95	99	103	108	113	118	124	131	137		
55	81	84	86	89	93	97	101	106	112	117	124	130	137			
60	82	84	88	91	95	100	105	110	116	123	129	137				
65	82	85	89	93	98	103	108	114	121	128	136					
70	83	86	90	95	100	105	112	119	126	134						
75	84	88	92	97	103	109	116	124	132							
80	84	89	94	100	106	113	121	129								
85	85	90	96	102	110	117	128	135								
90	86	91	98	105	113	122	131									
95	86	93	100	108	117	127										
100	87	95	103	112	121	132										

Likelihood of Heat Disorders with Prolonged Exposure or Strenuous Activity

Caution — Extreme Caution — Danger — Extreme Danger

Figure 43. NWS Heat Index Chart.[111]

Physiological Reactions to Extreme Heat

Show don't tell, right? When using heat in your story, you can show the effect by describing the physiological changes a character might go through under extreme heat. For example, your character might cramp after a long walk on a hot day and then get a headache. Maybe they're nauseated or their pulse is fast but weak. This could be a sign of heat exhaustion which would increase the tension in your reader, especially if they know that heat stroke may be imminent.

Symptoms of **Heat Cramps**: painful muscle cramps and spasms usually in legs and abdomen and heavy sweating.

Symptoms of **Heat Exhaustion**: heavy sweating, weakness or tiredness, cool, pale, clammy skin; fast, weak pulse, muscle cramps, dizziness, nausea or vomiting, headache, fainting.

Symptoms of **Heat Stroke**: throbbing headache, confusion, nausea, dizziness, body temperature above 103°F, hot, red, dry or damp skin, rapid and strong pulse, fainting, loss of consciousness.

Wind Chill Chart (from the National Weather Service)

Figure 44. NWS Wind Chill Chart.[112]

Physiological Reactions to Extreme Cold

Notice the time to **frostbite** in the above chart. Frostbite can happen in minutes, especially on fingers, toes, the nose, and ears. It can also happen on *any* exposed skin. Show this in your character through narration. When their survival mechanisms kick in, your character's circulation is going to be cut off and they may experience one of the following:

- First degree frostbite: Ice crystals form on the skin
- Second degree frostbite: Skin feels warm even though it's not defrosted
- Third degree frostbite: Skin turns red, pale or white
- Fourth degree frostbite: Pain lasts for more than a few hours and skin may develop dark blue or black patches

EXERCISE: The Temperature of a Scene

How do you describe hot or cold? Wet or dry? For each of the words below, write one complete sentence using the shown descriptor. For example, if the descriptor is "shape" you might write something about the wavy pattern of the air that happens with mirages in extreme heat (which can also be used as a visual descriptor). Try not to use the words "hot" or "cold" or "humid."

First, pick a temperature: ____°F (____°C)

For reference, 0°C = 32°F; 10°C = 50°F; 20°F = 68°F; 30°C = 86°F; 40°C = 104°F. The formulas for conversion are:

> Celsius to Fahrenheit: (°C x 9/5) + 32
> Fahrenheit to Celsius: (°F-32) x 5/9

Is it humid or dry? _____.

The next step will be to come up with an emotion that you might be going for in your narrative. Write that down. This will be your **emotional target**.

_____

_____

Find that emotion (or an associated one) on the chart below which has been reprinted under the Creative Commons Attribution License from Escobar, et al.

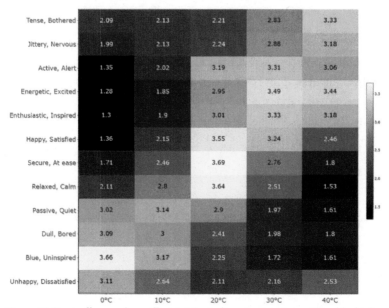

Figure 45. Heatwall map of overall association of temperature to emotion (the higher the number, the stronger the association).[113]

Describe[b] the temperature with...

...a shape

_____

_____

_____

...a color

_____

_____

_____

...a sound

_____

_____

_____

_____

[b] You may not be able to get all of these, especially shape and vision, since temperature is felt. But does the environment give an indication (e.g., a mirage, icy railings)?

...a tactile feel

_____

_____

_____

...a smell

_____

_____

_____

...an action verb

_____

_____

_____

Now, take what you've written above and see if you can put it into a paragraph. Again, try not to use the words "hot" or "cold" in your writing. If you can describe it well enough by tapping into the senses, you won't need to tell the reader. The reader will know.

_____

_____

_____

_____

_____

_____

_____

_____

_____

Next, determine the mood _you_ would feel in that situation. Is it the same as your emotional target? Transfer that mood to a character and let them play out a scene. There should be no mention by the characters (either through internal dialogue or in conversation with another) about how hot or cold the day/night is.

_____

_____

In the final, step, **remove the weather** and let someone else read it. Ask them what emotion is present. What do they, as a reader, feel? Then, with the weather put back in, ask your reader if anything has changed.

If there is an incongruency, your description of the weather worked. If there is not and your reader chose a different emotion from the one you intended, you might want to rework the description of the weather.

---

[97] Wharton, E. (1934). *A Backward Glance.* D. Appleton Century.

[98] Ruppelt, E.J. (1955). *The Report on Unidentified Flying Objects.* Doubleday & Company, Inc.

[99] Fagan, B. (2019). *The Little Ice Age: How Climate Made History 1300-1850.* Basic Books.

[100] Chari, S. (2018). *Shakespeare's Representation of Weather, Climate and Environment.* Edinburgh University Press.

[101] Chiari, S. (2017). Climate as Climax in Shakespeare's Plays. *Shakespeare in Southern Africa: Journal of the Shakespeare Society of Southern Africa, 29*, 1–15. https://doi.org/10.4314/sisa.v29i1.2

[102] Shakespeare, W. (1992). *King Lear.* C. Watts & K. Carabine (Eds.). Wordsworth Editions. (Original work published 1597).

[103] Doyle, A. C. (1893). The Adventure of the Cardboard Box. *The Strand Magazine, 5*(25).

[104] Reed, T. B. (1885). *Reginald Cruden.* First published in book form in 1903 by The Religious Tract Society.

[105] Barbosa Escobar, F., Velasco, C., Motoki, K., Byrne, D. V., & Wang, Q. J. (2021). The temperature of emotions. *PloS one, 16*(6), e0252408. https://doi.org/10.1371/journal.pone.0252408

[106] Ding, N., Berry, H. L., & Bennett, C. M. (2016). The Importance of Humidity in the Relationship between Heat and Population Mental Health: Evidence from Australia. *PLOS ONE, 11*(10), e0164190. https://doi.org/10.1371/journal.pone.0164190

[107] Deng, X., Brotzge, J., Tracy, M., Chang, H. H., Romeiko, X., Zhang, W., Ryan, I., Yu, F., Qu, Y., Luo, G., & Lin, S. (2022). Identifying joint impacts of sun radiation, temperature, humidity, and rain duration on triggering mental disorders using a high-resolution weather monitoring system. *Environment International, 167*, 107411. https://doi.org/10.1016/j.envint.2022.107411

[108] Barbosa Escobar, F., Velasco, C., Motoki, K., Byrne, D. V., & Wang, Q. J. (2021). The temperature of emotions. *PloS one, 16*(6), e0252408. https://doi.org/10.1371/journal.pone.0252408

[109] Attwell, S.Z. (2021). *Aestus, Book 1: The City.* https://szattwell.com/

[110] See also: Noelke, C., McGovern, M., Corsi, D. J., Jimenez, M. P., Stern, A., Wing, I. S., & Berkman, L. (2016). Increasing ambient temperature reduces emotional well-being. *Environmental research, 151*, 124–129. https://doi.org/10.1016/j.envres.2016.06.045

[111] National Weather Service. *Heat Forecast Tools*. https://www.weather.gov/safety/heat-index

[112] National Weather Service. *Wind Chill Chart*. https://www.weather.gov/safety/cold-wind-chill-chart

[113] Barbosa Escobar, F., Velasco, C., Motoki, K., Byrne, D. V., & Wang, Q. J. (2021). The temperature of emotions. *PloS one, 16*(6), e0252408. https://doi.org/10.1371/journal.pone.0252408

SOWING THE WIND

And as she stood looking towards London, Diamond saw that she was trembling.

"Are you cold, North Wind?" he asked.

"No, Diamond," she answered, looking down upon him with a smile; "I am only getting ready to sweep one of my rooms. Those careless, greedy, untidy children make it in such a mess."

—George MacDonald, *At the Back of the North Wind* (1871)[114]

UNLIKE FOG, WIND DOES NOT COME IN ON LITTLE CAT FEET. IT comes in like a 150-pound Anatolian shepherd chasing a sheep thief tumbling down a steep hill. And just like clouds and emotion go hand-in-hand (with respect to literature, anyway), so does wind and emotion.

Weather, as you know, moves. That is to say those clouds you see over there will be over here later. Probably. Unless they aren't. Then they might be somewhere else. Wind plays a part in that movement and it can play a very important part in your settings. As I mentioned in the introduction, wind goes up, down, around a corner and sneaks up a mountainside before falling back (and warming as it does so). Wind blows fences over, uproots trees, and ruins picnics.

Winds bring **anxiety**.

Think about the following scenario (which may or may not be auto-biographical):

A ten-year-old boy is sitting in the back seat of his parents' van. They are on a vacation, an **exciting** thing to be sure. While traveling between Tucson and Phoenix, the family notices a wall of dust approaching from the west. It is huge—a gigantic billowing brown cloud—and it's bearing down on their little van.

Knowing the appropriate thing to do in situations like this, the father moves the van under an overpass and parks. Dust storms (haboobs) are common in the deserts of Arizona, and getting caught in them while driving can be hazardous to your health (or others, if you run into them with your vehicle). The best thing to do is to seek shelter wherever that might be. So, with the van now parked, the boy watches from the safety of the back seat as the cloud of dust approaches. He is **fascinated** by the weather.

A truck driver, also knowing the appropriate thing to do in situations like this, moves his rig under the same overpass, now between the van and the approaching dust. The boy is **upset**. He can't see what's coming. He doesn't know how long he has before the wind reaches them, and now he is **anxious**.

He does, however, know when the wind arrives. The big rig next to the van begins to shake violently. Eddies formed on the backside of the trailer pummel the van and it, too, rocks back and forth. The wheels feel like they're about to come off the ground as the wind relentlessly batters the vehicles under the bridge. The trailer is sure to tip over. The boy is **nervous**.

The visibility drops. The boy cannot see the trailer outside the window, but he knows it's there. The van is going to tip over. The rig is going to do the same and smash the little boy under its weight. All this is happening and it's pitch black outside, the world swallowed up by dust. The boy is **scared**.

As you can see, emotion played a big role in that little story, and that emotion was driven by the wind. You can use the same weather in your own work if you want to increase anxiety, ramp up confusion, or cause your characters to lose their bearings as fear grips them.

Or you can go another way. A sea breeze, for example, can set a rather romantic mood for two lovers on a beach, especially if you describe the gentle caress against the skin or the fragrant smell of salty air as it wafts by. However, along the Gulf Coast of the United States, sea breezes have a tendency to help create thunderstorms slightly inland. When the sun sets and a land breeze sets in, those thunderstorms will be pushed back out to sea (and over the two lovers) ruining the mood.

Analogous to some relationships, actually.

Name that Wind

WIND HAS CHARACTER. It can blow across open fields, up from canyon bottoms, down from thunderstorms or across mountains. As it moves, atmospheric dynamics and interactions with the terrain alter the wind and that, in turn, alters the weather. Wind can warm as it travels down a mountain heating the plains or it can push a cold dome of air off a peak and plummet the temperature in a tiny village below. It can swirl in eddies at flight level and tip planes over, or it can slam into the ground from thousands of feet up, pick up agricultural dust and spread out across a landscape wreaking havoc on the world.

Figure 46. A haboob in the desert.

In 1997, I stood on the western edge of a town and snapped the above picture of a dust wall headed for me. It was tall, maybe 1,000 feet high, and moving around 35 to 45 knots (40 to 46 miles per hour). For those unaware, dust walls like these—**haboobs**, as they are colloquially known—are relatively common, occurring once, twice, or maybe three times a year in picturesque ways. Formed by the expulsion of the guts of thunderstorms as upward vertical motion ceases, they carry dust and grime from the land below and move outward in an ever-widening arc.

Not satisfied with seeing this wall from a distance, I put away my camera and decided to wait until it engulfed me. It wasn't the smartest move, but when you're in your twenties, you think nothing can really hurt you. Or maybe that was just me. For the record, agricultural dust hurts. It stings like needles or a million tiny bees stabbing you with their butts. Nevertheless, I thought it was **exciting**!

Dust storms like that can leave impressions, and if you're not careful, what's known as Valley Fever. Fast forward six years. I started a little story about a girl dying to learn her place in the world while fearing the same dust clouds. That picture—that event—became a character and my novel *Castles* was born.

Truth be told, the dust I inhaled that day which started that novel still sticks to my ribs.

Literally.

In 2006, while being evaluated for something else, the novel—or I should say the *impression* left by the genesis of the novel—was found inside of me. A CAT scan of my lungs revealed a "dot" in the upper left corner which turned out to be a nodule left behind by what's known as *coccidioidomycosis*, a fungal infection I received while standing in the above wall of dust. (If someone ever tells you that you can't inhale a novel idea, refer them to this book.)

The Aemoi

The ancient Greeks were fascinated with the wind, as they were fascinated with everything else in the natural world for that matter. The first "meteorological station" was erected in Athens in the 2nd Century BCE. Called the Tower of the Winds or the Clock of Andronicus Cyrrhestes, the tower once held a large water clock and had no fewer than nine sundials on its outer walls. Triton served as the weathervane and would point to one of eight gods depending on the direction of the wind.

Figure 47. The Tower of the Winds in Athens, Greece.[115]

Each of the wind gods had a character, some of which was derived from expectations of weather or the season in which they typically blew. Alexander Pope used the four main wind gods in a recipe for creating a tempest in an "Epick" poem. This could easily hold true for writing a novel in the 21st Century.

> For a Tempest. Take Eurus, Zephyr, Auster and Boreas, and cast them together in one Verse. Add to these of Rain, Lightning, and of Thunder (the loudest you can) quantum suffice. Mix your Clouds and Billows well together till they foam, and thicken your Description here and there with a Quicksand. Brew your Tempest well in your Head, before you set it a blowing.[116]

Boreas, or the North wind, is represented as a bearded man holding a shell trumpet. The god of winter and cold winds, Boreas has been depicted as a winged god with purple feathers. Homer noted the chill in the air in the *Iliad*.

> Now they were all pouring out from the camp, thick
> and fast, helmets gleaming bright, bossy
> shields, strong-plated corselets, lancewood spears;
> their sheen filled the sky—all the earth laughed
> with the glittering metal, the tramp of men resounded
> under their feet. It was like one great snowstorm,
> when the flakes fly thick and fast through the air, icy
> cold in the clear blast of Boreas.[117]

Kaikias, or the Northeast wind, is another bearded man holding a shield full of hailstones which he gleefully pours on people below. Kaikias is associated with violent summer storms, thunder and hail. While some have said the name comes from the Greek word for badass, I'm inclined to believe that καικίας really means "from the River Κάϊκος" which is where the wind blew over. It's too bad I couldn't verify the badass name.

Apeliotes, or the East wind (at least according to Aristotle), is depicted as a young man with a cloak full of fruit and grain. Apeliotes is claimed to be "nice" while Kaikias was bad. As such, his winds brought the gentle rains of spring and summer.

Euros, or the Southeast wind to Aristotle and the East wind to Homer[a], is yet another bearded man with a billowing cloak. He lounged around with the sun-god Helios and was associated with Autumn. This god could be warm, loud and raucous or calm. It's all in the perspective of the writer. (So, too, are the names of the winds in this case.)

Notus[b], or the South wind, is young man emptying an amphora of water. Bringing storms of late summer and early autumn, Notus lived in Ethiopia and was considered to be a destroyer of crops. In reality, Notus was ushering in a hot and humid world. The Roman name for Notus is Auster, and you may have noticed that Alexander Pope mixed the two in his recipe for an "Epick" poem. In Hesiod's old timey farmer's almanac *Works and Days*, he urges mariners to rush back to shore before Notus arrives.

> Then trust in the winds without care, and haul your
> swift ship down to the sea and put all the freight no
> board; but make all haste you can to return home
> again and do not wait till the time of the new wine and
> autumn rain and oncoming storms with the fierce
> gales of Notus who accompanies the heavy autumn
> rain of Zeus and stirs up the sea and makes the deep
> dangerous.[118]

[a] Euros is used by Pope and many others to denote the East wind, while Aristotle and others in his circle had relegated Euros to the southeast. It was Eratosthenes who was said to have developed an eight-point compass on which the Tower of Winds was built. On the tower, Euros is the Southeast and Apeliotes is the East.

[b] When I was programming climatological applications for the (then) Air Force Combat Climatology Center, our servers were given names based on Greek and Roman gods. My primary server (and the one I called "my own") was Notus, intended to help build maps on the fly for various applications. There were times Notus would be the "destroyer" of my code.

Lips, or the Southwest wind, is a young man holding the stern of a ship. He is said to have either brought excellent winds for sailing or strong winds and storms that would ruin a sailor's day. When looking at the etymology of the name, there are different accounts. On the one hand, Lips could have meant "from Libya" (which is southwest of Greece) or from the root word λείβω ("pouring") because "it brought wet."[119]

Zephyrus, or the West wind, is a young man in a coat of flowers. The word zephyr has come to refer to a gentle breeze, and in the *Odyssey*, Homer mentioned that "Zephyrus with his gentle whistling breeze...comes up from the Ocean to refresh mankind."[120] When Zephyrus came with Boreas, however, the winds came "in a sudden gale, and roll[ed] up the dark water into crests, and far across the salt water scatters the seaweed."[121] So, either Zephyrus is gentle or he is not.

Skiron, or the Northwest wind, is represented by a bearded man with an overturned metal vase filled with hot coals meant to kill plants and burn people. Skiron is associated with violent storms just as his brother Kaikias. Although while Kaikias brings hail, Skiron brings summer heat and lightning. He is also said to bring the onset of winter, I guess because he's pouring out the hot coals.

Modern Winds

Just as in ancient Greece, there are a lot of different names for wind today. Unlike ancient Greece, the names of the winds do not typically evoke some godlike power. Some of these winds are familiar, and you've probably heard of them once or twice. **Santa Ana winds** and **Chinooks** are two of the most common examples spoken frequently in the United States. In many cases, the dynamics behind named winds are no different. They can be **katabatic** (or fall) winds, **anabatic** (or upward moving) winds, **foehn** winds (warm dry winds in the lee of any mountain range), **boras** (violent, dry, cold winds which blow from the north or northeast).

All over the world, winds of the same basic type are given many different names. For example, the **Loo**, in northern India and Pakistan is similar to the Chinook, but to get caught in one increases a person's potential for heatstroke. Foehn winds in Central Europe have been found to increase suicide and accidents by ten percent.[141] Boras can exceed 115 knots (132 mph) and cause a great deal of damage and fatalities.

It's important to get the name right. You wouldn't have a Santa Ana wind heat up the land in eastern Spain. There, you would need to research and find out what kind of wind that is (hint: it's called a **ponentà**).

The Wind in the Sails

WINDS GUIDE OUR weather, and our weather is made up of a lot of stuff (atmosphere). There are winds that you know of which blow you around or knock your fences over, and there are winds in the upper atmosphere (i.e., anything over your head). Earth is constantly in motion, but we can group these winds into three general categories: primary winds, secondary winds, and (you guessed it) tertiary winds.

Primary Winds/General Circulation

You can thank Earth's rotation for the majority of our winds. If the planet did not rotate, air would rise over the equator as it was heated, flow north and south and eventually sink near the poles as it cooled. It would be rather boring. But Earth *does* rotate toward the east at approximately 1,028 mph (1,654 km/h) (at the equator) and takes 23 hours, 56 minutes and 4.09053 seconds to go around once. As the latitude increases (north or south), the rotational speed slows. For example, at 45°N latitude, the speed is about 733 mph (1,180 km/h) and at the poles it is essentially stationary (although Earth does wobble, so this isn't exactly true). This difference in speed is what makes all the following wind discussion possible.

But wait! There's more. If you grab an old record from your grandparents and spin it right 'round, right 'round, then draw a line with chalk from the center to the outside edge, will the line be straight? Not at all. This is what's called the **Coriolis effect** and explains the deflection of our winds. As winds move north (they heat up at the equator, rise, and decide it's time to head to colder climates), the winds shift to the right. South of the equator, this effect is reversed (winds shift to the left as they make their way to the land of penguins). While this is going on, subtropical semi-permanent high pressure areas attempt to return the wind whence it came.

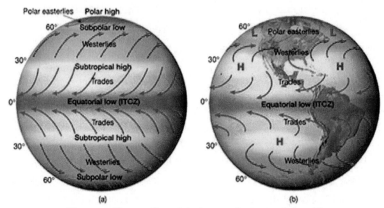

Figure 48. Three-cell model of atmospheric circulation.[122]

Wind goes up, moves, sinks, attempts to return to the equator because it's too cold, then repeats. This action creates the primary winds. Without getting into Hadley, Ferrell, or Polar cells and whole bunch of other stuff regarding atmospheric circulation, here's a basic rundown.

Trade Winds

About 5° north and south of the equator to about 30° latitude, the trade winds dominate. They are mostly northeasterly winds in the Northern Hemisphere and southeasterly in the Southern Hemisphere. They were once a popular route for sailing vessels...you know..."trading" goods.

Westerlies

The Westerlies or Prevailing Westerlies are where we hang out (most of us, anyway). The flow is typically from the west (regardless of hemisphere), which is why you'll find storm systems moving from the west to the east. You can thank the clash between the Prevailing Westerlies and Polar Easterlies for most of the weather in this region (e.g., fronts, storms, snow, rain).

Polar Easterlies

When the air reaches the poles, it sinks and tends to move easterly (westward). This creates a high pressure area with weak and irregular winds. Polar Easterlies are found north and south of 60° latitude.

Horse Latitudes

The horse latitudes are calmer. Some of the warm air that rose at the equator and attempted to make it to the poles gets tired and sinks around 30° latitude. These are where semi-permanent high pressure systems hang out. Skies are typically less cloudy, and the winds don't do much for ships. I don't write history, but you might have wondered why this region of the globe got the name. There are three theories about this, but my favorite (?) centers around the ships carrying horses which got stuck in this region. The sailors would run out of food and water, eventually tossing the animals (horses) overboard.[123]

Doldrums

On the equator, warm air rises and leaves a void, if you will. This area tends to have little if any surface wind and is therefore of no use to ships that would have to traverse it. It's a doldrum (more properly referred to as the Intertropical Convergence Zone or ITCZ). Tropical systems are most likely to form in this area and storms which build overland may come with copious amounts of rain.

Secondary Winds

Secondary winds are periodic or seasonal and associated with a specific region.

Monsoons

There are a few monsoons throughout the globe (e.g., Australia, India, Europe, Africa, North America), but the most famous might arguably be in India. Winds blow from high pressure to low pressure. In the summer in the Northern Hemisphere, a strong low forms from intense heating in the Thar Desert and surrounding areas in northwest India and southeast Pakistan. As a result, the Trade Winds are pulled toward the north, picking up a bunch of moisture along the way, and deflecting to the right thanks to that Coriolis force we previously mentioned. This creates the southwest monsoon so notorious (yet welcome) in the region. Seventy-five percent of the rainfall in much of India occurs from July to September.[124] During the winter months, the reverse happens and a northeast monsoon forms.

The monsoon dominates many aspects of life in India. In fact, Indra was the god of rain on par with Zeus (and even had a thunderbolt). Where the monsoon brings most of the year's rain to India all at once, the rain seems very much like a sudden gift from a god. "No single event is more important to India than the coming of the monsoon," Khushwant Singh tells the *Los Angeles Times*. "It is depicted in all of our literature and song. It is the inspiration for half of our poetry and ragas (ancient melodies)."[125] As the article relates further:

> Practically everyone in India has some personal signal that the monsoon is coming: The delicious summer mangoes from Lucknow, southeast of New Delhi, lose their tartness. The large, black Indian ants become frantic in their search for food, massing over the scorched earth with a collective desperation. A locust-type insect swarms over light fixtures. The late afternoon sky turns a dirty yellow and the midnight heavens thunder impotently, like a god with a hacking dry cough.

The same thing happens in the Southwest United States. Sort of. Called the North American Monsoon, it is created by intense heating in the Sonoran Desert which forms a thermal low. Because again wind flows from high pressure to low pressure, moist air is advected from the semi-permanent high pressure area located in or around the Gulf of Mexico. This warm, humid air creates a monsoon which lasts from approximately July to September in places like northwest Mexico, Arizona, and New Mexico. The effects of the increased moisture and consequent increase in thunderstorms can affect Texas, Colorado, Utah and Nevada as well.

When I lived in Phoenix, the monsoon was a "countdown event" probably because it meant the oppressive heat would be slightly altered by a couple of raindrops. The news channels at the time (this was in the 80s before Internet) would count the number of days the dew point was 55°F (12.8°C) or greater.[c] Three days in a row was the magic number and the "official" monsoon would be underway. Soon, gullies would be filled with water, people would complain about the humidity, and summer would be underway.

---

[c] Dew points above 55°F (12.8°C) are conducive to severe thunderstorm development.

A recent study examining leaf wax found that the Pliocene era had stronger monsoon seasons. In terms of how this will affect the region as the climate changes, the study hypothesizes that a return to that ancient pattern is likely. This means more rain—good for the desert—but also more floods, stronger winds, more damage to the infrastructure, and the potential for more wildfires as plant growth is encouraged.[126]

Land & Sea Breezes

Land and sea breezes occur at the transition between water (sea) and land. Land heats and cools faster than water. During the day, land rapidly heats decreasing the pressure. Since the sea heats slower, a higher pressure exists over water and the wind flows from sea to land. This is a cool wind (not just because it's awesome but because the temperature is lower). At night, the land cools off faster and the opposite occurs. The pressure at sea becomes lower than the pressure over land and the wind shifts. This is a drier wind.

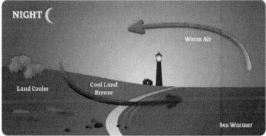

Figure 49. Sea Breeze (top) vs. Land Breeze (bottom).[127]

There are certain manmade features which can alter the meteorology near the coasts. In the Southern U.S., for example, I-10 runs east to west about five to ten miles away from the shore in places like Mississippi. Roadways like I-10 heat faster than the surrounding land. When the sea breeze sets up, the moist air is brought inland which helps to create thunderstorms north of the interstate and away from major cities like Biloxi and Gulfport. When the sea breeze is replaced by the land breeze, however, those thunderstorms move back toward the coast and over the cities. In a relatively unchanging airmass, you can pretty much set your clock by the storms.

Mountain & Valley Breezes

Mountain and valley breezes are much like land and sea breezes. During the day, the sun will heat up mountains faster than the valley creating a pressure difference. The wind will rise up from the valley floor. At night, the opposite happens.

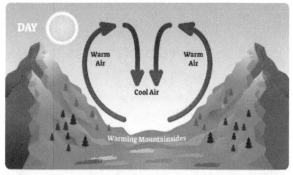

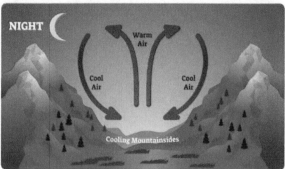

Figure 50. Valley Breeze (top) vs. Mountain Breeze (bottom).[128]

All of this assumes there are no major synoptic scale events going on at the time (e.g., fronts). Mountain and valley breezes are light and often depicted in literature as "soft" or "fresh" or "cool," which in fact, they typically are.

Tertiary Winds

Tertiary winds are related to a time of day or year in a relatively small area. Below are just a few examples of modern named tertiary winds and their impact on life. There are many (many) others which are listed for you in a handy table near the end of this chapter, but these few will get you started. As you read through the list, consider your setting (e.g., Europe, Africa, South America) and then ask yourself how you might use each to set the mood for scene.

Haboobs are typically formed from the collapse of a thunderstorm and bring large walls of dust. While often associated with Africa, they are common in many desert regions of the world, to include Australia, where they are related more to cold frontal passages than thunderstorm dissipation. In the United States, some of the more dramatic examples of storms during the Dust Bowl in the 1930s were also associated with frontal passages.

> The wind grew stronger, whisked under stones, carried up straws and old leaves, and even little clods, marking its course as it sailed across the fields. The air and the sky darkened and through them the sun shone redly, and there was a raw sting in the air. During a night the wind raced faster over the land, dug cunningly among the rootlets of the corn, and the corn fought the wind with its weakened leaves until the roots were freed by the prying wind and then each stalk settled wearily sideways toward the earth and pointed the direction of the wind.
>
> The dawn came, but no day. In the gray sky a red sun appeared, a dim red circle that gave a little light, like

dusk; and as that day advanced, the dusk slipped back toward darkness, and the wind cried and whimpered over the fallen corn.[129]

From the Arabic word for "fifty," **khamsin** (or khamaseen in Egypt) blow during a 50-day period between March and May in places like North Africa. The wind speed can be as much as 75 knots (86 mph) and with the sand comes dry, hot weather. These storms were said to impede Napoleon as well as conflicts between the Germans and Allies during World War II. In the Book of Exodus, it is said that this "east wind" parted the Red Sea.[d] This wind is similar to the **ghibli** in Tunis, the **sirocco**, and **simoom**. Because of its occurrence around April, it is often used in literature set in Egypt to denote a season.

In Asia, the **buran** (or **purga** when blowing over the tundra) is a powerful and cold northeasterly wind full of ice and snow that causes blizzard conditions. Most frequently, the buran occurs in Mongolia and Siberia. The buran is to be feared and can last for weeks.

> "It is a scientific fact that the sands march. During the kara burans or black wind-storms they will progress many feet a day. Sungan was built on the great caravan route from China to Samarcand and Persia, many centuries ago. Marco Polo followed this route when he visited the court of Kubla Khan... Sungan has been buried by the marching sands. Only the towers remain."[130]

A strong katabatic (fall) wind that blows across the Kanto Plain in Japan is called the **oroshi**. The wind blows down from the mountains and brings with it a rapid temperature decrease of several degrees.[131] High pressure to the west and low pressure to the east causes the winds to blow

---

[d] Exodus 14:21 (KJV): "And Moses stretched out his hand over the sea; and the Lord caused the sea to go back by a strong east wind all that night, and made the sea dry land, and the waters were divided."

across and up various mountains and then down the other side.

The **loo** is a hot wind which blows over the plains of India and Pakistan. This dry wind, typically occurring between May and June, brings very high temperatures (up to 120°F or 48.9°C). Plants dry out, the humidity lowers, and people and pets suffer from heat strokes. To give you an example of the power of the loo, here's a passage from *Twilight in Delhi* by Ali Ahmed.

> The temperature rose higher and higher until it reached one hundred and fifteen in the shade. From seven in the morning the loo began to moan, blowing drearily through the hopeless streets. The leaves of the henna tree became seared and wan, and the branches of the date palm became coated with sand. The dust blew through the unending noon; and men went out with their heads well-covered and protected....The sky lost its colour and became dirty and bronzed. The loo did not even stop at night. The stars flickered in the sky behind the covering layer of dust. The sand rained down all night, came between the teeth, covered the beds, and sleep did not come near parched humanity.
>
> Tempers rose and from all around came the loud voices of women quarrelling, husbands beating their wives, other their children, and there seemed no rest for man.[132]

In Argentina and Uruguay there is a severe line squall that occurs over the Pampas. This is called a **pampero** and denotes the passage of a cold front. There are two parts: first, the temperature drops considerably, humidity rises, and severe thunderstorms occur. Following this, however, is a cold, dry, gusty wind from the south or southwest which brings dust.

Jules Verne talked about the Pampero in his novel *In Search of Castaways*. I will not argue the use of "hurricane" here. It's Verne.

The sun's rays were extremely scorching, and when evening came, a bar of clouds streaked the southwest horizon—a sure sign of a change in the weather. The Patagonian pointed it out to the geographer, who replied:

"Yes, I know;" and turning to his companions, added, "see, a change of weather is coming! We are going to have a taste of PAMPERO."

And he went on to explain that this PAMPERO is very common in the Argentine plains. It is an extremely dry wind which blows from the southwest. Thalcave was not mistaken, for the PAMPERO blew violently all night, and was sufficiently trying to poor fellows only sheltered by their ponchos. The horses lay down on the ground, and the men stretched themselves beside them in a close group. Glenarvan was afraid they would be delayed by the continuance of the hurricane, but Paganel was able to reassure him on that score, after consulting his barometer.

"The PAMPERO generally brings a tempest which lasts three days, and may be always foretold by the depression of the mercury," he said. "But when the barometer rises, on the contrary, which is the case now, all we need expect is a few violent blasts. So you can make your mind easy, my good friend; by sunrise the sky will be quite clear again.[133]

Competing for the top prize for the best name, a **williwaw** is a violent and sudden cold katabatic (fall) wind which descends from a mountainous coast to the sea. Williwaws occur commonly in the Strait of Magellan or the Aleutian Islands. Williwaws have a rich literary tradition. After all, Gore Vidal named a book after it.

> He turned around to speak to Evans and at that moment the williwaw hit the ship.

> Martin was thrown across the wheelhouse. There was a thundering in his ears. He managed to grasp the railing and, desperately, he clung to it.

> The wheelhouse hit the water with a creaking smack. For a minute the deck of the wheelhouse was at a right angle with the water. Then, slowly, the ship righted herself.

> Evans, he saw, lay flat on the steep deck. The man who had been at the wheel was huddled near the companionway. The wheel was spinning aimlessly.

> The ship shuddered as tremendous waves lifted her high in the air. Martin, confused and helpless, shut his eyes and wished that the huge sound of the wind would go away.

> When he opened his eyes again he saw Evans crawling on hands and knees across the deck. Martin watched him move closer and closer to the wheel. A sudden lunge of the ship and Evans was thrown against it. Quickly he caught the wheel. Martin watched as Evans fought grimly to keep on course.[134]

Depending on the region, **Chinooks** are warm and dry winds coming off the Rocky Mountains *or* warm and *wet* winds coming off the ocean. In the Pacific Northwest, a Chinook (pronounced "CHIN"-ook) brings in moisture as both rain on the coast and snow in the mountains. This moisture is what allows the rainforests of this region to be what they are (i.e., rainy, wet). A Chinook (pronounced "SHIN"-ook) is a warm dry foehn wind that comes off the Rockies into the Great Plains of the United States. The Blackfoot call these winds "snow eaters" as they have been known to make a foot of snow disappear in a day.[135] A Chinook like this can raise the temperature upwards of 70°F (40°C) in hours. In fact, here are two world records for you.

- The most extreme 24-hour change: January 25, 1972, Loma, Montana—from -54°F (-47.8°C) to 49°F (9.4°C), a 103°F (57.2°C) difference.[136]

- The fastest increase in temperature: January 22, 1943, Spearfish, South Dakota—from -4°F (-20°C) to 45°F (7.2°C) in 2 minutes.[137]

The **Santa Ana winds** of Southern California are katabatic (fall) winds. These strong winds are warm and dry and are known to make fires much worse. They are created as air is pulled from higher pressure in the Great Basin to lower pressure off the coast. The wind flows through mountain passes and increases in speed. When the wind descends to lower elevations, the temperature increases, and moisture decreases. Since much of the moisture had already been wrung out by orographic lift (rising into the mountains), the result is a very strong, very warm, very dry wind slamming into high population centers like Los Angeles and San Diego.

Many of Southern California's wildfires are exacerbated by Santa Ana winds, which can gust up to 152 knots (175 mph).[138] That speed can cause a host of other problems to include destroying orchards, damaging buildings, and carrying coccidioidomycosis, otherwise known as Valley Fever.

In one of those books that begin with the weather, Raymond Chandler (of Philip Marlowe fame) writes:

> There was a desert wind blowing that night. It was one
> of those hot dry Santa Anas that come down through
> the mountain passes and curl your hair and make your

nerves jump and your skin itch. On nights like that every booze party ends in a fight. Meek little wives feel the edge of the carving knife and study their husbands' necks. Anything can happen. You can even get a full glass of beer at a cocktail lounge.[139]

The Emotional Connection

BY FAR, IMAGES (or thoughts) of wind evoke feelings along the spectrum of **fear** (terror, apprehension, awe, submission). In the survey on weather and emotions, images depicting wind were associated with these emotions 26% of the time, far more than the next closest emotional spectrums of **disgust** (loathing, boredom, contempt, remorse) and **anger** (rage, annoyance, aggressiveness, contempt), both of which received 15% each.

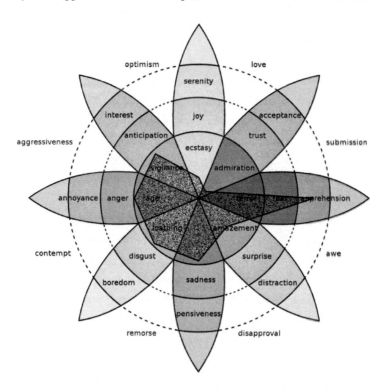

Figure 51. Wind mapped to emotions.

However you use wind in your stories, consider the emotion that you want to arouse in your reader. If it's a fear of what's to come, a cold wind sure will help. If it's excitement coupled with a fear of the present, you might want to consider a hot wind or haboob.

You can also use wind in an allegorical way. Just as rain can wash things away, wind can do the same. It can be cleansing, or it can portend the advent of something awful happening. It can be the difference between one state of being (calm) and another (tumultuous). Here in my part of the world, the wind picks up in intensity a few hours before snow as a cold front moves through. I find myself highly anxious when I hear the wind blow, yet I would rather be inside than out. In *Moby Dick*, Ishmael comments on the difference between being inside when the wind blows "with his feet on the hob quietly toasting for bed" or outside. Through the use of the wind storm (a Euroclydon), we see the vast difference between wealth and poverty.

> It was a queer sort of place—a gable-ended old house, one side palsied as it were, and leaning over sadly. It stood on a sharp bleak corner, where that tempestuous wind Euroclydon kept up a worse howling than ever it did about poor Paul's tossed craft. Euroclydon, nevertheless, is a mighty pleasant zephyr to any one indoors, with his feet on the hob quietly toasting for bed. "In judging of that tempestuous wind called Euroclydon," says an old writer—of whose works I possess the only copy extant—"it maketh a marvellous difference, whether thou lookest out at it from a glass window where the frost is all on the outside, or whether thou observest it from that sashless window, where the frost is on both sides, and of which the wight Death is the only glazier."...Poor Lazarus there, chattering his teeth against the curbstone for his pillow, and shaking off his tatters with his shiverings, he might plug up both ears with rags, and put a corn-cob into his

mouth, and yet that would not keep out the tempestu-
ous Euroclydon. Euroclydon! says old Dives, in his
red silken wrapper—(he had a redder one afterwards)
pooh, pooh! What a fine frosty night; how Orion glit-
ters; what northern lights! Let them talk of their orien-
tal summer climes of everlasting conservatories; give
me the privilege of making my own summer with my
own coals.

But what thinks Lazarus? Can he warm his blue hands
by holding them up to the grand northern lights?
Would not Lazarus rather be in Sumatra than here?
Would he not far rather lay him down lengthwise
along the line of the equator; yea, ye gods! go down to
the fiery pit itself, in order to keep out this frost?[140]

WIND CAN MAKE you crazy. I know this for a fact. As I sit in my office and
write this, the winds are howling outside. Early in the morning, a speed
of 91 knots (105 mph) was recorded at an observing station nearby.
Winds like this blow fences over and make me want to put earphones on
and listen to something calming like Iron Maiden or Black Sabbath. The
dogs refuse to go outside. The waste truck has decided to wait a day. A
truck just flipped over on the freeway.

In case you're not sure if the wind can really have an effect on the
emotional state of humans, consider the following. Researchers in Swit-
zerland analyzed records of patients in a psychiatric hospital near an area
which is frequently beset by foehn winds. **Foehn winds** occur in the Swiss
alps, descending from the tops of the mountains into the valleys, warming and drying the air. They are often severe and reach speeds upwards
of 109 knots (125 mph). Looking at records from 2013 through 2020, the
study concluded that foehn winds increased distress and negatively impacted more unstable individuals leading them to seek hospitalization in
a psychiatric clinic, stating "at the time of admission, foehn episodes
might have a negative influence on several specific psychopathological

dimensions, namely, obsession–compulsion, interpersonal sensitivity, depression, anxiety, phobic anxiety, and paranoid ideation."[141] It was not immediate, however. The negative effects were found to lag two days behind the wind event.

While the study was limited to those with mental disorders or those who were unstable enough to have sought psychiatric treatment, the effect of wind is not limited to this population. Many notable people in history have complained in some way about the wind, from Darwin to Columbus to Michelangelo to Milton to Wagner. For Voltaire, a wind coming from the east was particularly disastrous.

> This east wind, is responsible for numerous cases of suicide...Black melancholy spreads over the whole nation. Even the animals suffer from it and have a dejected air. Men who are strong enough to preserve their health in this accursed wind at least lose their good humor. Everyone wears a grim expression and is inclined to make desperate decisions. It was literally in an east wind that Charles I was beheaded and James II deposed.[142]

Some of the differences in our reactions to wind are gender-biased. Women tend to seek shelter from strong wind, while men become exceedingly restless. I'm sure there are theories on why this is, but the physiology is the same: adrenaline increases, large blood vessels dilate, and pupils widen—all precursors to your sympathetic nervous system's fight or flight responses.

On the side of fight, Lyall Watson writes that in 1968, statistics of homicides were reviewed in Los Angeles county and found that on 34 of 53 days affected by Santa Ana winds between 1964 and 1965, there were more deaths. In one week during October 1965, the murder rate was 47 percent higher than in any other week.[143] Incidentally, the Santa Ana winds are either named from the pass through which they travel or from a Native American word meaning "devil wind." I'm going to go with the latter, here.

Looking back at the survey on weather and emotions, wind evokes feelings along the spectrum of **fear** (terror, apprehension, awe, submission), which is consistent with the Swiss study that found an increase in depression, anxiety, and paranoia. It is more common for the wind to make people crazy than it is for it make them feel safe, calm, or even loved. With that in mind, you could highlight a character's instability by putting them in a strong wind (named based on the area in which the story is set) and then showing the reader their breakdown. You could also reverse that for a strong character and show their resilience in the face of an unrelenting gale. It's up to you.

The Gust of Wind by Jean-François Millet (1871-73)

A Handy Table of Localized (Tertiary) Winds[144]

USE THIS TABLE if you want to bring in a little local flair to your story. There are likely many other local winds out there, some only known by a few residents but named, nonetheless. This is just a start.[e]

Continent	Region/ Country	Wind	Distinct Features
Africa	S. Africa	berg	A katabatic wind blowing down the Great Escarpment from the high central plateau to the coast in South Africa.
Africa	S. Africa	Cape Doctor	often persistent and dry SE wind that blows on the South African coast from September to March
Africa	Canary Islands	calima	a hot, oppressing dust and sand-laden, S to SE, sometimes E wind in the Canary Islands region
Africa	Libya	ghibli	a hot, dry, usually S to SE dust-bearing desert wind, that occurs throughout the year, but most frequently in spring and early summer; a local name for sirocco
Africa	Sudan	haboob	a sandstorm with fast moving wind which decreases the temperature over the area it passes
Africa	Sahara	harmattan	a dry wind that blows from the NE, bringing dust from the Sahara Desert south toward the Gulf of Guinea

---

[e] Every effort has been made to determine the capitalization of these winds. However, I encourage you to do your own research to find out if a name is proper or not.

Continent	Region/ Country	Wind	Distinct Features
Africa	N. Africa	khamsin	an oppressive, hot, dry and dusty S or SE wind occurring in N. Africa, E. Mediterranean and the Arabian Peninsula; occurs intermittently in late winter and early summer, but most frequently between April and June
Africa	Saudi Arabia, Syria	simoom	a very hot, dry, suffocating, and dust-laden wind that blasts across the African deserts, notably in Saudi Arabia, Syria, and neighboring countries; generated by the extreme heat of the parched deserts or sandy plains
Africa	N. Africa	sirocco	any hot and subsequently humid SE to SW wind originating as hot, dry desert-air over Northern Africa, flowing N into the southern Mediterranean basin
Asia	India	Kali Andhi	the "black storm"; a violent, squally dust storm occurring in late spring in NW India; the Andhi heralds the imminent arrival of the monsoon
Asia	Philippines	Amihan	NE wind across the Philippines
Asia	Indonesia	barat	a squally and strong W to NW wind occurring from December to February along the northern coasts of the Celebes (Sulawesi), Indonesia
Asia	Russia	Barguzin	steady, strong wind on Lake Baikal in Russia

Continent	Region/ Country	Wind	Distinct Features
Asia	Mongolia, Siberia	buran	A strong cold NE wind creating extreme blizzard conditions during winter
Asia	India	Elephanta	strong S or SE wind on the Malabar coast of India
Asia	Azerbaijan Republic	gilavar	S wind in the Absheron Peninsula of the Azerbaijan Republic
Asia	Philippines	Habagat	SW wind across the Philippines
Asia	Central Asia	karaburan	"power storm"; a spring and winter katabatic wind of Central Asia
Asia	Japan	karakkaze	strong cold mountain wind from Gunma Prefecture in Japan
Asia	Caspian Sea	khazri	cold, coastal gale-force wind of the northern Caspian Sea
Asia	India, Pakistan	loo	hot wind which blows over the plains of India and Pakistan
Asia	Persian Gulf	n'aschi	NE wind on the Iranian coast of the Persian Gulf, and on the Makran coast
Asia	Japan	oroshi	strong katabatic wind across the Kanto Plain
Asia	Persian Gulf	quas, kaus, cowshee	a moderate to gale-force SE wind in the Persian Gulf, most frequent between December and April, when eastward traveling winter depressions from the Mediterranean Sea moving across the Middle East become reinvigorated over warm Persian Gulf waters

Continent	Region/Country	Wind	Distinct Features
Asia	Iraq	Rashabar	a strong wind in the Kurdistan Region of Iraq, particularly in Sulaimaniya
Asia	Lake Baikal	Sarma	a cold, strong wind on the western shore of Lake Baikal
Asia	Iraq	shamal	a summer NW wind blowing over Iraq and the Persian Gulf states
Asia	Middle East	sharqi	seasonal dry, dusty Middle Eastern wind coming from the S and SE
Asia	Kazakhstan	sukhovey	hot dry wind in the steppes, semi-deserts, and deserts of the Kazakhstan and the Caspian region
Asia	Iran	Wind of 120 Days	a strong summer wind occurring from late May to late September in the east and southeast of the Iranian Plateau
Central America & the Caribbean	Cuba	bayamo	violent wind on Cuba's southern coast
Central America & the Caribbean	Baja California	Coromuel	S to SW wind in the La Paz area of the Baja California peninsula and the Gulf of California
Central America & the Caribbean	Mexico	Norte	Strong, cold NE wind; primarily affects the states along the coast, including: Tamaulipas, Veracruz, Tabasco, Campeche, and Yucatán
Central America & the Caribbean	Nicaragua, Costa Rica	Papagayo jet	periodic wind which blows across Nicaragua and Costa Rica and out over the Gulf of Papagayo

Continent	Region/ Country	Wind	Distinct Features
Central America & the Carib- bean	Mexico	Tehuante- pecer, Tehuano	a violent, squally N or NE mountain-gap wind in the Gulf of Tehuantepec on the Pacific coast of southern Mex- ico
Europe	Britain	Helm	a strong NE wind which blows down the SW slope of the Cross Fell escarpment
Europe	France	autan, antane, autune	a SE, foehn-type wind starting in the Mediterranean and blowing across the Languedoc into the Tarn and Garonne valleys affecting the Lauragais and the Toulouse area
Europe	Switzer- land, France	Bise	a cold, vigorous and persistent N or NE wind blowing from the alpine mountains
Europe	C. Europe	böhm, Bohemian Wind	cold, dry wind in Central Eu- rope
Europe	Adriatic Sea	bora	a cold and typically very dry and often gusty katabatic wind from the NE
Europe	France	burle	N wind which blows in the winter in south-central France
Europe	France	Cers	strong, very dry NE wind in the bas-Languedoc region in southern France
Europe	Spain	ciezro	cool N or NW wind on Ebro Valley in Spain
Europe	C. Europe	crivăț	strong, very cold NE wind in Moldavia, Dobruja, and the Bărăgan Plain parts of Roma- nia

Continent	Region/ Country	Wind	Distinct Features
Europe	Greece	Etesian, meltem	prevailing summer winds, blowing over large parts of Greece, the Aegean Sea and eastern Mediterranean
Europe	Mediterra- nean	Eurocly- don	a cyclonic strong NE wind in the Mediterranean; see Acts 27:14 "But not long after there arose against it a tempestuous wind, called Euroclydon."[145]
Europe	Italy	foehn, föhn	a warm, dry, S wind off the northern side of the Alps and North Italy
Europe	Malta	gregale	a Mediterranean wind that can occur during times when low pressure moves through the area to the south of Malta, cre- ating a strong, cool, NE wind to affect the island
Europe	C. Europe	halny	a foehn wind that blows in southern Poland and in Slo- vakia in the Tatra Mountains of the Carpathians
Europe	Bulgaria	karajol, qarajel, quara	a W wind on the Bulgarian coasts; typically follows a pe- riod of rain and persists for 1 to 3 days
Europe	Serbia	košava	a strong, cold SE seasonal wind in Serbia
Europe	Strait of Gibraltar	levante, levanter	a warm, E to NE wind that flows from the Alboran Chan- nel and is funneled through the Strait of Gibraltar

Continent	Region/Country	Wind	Distinct Features
Europe	Corsica	libeccio, leveche	the W or SW wind which predominates in northern Corsica all year round
Europe	Strait of Gibraltar	llevantades	an intense form of the levante
Europe	Aegean Sea, Turkey	lodos	strong SW wind may predominate episodically in the Aegean Sea and Marmara Sea as well as the Mediterranean coast of Turkey
Europe	France, Italy	Lombarde	E to NE wind that predominates the French-Italian borders
Europe	Adriatic Sea	maestro	an anabatic sea-breeze wind which blows in the summer when the east Adriatic coast gets warmer than the sea
Europe	Germany	moazagoatl	a foehn type wind; marked by a lee wave rotor cloud, a stationary bank of cirrostratus marking the upper portion of the system of lenticular clouds produced by flow across the Sudeten Mountains in southeastern Germany
Europe	France	Marin	a warm, moist wind in the Gulf of Lion of France, blowing from the SE or SSE onto the coast of Languedoc and Roussillon

Continent	Region/ Country	Wind	Distinct Features
Europe	Spain, Italy	mistral	Strong, cold, dry and squally N wind that blows offshore with great frequency along the Mediterranean coast from northern Spain to northern Italy; frequent in the lower Rhone valley in SE France
Europe	Spain	Nordés	NE wind in Spain
Europe	Adriatic Sea	ostro, austro	S wind in the Mediterranean Sea, especially in the Adriatic
Europe	Spain, Strait of Gibraltar	poniente, ponentà, ponent	strong W to E wind formed by the wind tunnel effect of the Strait of Gibraltar; the opposite of the lavante
Europe	Mediterranean	solano	an E to SE wind; a regional variation or extension of the sirocco that refers to the relative position between the North African coast and southern Spain and not any of the other countries around the Mediterranean Sea
Europe	Spain, Italy	tramontana, garigliano	cold northwesterly from the Pyrenees or northeasterly from the Alps to the Mediterranean; similar to mistral
Europe	Macedonia	vardar	a cold NW wind blowing from the mountains down to the valleys of Macedonia
Europe	Morocco	vendavel	W wind that blows into the Mediterranean Sea around the Strait of Gibraltar and Morocco

Continent	Region/ Country	Wind	Distinct Features
North America	Canada	Alberta Clipper	fast-moving, frigid winter wind out of the central Canadian plains that swoops down across the U.S. Plains, Midwest and Great Lakes
North America	United States	Barber	a severe wind, generally blowing E to SE; carries sleet, snow, or spray at air temperatures close to the freezing point
North America	Oregon	Brookings Effect, Chetco Effect	off-shore wind on the SW Oregon coast
North America	United States	Chinook	warm dry W wind off the Rocky Mountains
North America	California	Diablo	hot, dry, offshore wind from the NE in San Francisco Bay
North America	California	Jarbo Gap Wind	a locally named wind in California's Jarbo Gap; contributes to the growth of local wildfires
North America	Nova Scotia	Le Seutes	high speed SE winds in western Cape Breton Highland
North America	New England	Montreal Express	an arctic cold air mass that sweeps across New England sometimes as far as Massachusetts
North America	Greenland	nigeq	a strong wind from the E
North America	United States, Canada	nor'easter	strong storm with winds from the NE on the NE coast of the U.S. (particularly New England states) and the east coast of Canada
North America	Greenland	Piteraq	cold katabatic wind on the east coast of Greenland

Continent	Region/ Country	Wind	Distinct Features
North America	United States	plough wind	straight line wind which precedes thunderstorms
North America	California	Santa Ana winds	dry downslope winds that affect coastal Southern California and northern Baja California
North America	California	Santa Lucia winds	a downslope wind affecting southern San Luis Obispo and northern Santa Barbara Counties, California
North America	Canada	squamish	strong, violent wind occurring in many of the fjords of British Columbia
North America	California	Sundowner	strong offshore wind off the California coast
North America	Texas	Texas Norther, Blue Norther	fast-moving, stormy Arctic cold front that strikes Texas in winter, dropping freezing rain or sleet
North America	Chicago	The Hawk	cold winter wind in Chicago
North America	Nevada	Washoe Zephyr	seasonal diurnal wind in parts of western Nevada
North America	Alaska	williwaw	strong, violent wind occurring in the Strait of Magellan, the Aleutian Islands, and the coastal fjords of SE Alaska
North America	Great Lakes	Witch of November	strong winds blowing across the Great Lakes in autumn
North America	New-foundland	Wreck-house	strong downslope winds off the Long Range Mountains in SW Newfoundland

Continent	Region/ Country	Wind	Distinct Features
Oceania	Australia	Black nor'easter	violent NE storm that occurs on the east coast of Australia usually between late spring and early autumn
Oceania	Australia	Brickfielder	hot and dry wind in S Australia that develops in the deserts in late spring and summer
Oceania	Australia	Fremantle Doctor, Freo Doctor	afternoon sea breeze from the Indian Ocean which cools Perth during summer
Oceania	New Zealand	Kaimai Breeze	turbulent wind with strong downdrafts in the Kaimai Range of North Island
Oceania	Hawaii	Kona	SE wind replacing trade winds, bringing high humidity and often rain

EXERCISE: Describing Wind

This exercise is a little different from the previous ones and comes in several steps. After all, how do you describe something that can't be seen? By the effect it has on something else?

First, determine the type of wind you want to describe (use the flow chart and the table above to help).

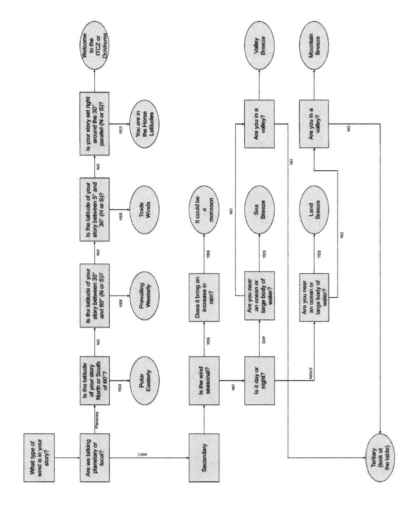

Figure 52. Wind Decision Tree

What type of wind did you come up with? _____

Briefly describe the characteristics of that wind (e.g., cold, warm, wet, dry). You can be clinical here.

_____

_____

_____

The next step will be to come up with an emotion that you might be going for in your narrative. Write that down.

_____

According to research, colors can consistently be linked to emotions across 30 different countries. With the emotion you selected in mind, look at the colors versus emotions chart shown below and pick a color or two that best corresponds to your emotion (e.g., anger is mostly red and black).

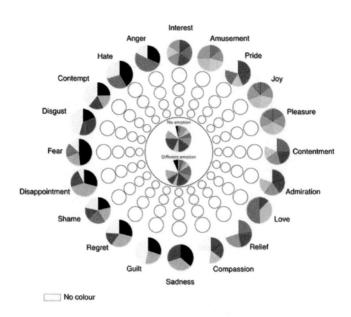

Figure 53. The most common colors associated with emotions.[146]

What color(s) did you select? _____

Now, for each of the words below, write one complete sentence using the stated descriptor. With some exceptions, you will most likely be describing the *object* upon which the wind is *having an effect*. Try not to use "wind" in your sentence.

Describe [your chosen wind] with...
...a shape (what is the wind affecting)

_____

_____

_____

...a color (use the colors you selected)

_____

_____

_____

...a sound

_____

_____

_____

...a tactile feel

_____

_____

_____

...a smell

_____

_____

_____

...an action verb

_____

_____

_____

Take what you've written above and see if you can put it into a paragraph. Again, try not to use the word "wind" in your writing. Like the other exercises, the trick is to describe the wind by tapping into the senses.

_____
_____
_____
_____
_____
_____
_____
_____
_____

Look at your description. If your setting is outside, how is the wind affecting the scenery? Are the trees swaying or is the grass in a field waving? If your setting is inside, how does the wind sound? What's happening to the windows, walls, roof, doors? Rewrite your paragraph, doing your best to avoid any character description or reaction.

_____
_____
_____
_____
_____
_____

Now, invite a character or two onto the stage and let them play out a scene. There should be no mention by the characters (either through internal dialogue or in conversation with another) about the wind.

_____
_____
_____
_____
_____
_____

In the final, step, **remove the weather** and let someone else read it. Ask them what emotion is present. What do they, as a reader, feel? Then, with the weather put back in, ask your reader if anything has changed.

If there is an incongruency, your description of the weather worked. If there is not and your reader chose a different emotion from the one you intended, you might want to rework the description of the weather.

114 MacDonald, G. (1871). *At the Back of the North Wind.*

115 Raddato, C. (2017, March 30). *Tower of the Winds (Athens).* World History Encyclopedia. https://www.worldhistory.org/image/6462/tower-of-the-winds-athens/

116 Pope, A. (1714, June 10). *The Guardian,* Volume I, Number 78.

117 Homer. (2015). *The Iliad* (S. L. Schein & A. Nicholson, Eds.; W. H. D. Rouse, Trans.). Signet.

118 *Hesiod, the Homeric Hymns, and Homerica (Loeb Classical Library No. 57)* (H. G. Evelyn-White, Trans.). (1914). Harvard University Press.

119 Valpy, F.E.J. (1860). *The Etymology of the Words of the Greek Language.*

120 Homer. (2015). *The Odyssey* (D. Steiner & A. Nicholson, Eds.; W. H. D. Rouse, Trans.). Signet.

121 Homer. (2015). *The Iliad* (S. L. Schein & A. Nicholson, Eds.; W. H. D. Rouse, Trans.). Signet.

122 Lyndon State College Atmospheric Sciences Department. Extended Hadley Cells. "Three-Cell Model of the General Circulation" https://apollo.nvu.vsc.edu/classes/met130/notes/chapter10/three_cell.html.

123 "Horse Latitudes." (2003). The Columbia Electronic Encyclopedia, Sixth Edition. New York: Columbia University Press.

124 Ahmad, L., Kanth, R.H., Parvaze, S., Mahdi, S.S. (2017). *Experimental Agrometeorology: A Practical Manual.* Springer.

125 Tempest, R. (2019, March 12). Cultural Mainstay : Monsoon: It's More Than a Rain for India. *Los Angeles Times.* https://www.latimes.com/archives/la-xpm-1987-07-18-mn-712-story.html

126 Bhattacharya, T., Feng, R., Tierney, J. E., Rubbelke, C., Burls, N., Knapp, S., & Fu, M. (2022). Expansion and Intensification of the North American Monsoon During the Pliocene. *AGU Advances, 3*(6). https://doi.org/10.1029/2022av000757

127 VectorMine. (Illustrator). *Land vs sea breeze vector illustration* [digital image]. Retrieved from https://www.shutterstock.com/

128 VectorMine. (Illustrator). *Valley breeze vector illustration.* [digital image]. Retrieved from https://www.shutterstock.com/

129 Steinbeck, J. (1939). *The Grapes of Wrath.* The Viking Press-James Lloyd.

130 Lamb, H. (1920). *Marching Sands.* D. Appleton and Company.

131 Takimoto, I. (2022). Case study of the downslope wind of Japan "Rokko-oroshi". *Atmospheric Science Letters, 23*(9), e1097. https://doi.org/10.1002/asl.1097

132 Ahmed, A. (1994). *Twilight in Delhi.* New Directions Publishing.

133 Verne, J. (1867). *In Search of the Castaways.* Pierre-Jules Hetzel.

134 Vidal, G. (1946). *Williwaw.* E.P. Dutton & Company, Inc.

135 Ahrens, C. Donald; Henson, Robert (January 2015). *Meteorology Today : An Introduction to Weather, Climate, and the Environment* (11th, student ed.). Boston, MA: Cengage Learning.

[136] Lyons, Walter A (1997). *The Handy Weather Answer Book* (2nd ed.). Detroit, Michigan: Visible Ink Press.

[137] National Weather Service. (1943, January 22). *The Black Hills Remarkable Temperature Change of January 22, 1943.* https://www.weather.gov/unr/1943-01-22

[138] Burt, C. C. (2011, December 4). *Big Winds in the West, Possible Wind Gust Record in California | Weather Extremes.* Weather Underground. https://www.wunderground.com/blog/weatherhistorian/big-winds-in-the-west-possible-wind-gust-record-in-california.html

[139] Chander, R. (1946). *Red Wind.* World Publishing Company.

[140] Melville, H. (1851) *Moby Dick; or, The Whale.* New York, Harper & Brothers.

[141] Mikutta, C. A., Pervilhac, C., Znoj, H., Federspiel, A., & Müller, T. J. (2022). The Impact of Foehn Wind on Mental Distress among Patients in a Swiss Psychiatric Hospital. *International Journal of Environmental Research and Public Health, 19*(17), 10831. https://doi.org/10.3390/ijerph191710831

[142] Review of Lettres Inédites de Voltaire, by M. de Cayrol, M. A. François, & M. S.-M. Girardin]. (1865). *The North American Review, 100*(207), 347–389. http://www.jstor.org/stable/25107797

[143] Watson, L., & Hunt, N. (2019). *Heaven's Breath: A Natural History of the Wind.* Adfo Books.

[144] Compiled from multiple sources, including Weather Online (UK) https://www.weatheronline.co.uk/reports/wind/

[145] *King James Version.* (1611). Bible Hub. https://biblehub.com/acts/27-14.htm

[146] Jonauskaite, D., Abu-Akel, A., Dael, N., Oberfeld, D., Abdel-Khalek, A. M., Al-Rasheed, A. S,...Mohr, C. (2020). Universal Patterns in Color-Emotion Associations Are Further Shaped by Linguistic and Geographic Proximity. *Psychological Science, 31*(10), 1245–1260. https://doi.org/10.1177/0956797620948810

LIGHTNING COMING OUT OF THAT ONE

Il y a des grands seigneurs dont il ne faut approcher
qu'avec d'extrêmes précautions; le tonnerre est de ce
nombre.[a]

—François-Marie Arouet, known as Voltaire[147]

THUNDERSTORMS ARE NATURE'S ATTEMPTS TO RESTORE BALANCE
to an unstable atmosphere. What's that you say? Restore balance? Unstable atmosphere? Yes! The way nature uses thunderstorms to restore balance to an unstable atmosphere is akin to the way a plot is intended to resolve a conflict. More on that in a minute.

You may be wondering why I titled this chapter LIGHTNING COMING OUT OF THAT ONE. If you're not, then I'll mention it anyway. On August 2, 1985 Delta Airlines Flight 191 crashed on approach to Dallas/Fort Worth International Airport (DFW). The captain and copilot had noticed an isolated thunderstorm ahead, but decided to proceed through it anyway, which resulted in the aircraft getting caught up in a microburst. The National Transportation Safety Board's (NTSB) accident team determined that the cause of the incident was wind-shear associated with an intense thunderstorm downdraft that occurred at the north end of the airport.[148]

---

[a] Translation: "There are great lords whom it is necessary to approach only with extreme precautions; thunder [lightning] is of this number."

According to the cockpit voice recorder, one of the final exchanges between the Captain and copilot went like this:

18.04:18 CAM-2 Lightning coming out of that one
18.04:19 CAM-1 What?
18.04:21 CAM-2 Lightning coming out of that one
18.04:22 CAM-1 Where?
18.04:23 CAM-2 Right ahead of us[149]

When I taught convective and nonconvective severe weather at the U.S. Air Force Weather Training Center, I would add to my lessons snippets of cockpit voice recordings to show that the weather mattered. Ice on the wings? Air Florida Flight 90. Turbulence? United Airlines Flight 585. While this might be considered morbid, the message was well-received. The folks I was instructing were going to go out into the world and specifically write forecasts and flight briefings for pilots who might find themselves in the same situations as the crews of these doomed flights.[b] I wanted people to be prepared.

In the years leading up to the crash of Flight 191, the study of microbursts (a smaller but much more intense downdraft) had not advanced as far as other types of severe weather. Yet microbursts have been documented back to the 1600s. In a 1993 article in the *Bulletin of the American Meteorological Society*, Randall Cerveny proposes that Homer may very well have been the first to accurately describe a microburst.[150]

> [Poseidon] grasped his trident, stirred it round in the sea, and roused the rage of every wind that blows till earth, sea, and sky were hidden in cloud, and night sprang forth out of the heavens. Winds from East, South, North, and West fell upon him all at the same time, and a tremendous sea got up...[151]

---

[b] If there are any of my former weather students reading this book: a) Hi!; and b) Get to writing!

Some of the outcomes of the Delta accident included an increased study of microbursts and the installation of Terminal Doppler Weather Radar (TDWR) at over 45 airports in the United States and Puerto Rico. TDWR, operated by the Federal Aviation Administration (FAA) is capable of examining the atmosphere at a much greater detail than the current WSR-88D radars which are used by the National Weather Service. In addition to adding protection to airports, the FAA ordered all commercial aircraft to have on-board wind shear detection systems installed.

So now when I see lightning coming out of a cloud, I immediately think to myself "Lightning coming out of that one." It's a reminder that the beautiful cumulonimbus in front of me is extremely dangerous, even at a distance. Lightning can strike over 25 miles from a storm—a true "bolt from the blue." Hail can damage crops and even kill people. Flash flooding can wipe out towns from storms miles away. Downbursts from collapsing thunderstorms can ravage cities, slam aircraft into the ground, flip over semitrucks, and knock over fences. And of course, many thunderstorms are capable of producing that most awe-inspiring of meteorological phenomena—the tornado.

The Dynamics of Thunderstorms

THUNDERSTORMS ARE OFTEN what we think of when we talk about weather. They are awesome, and I've been in my fair share both on the ground and in the air. I'm sure you have, as well. I've always loved the dynamics behind thunderstorms from a meteorological standpoint. Recently, however, I've also been seeing parallels to the standard plot curve many writers have been taught.

Thunderstorm Stages

Before I get into how I think thunderstorms mirror that plot curve (and how they can be used to provide structure to any story), I'd like to relay some basics. (Some *very* basic, basics). There are many good books that have been written about thunderstorm dynamics, and this is *not* one of them. My intent is to explain a few things that may be of use to you in your *story*, not to go into incredible detail on things like CAPE, hodographs, the planetary boundary layer, Skew-T indices, or a whole semester's worth of physics.

With that said, thunderstorms can be broken down into 3 stages as depicted in the image below.

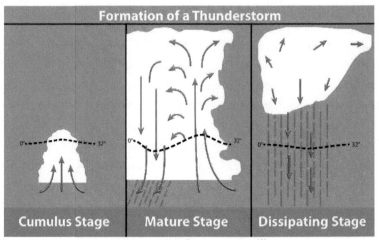

Figure 54. Thunderstorm stages.[152]

In the **Cumulus Stage**, you see the happy cloud. Moisture and air is drawn up toward what's called the "convective condensation level" where clouds form. If there is enough instability in the air, the parcels continue to rise, the moisture continues to condense, and the clouds get bigger.

During the **Mature Stage**, what goes up, must come down. The rising air has pushed our happy cloud to the limit and it peeks above the freezing level. As ice crystals high within the cloud flow up and down in the turbulent air, they crash into each other. Small negatively charged electrons are knocked off some ice and added to other ice as they crash past each other, separating the positive and negative charges of the clouds. When the top of the cloud becomes positively charged and the base of the cloud becomes negatively charged, lightning flashes. Moisture droplets merge and form hail which is then sucked up and down within the cloud. As the hail falls below the freezing level, it melts and rain falls.

More stuff happens, and tornadoes come.

Finally, when all the downward motion overtakes the upward motion, the thunderstorm moves into the **Dissipating Stage**. Rain continues to fall, the cloud falls apart, and it's pretty much over.

In order for all of this to happen, three elements are needed:

- moisture
- instability, and
- a lifting mechanism

One way to create instability is to place cold air (which sinks because it's heavy) over warm air (which rises because it's lighter). The cold over warm creates an atmospheric COW. Because the atmosphere is always trying to maintain a certain equilibrium, violent things must happen. That's what I meant when I said earlier that thunderstorms are nature's attempts to restore balance to an unstable atmosphere.

It's that instability you want to use in your fiction. Most likely, you already have it: your conflict.

A Recipe for a Thunderstorm

As with a cake, a gumbo, or a pizza, there is a recipe for thunderstorms. As mentioned above, three things are needed: moisture, instability, and lift. When wind shear is added (a change in direction of the wind with height), the thunderstorm may become more severe.

Moisture

A certain amount of moisture is required in the atmosphere. When surface dew points are 55°F or higher, then severe thunderstorm development is possible. That doesn't mean that thunderstorms cannot form if the surface dew point is lower, just that the severe development can be hindered.

Instability

The second ingredient is instability, a condition in which air will rise on its own due to positive buoyancy such as a balloon brought to the bottom of a pool. The balloon rises because the air inside is less dense than the surrounding water. How fast the balloon rises depends on the density difference. As thunderstorms require rising air, they require instability.

Lift

The final ingredient in thunderstorm development is lift. Something has to force air to rise. Even if a balloon is more buoyant at the bottom of the pool, you have to let it go for it to rise. There are several different ways lift can happen:

- along a front, a dry line, or an outflow boundary from a previous thunderstorm that is dissipating;
- warm air being brought in at the lower levels of the atmosphere (as warm air will want to rise);
- flow that goes uphill (orographic lift);
- differential heating between soil, vegetation, manmade features;
- the winds in the upper atmosphere diverging which creates a void that nature wants to fill from below

Wind Shear (supercell, multicell, airmass)

The more the wind changes direction as air is lifted, the more vertical directional shear will occur. If the wind changes clockwise with height (the more it veers), the more warm air is advected into the storm, the more the severity of a thunderstorm will increase. If the speed also increases as the direction veers, this will also increase the severity. Thus, directional and velocity changes of the wind with height is important for the severity of the storm.

Air going up will reach a point before it wants to go down. Up is the updraft, and down is the downdraft. If the downdraft is over the updraft because wind shear is light, the thunderstorm's development will be cut off quickly. You might recognize these thunderstorms as daily ones that spit a bolt of lightning or two, rain a bit, then quickly go away. Those are called **airmass** thunderstorms.

If the wind speed increases with height but the direction not so much, the storm will move. The updraft will tilt so that it's no longer capable of being cut off by the downdraft. This keeps the storm alive. Under these conditions you might find storms that form into lines. As the storm moves, the outflow produced creates lift that enables new storms to grow on the edges. Do this long enough, and a line results. These are **multicell** storms and can produce small hail, weak tornadoes, and heavy rain.

If *both* the direction and the speed changes with height, then the updraft will tilt and begin to rotate. The downdraft is no longer over the updraft and conditions are right for **supercell** development, to include tornadoes, large hail, and heavy rain.

The Supercell

Supercells are very large, severe, and dangerous storms and come with a few features that normal thunderstorms do not. In the two diagrams below, the location of the wall cloud, the shelf cloud, the updrafts, downdrafts, and rotation are shown. This very simple diagram can help you decide where best to put your character if you want them to be beaten by an outflow boundary or come face to face with a tornado. You can also see how wind shear has tilted the updraft and helped to create rotation leading to a mesocyclone and tornado. Note the direction of the storm, the location of mammatus, and how the top of the thunderstorm has reached the tropopause (the layer of atmosphere between the troposphere and the stratosphere). Thunderstorms of this magnitude are extraordinarily dramatic and most of what you'll run across in narratives.

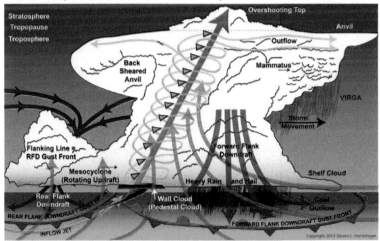

Figure 55. Anatomy of a Supercell Thunderstorm.[153]

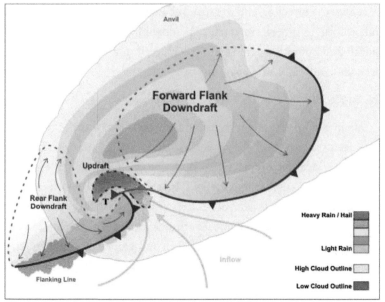

Figure 56. Overhead view of a supercell thunderstorm.[c]

Supercell thunderstorms have very tall tops as they exceed the tropo-pause which is, on average, around 20,000 feet near the poles and 60,000 feet near the equator (based on the U.S. Standard Atmosphere).[154] At-mospheric dynamics determine the actual height. The temperature in the troposphere decreases with height while in the stratosphere it increases with height. The tropopause marks that boundary.

The traditional anvil you see with thunderstorms denotes the height of the tropopause as the stable layer in the stratosphere above inhibits the growth of the storm. The stronger the storm, the more it will "punch through" the tropopause and into the stratosphere. The tops of these storms can grow upwards of 65,000 feet. Near the equator, that could be nearly 75,000 feet (or 14 miles) up.

Hail

When water droplets are caught in an updraft inside a thunderstorm,

---

[c] The rotation within a thunderstorm is cyclonic (counterclockwise) in the Northern Hemisphere. This rotation creates lower pressure and essentially a tiny frontal sys-tem as depicted in this image.

hail forms. As the air rises, the droplets reach above the tropopause and near temperatures close to -112°F (-80°C). Frozen balls of ice fall, collecting more water as they do. If the updraft is strong enough, the hailstones may be thrown back into the air again and again like a popcorn maker getting larger each time until gravity wins and the now large balls of ice fall to the ground.

Hail can destroy crops, clog drains causing floods, and even kill livestock and people. It can be Biblical, as in the Book of Joshua when "there were more who died because of the hailstones than the sons of Israel killed with the sword."[155] In Exodus, Moses is said to have "stretched out his staff toward heaven, and the LORD sent thunder and hail, and lightning struck the earth. So the LORD rained down hail upon the land of Egypt...It was the worst storm in all the land of Egypt since it had become a nation."[156] In 1360, hundreds of English army troops were killed by hailstones the size of goose eggs forcing King Edward III to sign the Treaty of Brétigny. In the Himalayas in 1853, hail killed 84 people and 3,000 oxen and in New Delhi, India in 1888, 246 people and over 1,600 cattle, sheep, and goats were killed by hailstones the size of "cricket balls" (nearly 3 inches in diameter).[157]

Hail can even be apocalyptic. In the past few years, there have been news reports of "apocalyptic" hail in many parts of the world from France to Tennessee. While large and damaging in scope, the stones don't come near the size of those prophesized to fall in the Book of Revelations when the Seventh Bowl of Wrath is poured out. "From the sky huge hailstones, each weighing about a hundred pounds, fell on people. And they cursed God on account of the plague of hail, because the plague was so terrible."[158]

Hail can be large or small and often have layers like an onion. Hail falls from cumulonimbus—thunderstorms. Period. It is not uncommon for hail to clump together, making even bigger stones (and larger dents in cars). The largest recorded hailstone was 8 inches in diameter and fell in Vivian, South Dakota in 2010. That stone weighed approximately 1.9 pounds.[159]

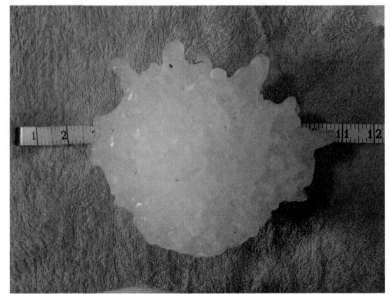

Figure 57. A record-setting hailstone that fell in Vivian, South Dakota on July 23, 2010.

Using the terminal velocity formula[160], a hailstone with a diameter of this size would fall to Earth at 201 mph (323 km/h). Imagine one of your characters being hit with that.

Tornadoes

A **tornado** is a column of air which violently rotates in a counterclockwise direction (in the Northern Hemisphere). The column descends from a thunderstorm and contacts the ground. They can last minutes or hours and travel feet or miles. The damage they cause can be incredible.

While the United States is known to have its share of tornadoes, they have been recorded on every continent, mostly in mid-latitudes where there is the potential for a clash between colder polar air and warmer oceanic moisture that is advected inland. With this is mind, check the setting of your story. Does it fall in one of the shaded areas on this map?

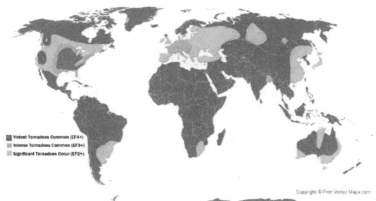

Figure 58. Global distribution of tornadoes.[161]

Most tornadoes in the United States occur between April and June, primarily in the central part of the country thanks to abundant moisture from the Gulf of Mexico clashing with cold polar air from Canada. There are approximately 1,300 tornadoes in the United States each year. From 1940 to 2021, 7,866 people were killed by tornadoes at an average of 71 deaths per year. A record 553 occurred in 2011 alone.[162]

The funnel of a tornado is made of moist air, which condenses into water droplets as it descends. These droplets make the funnel visible and take on the color of the cloud. Once debris is picked up, the color of the tornado changes (e.g., red when red dirt is picked up, black if most of the dirt is black).

The first assumed sighting of a tornado in what would eventually become the United States was recorded by John Winthrop on July 5, 1643. The below record could have been straight-line winds (sometimes referred to as a **derecho**[d]), but the specific mention of the meeting house being "lifted up" convinced historians otherwise.

---

[d] A derecho ("deh-REY-cho") is a widespread, long-lived wind storm associated with fast-moving thunderstorms. The term "straight-line wind damage" sometimes is used to describe its impact. A derecho is classified as such if the damage extends more than 240 miles and the winds are greater than 50 knots (58 mph). Given the swatch of destruction required, derechos occur every few years from the plains of the United States eastward to the Atlantic coast where mountains will not impede the flow.

There arose a sudden gust at N.W. so violent for half
an hour as it blew down multitudes of trees. It lifted
up their meeting house at Newbury, the people being
in it. It darkened the air with dust, yet through God's
great mercy it did no hurt, but only killed one Indian
with the fall of a tree. It was straight between Linne
[Lynn] and Hampton.[163]

The first known photograph of a tornado was taken on April 23, 1884
in Anderson County, Kansas. That picture (as seen below) showed many
Americans for the first time what a tornado looked like.

Figure 59. First known photograph of a tornado, taken in 1884.[164]

Theodore "Ted" Fujita from the University of Chicago developed a scale in 1971[e] for classifying the strength of tornado based on wind speed and damage. The Fujita—or F—Scale was in use until 2007 when an enhanced scale replaced it (the EF Scale). The EF scale uses 28 damage indicators such as building type, structure, the type of trees in the area, etc. to classify tornadoes. The table below shows a comparison between the original F Scale and the EF Scale.

Original F Scale		Enhanced F Scale	
Rating	3 second gust (mph/km/h)	Rating	3 second gust speed (mph/km/h)
F0	45/72-78/126	EF0	65/105-85/137
F1	79/127-117/188	EF1	86/138-110/177
F2	118/189-161/259	EF2	111/178-135/217
F3	162/260-209/336	EF3	136/218-165/266
F4	210/337-261/420	EF4	166/267-200/322
F5	262/421-317/510	EF5	>200/322

Of course, the most famous of tornadoes occurred in Kansas in 1939.

> The house whirled around two or three times and rose slowly through the air. Dorothy felt as if she were going up in a balloon...The north and south winds met where the house stood, and made it the exact center of the cyclone...Toto did not like it.[165]

An interesting observation was made by John Fricke in an article written for the Oz Museum. In it, he recalls a story behind the use of the word "cyclone" (which is technically wrong).

---

[e] It is interesting (to me, anyway) to know that "Mr. Tornado" as he was known did not actually see a tornado until 1982. See: Lerner, L. (2020, October 22). *How one scientist reshaped what we know about tornadoes*. University of Chicago News. https://news.uchicago.edu/story/how-one-scientist-reshaped-what-we-know-about-tornadoes

"Cyclone" is the word L. Frank Baum chose to describe the Kansas storm in his story, although he clearly meant "tornado." Shortly after THE WIZARD OF OZ book first appeared in 1900, Professor Willis L. Moore, then Chief of the United States Weather Bureau, wrote Baum's publishers to urge them to correct the inaccurate usage. He received a response from Frank K. Reilly of The George M. Hill Company, offering that the change would be made in the next edition. This, however, was never done, and any who purchase a copy of THE WIZARD OF OZ reprinting Baum's original language will find that "cyclone" remains, again and again – as colloquial and as factually incorrect as ever.[166]

In one of the first time travel books I fondly recall reading, *The Lost City* by Joseph E. Badger, Jr., the estimable Professor Featherwit (great name) corrects the reader.

"We would be all at sea," quickly interposed the professor, the fingers of one hand vigorously stirring his gray pompadour, while the other was lifted in a deprecatory manner. "At sea, literally as well as metaphorically, my dear Bruno; for, correctly speaking, the ocean alone can give birth to the cyclone."

"Why can't you remember anything, boy?" sternly cut in the roguish-eyed youngster, with admonitory forefinger, coming to the front. "How many times have I told you never to say blue when you mean green? Why don't you say Kansas zephyr? Or windy-auger? Or twister? Or whirly-gust on a corkscrew wiggle-waggle? Or—well, almost any other old thing that you

can't think of at the right time? W-h-e-w! Who mentioned sitting on a snowdrift, and sucking at an icicle?
Hot? Well, now, if this isn't a genuine old cyclone
breeder, then I wouldn't ask a cent!"

Waldo Gillespie let his feet slip from beneath him, sitting down with greater force than grace, back sup-
ported against a gnarled juniper, loosening the clothes
at his neck while using his other hand to ply his crumpled hat as a fan."

...Bruno laughed outright at this characteristic anticli-
max, while Professor Featherwit was obliged to smile,
even while compelled to correct.

"Tornado, please, nephew; not cyclone."[167]

Good for the Professor, although I have to say the other names for a
tornado listed by little Waldo Gillespie—a Kansas zephyr, a windy-auger,
a twister, and (my favorite), a "whirly-gust on a corkscrew wiggle-waggle"—are better. This of course prompted me to look up all the various
synonyms for a tornado. There are plenty of incorrect ones that would
chaff my hide if I read them: squall, gale, cyclone (of course), gustnado[f],
dust devil[g], steam devil, winder, etc. A tornado is a tornado. At the same
time, however, I believe colloquialisms and regional dialects are good
provided they are consistent with the narrative. So if your character on
the U.S. plains is running from a Kansas zephyr, it would fit.

---

[f] Yes, there is a gustnado, but it is not a tornado. A gustnado is surface-based and does
not connect to the cloud above it.

[g] A dust devil is a vortex formed from intense heating which creates a tiny area of low
pressure.

A Few Words About Lightning

First and foremost (as the grammar nerd in me requires): it is *lightning*, not lightening or lighting. Reading either of the latter two in books when referring to what comes out of a thunderstorm is like seeing "your" for "you're" or "there" for "they're" on a tweet: I have a sickening urge to call it out, but of course, don't because, well, it's social media and that's where alien anthropologists will declare all human wars began.

With hazards such as flash flooding, hail, tornadoes, and lightning, all thunderstorms can be dangerous. In the United States, flash flooding killed an average of 88 people in the past 80 years or so, and hail causes approximately $1 billion in damages. Of all hazards, lightning killed the most people between 1940 and 2021, although it does not have the highest average. Almost 9,500 people died as a result of lightning strikes during that time, averaging 37 per year.[168]

Lightning can occur cloud to cloud, cloud to ground, in-cloud (that's a pretty sight), and cloud to air. Most strikes are cloud to cloud. Caused by the action of rising and descending air which is then affected by water and ice inside a storm, lightning occurs when electrical energy between positive and negatively charged areas is discharged. When the negative charges (electrons) in the bottom of the cloud are attracted to the positive charges (protons) in the ground, lightning happens. The electrons bolt toward a higher point where protons have clustered awaiting their lover's arrival (e.g., the top of a tree). That lover's meeting heats the air around the bolt to upwards of 54,000°F (30,000°C) which causes rapid expansion. We know this as **thunder**. That's about as scientific as I want to get for the purposes of this book.

There is a myth that lightning only happens when it rains (and another saying that claims "Thunder only happens when it's rainin'"). Not true. A "Bolt from the Blue" is a cloud-to-ground lightning flash that typically comes out of the back side of a thunderstorm but can also come from the front. These bolts can travel a relatively large distance in clear air *away* from the storm cloud and angle down to strike the ground.[169] Bolts like this have been documented to travel more than 25 miles away from the thunderstorm.[170]

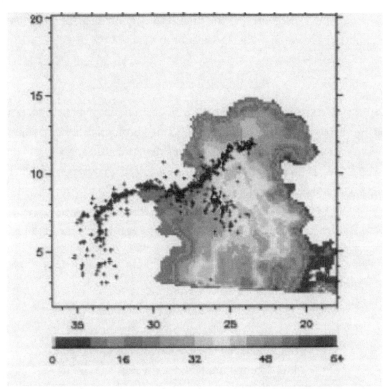

Figure 60. Radar cross-section of a thunderstorm with lightning superimposed.

How can you use this is your writing? Remember that story about the kids at the soccer game and the moments after in the chapter titled THAT ONE LOOKS LIKE A LLAMA RIDING A BICYCLE CHASING A PLATYPUS ON A SKATEBOARD? No? You should go back and read the ending of that story then ask if the danger is *really* over? The storm was gone, right? It moved on...what could possibly happen?

There are quite a few good books on lightning that I would encourage you to pick up. The most informative I've found is *All About Lightning* by Martin A. Uman, an American engineer who is considered one of the world's leading experts on lightning and lightning modeling. Originally written in 1971 and updated in 1986, Uman discusses lightning by answering questions. For example: What is heat lightning? Does lightning "never strike twice?" Are UFOs and ball lightning related? You'll get more out of this one book that you can use in your fictional narrative than in months of research on the Internet or in the library.

The Emotional Connection

THUNDERSTORMS ARE SYNONYMOUS with destruction, and I believe show up more often in literature than other meteorological phenomena. It would take an effort a few English interns to perform an analysis and develop a proper literature review, but I'm going to go out on a limb here and say that thunderstorms are king.

Just as an example, here is small passage from Thomas Hardy's[h] *Far from the Madding Crowd*, where Gabriel observes with concern an approaching storm.

> A hot breeze, as if breathed from the parted lips of some dragon about to swallow the globe, fanned him from the south, while directly opposite in the north rose a grim misshapen body of cloud, in the very teeth of the wind. So unnaturally did it rise that one could fancy it to be lifted by machinery from below. Meanwhile the faint cloudlets had flown back into the south-east corner of the sky, as if in terror of the large cloud, like a young brood gazed in upon by some monster.[171]

What follows is a rather long passage wherein Gabriel and Bathsheba are pummeled by a storm that "sprang from east, west, north, south, and

---

[h] A small note on Thomas Hardy. When I was in high school, one of the books we were required to read in an AP English class was Hardy's *Tess of the d'Urbervilles*, an excruciatingly long book that was severely censored when it came out in 1891. I tried to read it, honestly, but couldn't get past one overly descriptive passage about the Vale of Blackmoor. As I grew older, however, I returned to this prime example of 19th century literature and developed a new appreciation for all those descriptive passages. Editors today would have cut all that stuff out, saying (with a haughty tone), "if it doesn't advance the plot, you don't need it." If those editors were working with the greats of the past, most literature would have been in pamphlet form.

was a perfect dance of death." There is no doubt that Hardy uses the storm as a device to pull fear from the reader. Here is but one paragraph of description.

> Heaven opened then, indeed. The flash was almost too novel for its inexpressibly dangerous nature to be at once realized, and they could only comprehend the magnificence of its beauty. It sprang from east, west, north, south, and was a perfect dance of death. The forms of skeletons appeared in the air, shaped with blue fire for bones—dancing, leaping, striding, racing around, and mingling altogether in unparalleled confusion. With these were intertwined undulating snakes of green, and behind these was a broad mass of lesser light. Simultaneously came from every part of the tumbling sky what may be called a shout; since, though no shout ever came near it, it was more of the nature of a shout than of anything else earthly. In the meantime one of the grisly forms had alighted upon the point of Gabriel's rod, to run invisibly down it, down the chain, and into the earth. Gabriel was almost blinded, and he could feel Bathsheba's warm arm tremble in his hand—a sensation novel and thrilling enough; but love, life, everything human, seemed small and trifling in such close juxtaposition with an infuriated universe.[172]

When I ran my survey on weather and emotions, I did not specifically call out thunderstorms. Rather, I decided to group them in with extreme weather. The below radar graph superimposed on Robert Plutchik's Wheel of Emotions, shows how participants in the survey responded to images of extreme weather (most of which were, in fact, thunderstorms).

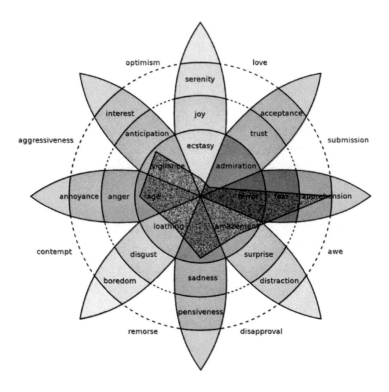

Figure 61. Extreme weather mapped to emotions.

As you might expect, the emotions most associated with thunder-storms (extreme weather) were **terror**, **fear** and **apprehension**. **Vigilance** and a little **rage** came in second. There was also a little **sadness**.

Take a look at the chart on the next page. It is a better look at the distribution of emotions. What does this tell us? Thunderstorms within the narrative can increase those particular emotions or at least mirror those emotions that are present in the characters. We know this. Leo Tolstoy was clear enough in his autobiographical *Boyhood*. "A thunderstorm always communicated to me an inexpressibly oppressive feeling of fear and gloom."[173]

Thunderstorms are often used for effect, and they have been for hundreds—if not thousands—of years. In Tablet 4 of the *Epic of Gilgamesh* said to have been written down around the 12th Century BCE, we read of the dreams of Gilgamesh and their meanings.

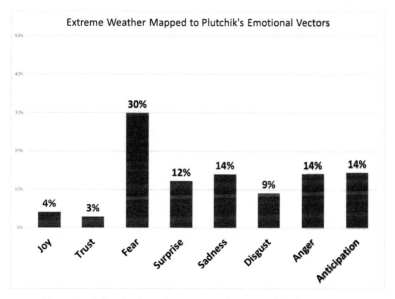

Figure 62. A distribution of extreme weather to emotional spectrums.

The heavens roared and the earth rumbled;
(then) it became deathly still, and darkness loomed.
A bolt of lightning cracked and a fire broke out,
and where(?) it kept thickening, there rained death.
Then the white-hot name dimmed, and the fire went
out,
and everything that had been falling around turned to
ash.

The best part of the translation of the clay tablet on which this was written comes next.

Let us go down into the plain so we can talk it over.
Enkidu heard the dream that he had presented and
said to Gilgamesh
(About 40 lines are missing here.)[174]

Argh! Someone needs to find the missing lines so we can get an interpretation of the dream.

The thunderstorm in *King Lear* by William Shakespeare mirrors the king's own descent into madness. That madness triggers **terror** in others as well as **apprehension**.

> LEAR
> Blow winds, and crack your cheeks! Rage, blow!
> You cataracts and hurricanes, spout
> Till you have drenched our steeples, drowned the
> cocks.
> You sulph'rous and thought-executing fires,
> Vaunt-couriers of oak-cleaving thunderbolts,
> Singe my white head. And thou, all-shaking thunder,
> Strike flat the thick rotundity o' th' world.
> Crack nature's molds, all germens spill at once
> That makes ingrateful man.[175]

Lightning within a thunderstorm can also be used to "reveal" horrors, something you often see in movies. In *Frankenstein or, the Modern Prometheus*, Shelly unveils the monster to Victor Frankenstein using lightning as a tool. (You might also recognize a portion of this passage was used as an example of **subjective joy** in the chapter on the weather and emotions experiment. In this case, I believe the **joy** followed quickly by **fear** is a sharp enough contrast to delight the reader.)

> ...I perceived in the gloom a figure which stole from
> behind a clump of trees near me; I stood fixed, gazing
> intently: I could not be mistaken. A flash of lightning
> illuminated the object, and discovered its shape
> plainly to me; its gigantic stature, and the deformity of
> its aspect more hideous than belongs to humanity, instantly informed me that it was the wretch, the filthy
> dæmon, to whom I had given life.[176]

Of course, a tornado—that ultimate destructive force which comes out of thunderstorms—can certainly evoke feelings of fear and vigilance. In *American Nomads*, Indie author N.L. McLaughlin writes an exciting scene replete with wind, hail, and driving rain that culminates in a tornado after several pages. The rising action leading to the climax (the tornado) of the chapter is what puts the reader on edge, arousing those familiar (and often unwanted) feelings of **apprehension, vigilance, fear,** and a real need to survive—the most basic of human experience.

> Gusts of wind whipped back and forth. The sky turned dark, olive green. The air became damp and heavy with humidity...
>
> Finn picked up his pack. "We should go now."
>
> Dark clouds swallowed up the sun. Lightning lit up the sky, followed by a low rumbling sound that reverberated all around. Large droplets of rain plummeted to the ground...
>
> Halfway through the field, tornado warning sirens went off...Lightning flashed. Thunder rumbled. He ran full speed, through the trees, emerging on the other side where the old farmhouse stood. A quick glance back assured him that his friends were holding their own. He pointed to the house, the others nodded and sprinted for shelter...
>
> Outside, the wind raged, causing the old house to creak and sway. Hail pounded against the metal roof. Bang, bang, bang—like firecrackers...A funnel formed in the clouds. Transfixed, he watched in awe as the finger stretched down to touch the ground, ripping trees out by their roots. Flinging them through the air

like toothpicks. Churning and swirling, the dark cloud moved slowly, picking up everything in its path.[177]

There is a different way to use a thunderstorm in literature (just as there are different ways to use any weather element): by juxtaposing. If you know a particular storm will create **fear**, for example, think of what might be opposite that. Perhaps **joy**? **Ecstasy**? Take this example of juxtaposition in the short story "The Storm" by Kate Chopin (1898). In the story, a thunderstorm rages on as two lovers act on their desires. Here, it is the **comforting** of the **fear** that Calixta has which prompts this act and you can clearly see how the emotions are opposite each other. The **fear** enhances the **desire**.

> "Calixta," he said, "don't be frightened. Nothing can happen. The house is too low to be struck, with so many tall trees standing about. There! aren't you going to be quiet? say, aren't you?" He pushed her hair back from her face that was warm and steaming. Her lips were as red and moist as pomegranate seed. Her white neck and a glimpse of her full, firm bosom disturbed him powerfully. As she glanced up at him the fear in her liquid blue eyes had given place to a drowsy gleam that unconsciously betrayed a sensuous desire. He looked down into her eyes and there was nothing for him to do but to gather her lips in a kiss. It reminded him of Assumption.[178]

The Thunderstorm Story Model

Now, let's get to what I hope is a simple way to incorporate a thunderstorm into your story. I'm calling this the Thunderstorm Story Model (queue copywrite notice) and it goes something like this.

Remember the plot curve we learned about in school? There's the exposition, the rising action, the climax, the falling action, and the dénouement. Not all stories follow this plot curve, but for the sake of this model, we'll assume yours does. If I were to break this up for the screen-writers out there, I might say something like this: there is a prologue, Acts 1 through 3 and finally the Epilogue.

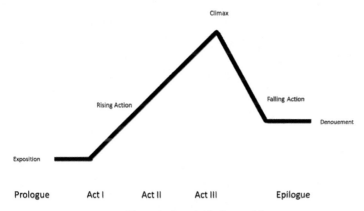

Figure 63. Standard plot model.

Harkening back to the basics of thunderstorm development, we can view the model this way:

- First, you need moisture and instability; this would be the characters and setting and make up our exposition.
- Next, we add in the lift, the trigger, or the inciting incident that gets our plot moving.
- Clouds build as your story builds (kind of like rising action)...
- ...bigger and bigger until, finally, we reach the dramatic moment, the climax of the story when a fully formed thunderstorm is raging all around. If you want to make it two climaxes, of course, you could then throw in a tornado. Maybe some hail. A wall cloud. Something dramatic.
- The storm (and climax) now over, things must dissipate (a true bit of falling action).
- Our thunderstorm goes away, and we're left with some cumulus fractus, a wet ground or destroyed town, and then the dénouement.

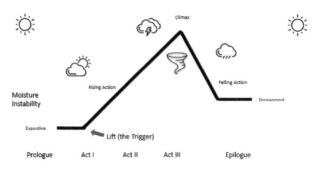

Figure 64. The Thunderstorm Story Model.

It's not the best model, but it works. Depending on the temporal scale of your story, you start with happy clouds and then build them throughout. As the rising action reaches the climax, you might have a true thunderstorm in the novel or some other weather that sparks the emotion you're after in your reader. Finally, at the end of the story, the storms could move on.

King Lear and the Fool in the Storm by William Dyce (1851)

EXERCISE: Describing Thunderstorms

Thunderstorms can conjure a variety of emotions. In this exercise, we'll start with the basic descriptive sentences as we have for the previous elements.

Describe a thunderstorm with...
...a shape

_____

_____

_____

...a color

_____

_____

_____

...a sound

_____

_____

_____

...a tactile feel

_____

_____

_____

...a smell

_____

_____

_____

...an action verb

_____

_____

_____

The most obvious emotion to apply to your description of a thunderstorm would be the ones people most associate with them: **fear** or **anger**. But rather than stick with that, try to write a description of a thunderstorm using emotions from all *eight* of the primary spectrums: **anger, fear, sadness, disgust, surprise, anticipation, trust,** and **joy**.

For each of the following emotions, **give a character an emotion**, and then have them describe how the thunderstorm looks to them. (Refer back to Plutchik's Wheel of Emotions for emotions along each spectrum.)

Anger

_____
_____
_____
_____
_____

Fear

_____
_____
_____
_____
_____

Sadness

_____
_____
_____
_____
_____

Disgust

_____
_____
_____
_____
_____

Surprise

_____
_____
_____
_____
_____

Anticipation

_____
_____
_____
_____
_____

Trust

_____
_____
_____
_____

Joy

_____
_____
_____
_____
_____

EXERCISE: Plotting a Storm

There is precedence for using a thunderstorm to mirror a plot. Using this worksheet, attempt to relate your plot development to the development of a thunderstorm using the model. For reference, you can refer back to the model earlier in this chapter.

Write a sentence or two for each of the stages of your plot keeping the stages of thunderstorms in mind. You can keep the same thunderstorm or spread it out over several days/weeks. I have provided connections for each stage of plot development.

Exposition (clear skies, ingredients for a storm)

_____

_____

_____

_____

_____

Conflict or **Inciting Incident** (that thunderstorm needs a trigger)

_____

_____

_____

_____

_____

Rising Action (building cumulus, moderate or towering cumulus)

_____

_____

_____

_____

_____

Climax (cumulonimbus with or without mammatus, a wall cloud, a shelf cloud, hail, or a tornado)

_____

_____

_____

_____

_____

_____

Falling Action (the thunderstorm is moving on or raining itself out)

_____

_____

_____

_____

_____

_____

Dénouement (return to a stable atmosphere)

_____

_____

_____

_____

_____

_____

_____

[147] Molloy, G. (1890). *Lightning, Thunder and Lightning Conductors*. The Humboldt Publishing Co.

[148] Bureau of Accident Investigation. (1986). *Aircraft Accident Report: Delta Air Lines, Inc., Lockheed L-101 L-385-1, N726da Dallas/Fort Worth - International Airport, Texas August 2,1985* (NTSB/AAR-86/05). National Transportation Safety Board.

[149] *Delta Airlines 191 CVR Transcript*. (n.d.). Cockpit Voice Recorder Database. https://tailstrike.com/database/2-august-1985-delta-191/

[150] Cerveny, R. S. (1993). Meteorological Assessment of Homer's Odyssey. *Bulletin of the American Meteorological Society, 74*(6), 1025–1034. http://www.jstor.org/stable/26230550

[151] Homer., Loomis, L. R., & Butler, S. (1944). *The Odyssey of Homer*. New York, Pub. for the Classics Club by W.J. Black.

[152] gstraub. (Illustrator). *Diagram of the formation of a thunderstorm* [digital image]. Retrieved from https://www.shutterstock.com/

[153] (for both figures) Haby, J. (n.d.). *Thunderstorms*. https://www.weather.gov/source/zhu/ZHU_Training_Page/thunderstorm_stuff/Thunderstorms/thunderstorms.htm

[154] National Oceanic and Atmospheric Administration. (1976). *U.S. Standard Atmosphere, 1976* (NOAA-S/T-76-1562). U.S. Government Printing Office. https://ntrs.nasa.gov/citations/19770009539

[155] *New International Version*. (1973). Bible Hub. https://biblehub.com/joshua/10-11.htm

[156] *New International Version*. (1973). Bible Hub. https://biblehub.com/exodus/9-23.htm

[157] Dennis, J., & Wolff, G. (1993). *It's Raining Frogs and Fishes: Four Seasons of Natural Phenomena and Oddities of the Sky* (First Printing). HarperPerennial.

[158] *New International Version*. (1973). Bible Hub. https://biblehub.com/revelation/16-21.htm

[159] National Weather Service. (n.d.). *Record Setting Hail Event in Vivian, South Dakota on July 23, 2010.* https://www.weather.gov/abr/vivianhailstone

[160] *Fluid Friction*. (n.d.). http://hyperphysics.phy-astr.gsu.edu/hbase/airfri2.html

[161] @scienceoutthere (n.d.) *Worldwide tornado frequency map*. https://www.reddit.com/r/MapPorn/comments/v3eze5/worldwide_tornado_frequency_map_derived_by/

[162] National Weather Service. (n.d.). *Weather Related Fatality and Injury Statistics.* https://www.weather.gov/hazstat/

[163] Kovalchik, K. (2011, June 2). *Not-So-Famous Firsts: Tornado Edition*. Mental Floss. https://www.mentalfloss.com/article/27887/not-so-famous-firsts-tornado-edition

[164] Adams, A. A. (1884, April 23). *Tornado, Anderson County, Kansas*. Kansas Historical Society. https://www.kansasmemory.org/item/209199

[165] Baum, L. F. & Denslow, W. W. (1900) *The Wonderful Wizard of Oz*. George M. Hill Company.

[166] Fricke, J. (n.d.). *"WE MUST BE UP INSIDE THE CYCLONE!"* OZ Museum / Columbian Theatre. https://ozmuseum.com/blogs/news/we-must-be-up-inside-the-cyclone

[167] Badger, J.E. (1898). *The Lost City*. Dana Estes & Company.

[168] National Weather Service. (n.d.). *Weather Related Fatality and Injury Statistics.* https://www.weather.gov/hazstat/

[169] Tamurian, Z. N. (2012). Determining the Characteristics of Anvil and Thunderstorm Lightning for Use in the Lightning Launch Commit Criteria at Cape Canaveral Air Force Station and Kennedy Space Center. Retrieved from http://purl.flvc.org/fsu/fd/FSU_migr_etd-5223

[170] National Weather Service. (n.d.). *NWS Pueblo Lightning Page - Bolts from the blue.* https://www.weather.gov/pub/lightningBoltBlue

[171] Hardy, T. (1874). *Far from the Maddening Crowd*.

[172] Hardy, T. (1874). *Far from the Maddening Crowd*.

[173] Tolstoy, L. (1854). *Boyhood*. Sovremennik.

[174] Kovacs, M. G. (1989). *The Epic of Gilgamesh* (1st ed.). Stanford University Press.

[175] Shakespeare, W. (1992). *King Lear*. C. Watts & K. Carabine (Eds.). Wordsworth Editions. (Original work published 1608).

[176] Shelly, M.W. (1818). *Frankenstein; or, the Modern Prometheus*. Lackington, Hughes, Harding, Mavor & Jones.

[177] McLaughlin, N.L. (2021). *American Nomads*. Twisted Sky, LLC. Kindle Edition. https://www.nancylmclaughlin.com/

[178] Chopin, K. (1969). The Storm. In P. Seyersted (Ed.). *The Complete Works of Kate Chopin (Southern Literary Studies)*. LSU Press.

THE SUN IS HOT! SO IS ITS WEATHER

the red, blazing red,
of the pitiless sun – yet
autumn in the wind
      —Matsuo Bashō (1644-1694)[179]

W HEN I WAS A YOUNGER LAD, I HAD AN OPPORTUNITY TO SHIFT my airfield weather focus to something a little more "out there"—solar weather observation and forecasting. What kept me from joining those illustrious ranks of others who had gone before was this: a lot of other people wanted that job, too.

It was in Australia, mate.

Talk about your adventure. As I said, I didn't get the job, but that didn't damper my attitude toward solar weather. After all, the fact that we have weather in the first place—and the fact that we exist at all—is because of that big ball of gas in the sky.

Solar weather is not the best term to use, though. The field studies the composition of the sun, its gaseous atmosphere, and the impact of storms on the surface of the sun on our own planet, our lives, and our technology. The "official" term is **space weather**, a branch of **heliophysics**, which sounds so much cooler than solar weather. I mean, why not call it geo-solar-impactfulness?

Space weather is all about the interaction of the sun and Earth. Earth's atmosphere is made of several layers, each of which is affected by the sun: the troposphere (where we live), the stratosphere, the mesosphere, the thermosphere (where the ionosphere and magnetosphere begin), and the exosphere.

The sun is a ball of hot plasma, heated by nuclear fusion which converts hydrogen to helium and matter into energy. That energy travels across the solar system, eventually impacting the planets. When the moon covers the sun, we can see the sun's own atmosphere: the chromosphere, the transition region, the corona and the heliosphere.

Figure 65. The sun's corona.[180]

There's a lot out there on the composition of the sun, its dynamics, and a bunch of formulas that I don't understand. What I *do* understand is how the sun can play a part in writing, not only as an obvious source of light, but also as a literary device all its own. Its interplay with Earth can drive plots.

The sun can do some real damage to our own little part of the universe. It can also give us some **awe-inspiring** celestial displays which, when used effectively, can enhance the narrative of our writing.

Cool Sun Stuff

WITHOUT DIGGING TOO much into heliophysics, I do want share some basics, things you may remember from Earth Science (or Astronomy, if your high school was cool enough to have that as an elective). Perhaps you've learned a little about the sun through decades of standing in it and being burned. Whatever the case, here's a few things that I believe are important for writers to know if they might be thinking about using the sun in their narratives more than just "The sun rose" or "It was sunset and Cletus had enough of the farm."

Solar Cycle and Rotation

The sun has a solar cycle that lasts an average of 11 years with both a maximum and a minimum. This cycle occurs due to the sun changing its polarity, which causes an increase in solar flare activity. Because the sun is a ball of gas, it does not rotate uniformly at all latitudes—it is faster at the equator than at the poles. The equator completes a full rotation in about 25 days while the poles take about 30 days to complete a rotation. The average is about 27 days. This differential rotation adds to the volatile state of the sun.

What volatile state you ask?

Solar Features and Effects

Sunspots

Sunspots are dark patches or spots that are seen when one projects an image of the sun onto an object. Sunspots often appear in groups and are caused by strong magnetic fields on the sun. They appear dark because they are slightly cooler at 7,100°F (3,927°C) than the surrounding photosphere which is around 10,000°F (5,704°C). Sunspots are more numerous during solar maxima and appear less during solar minima.

Flares

A flare is a temporary intense explosion of energy on the sun. They generally occur in the vicinity of sunspots in areas of complicated magnetic fields. Though appearing small, they are greater than Earth-size. A large flare would produce energy equivalent to 10 billion 1-megaton nuclear bombs.[181]

Filaments & Prominence Features

Filaments appear as a dark ribbon-like features visible against the brighter solar disk. A prominence is the same as a filament, but it is located on the limb or edge. They are held suspended above the surface by the sun's magnetic field. They can persist for long periods of time or disappear within minutes. When they erupt, they can send a large particle stream into interplanetary space. If Earth is in the right location to interact with the particle stream, the electrically charged gas cloud can affect Earth's magnetic field for a period of 20 to 40 hours.

Coronal Holes

Coronal holes are breaks in the sun's magnetic field lines caused by excessive pressure exerted by the corona in other areas. Imagine a balloon. You squeeze it and it expands outward. These weaker areas in the corona (like the balloon) eventually burst open. The result is a high-speed stream of coronal material released into the solar wind. This phenomenon is strongest during solar minima because it requires time and a stable environment to build into this state.

Solar Activity and Impact

THE SUN EMITS a vast spectrum of electromagnetic radiation, from gamma rays to radio waves. Gamma ray radiation is the most "energetic." Radioactive substances emit these rays as well. You're probably familiar with x-rays and if you've been burnt by the sun, you know that ultraviolet radiation is not your best friend. Light is what we see in the visible spectrum, while infrared radiation is used in heaters, certain cooking tools, your television remote, and weapons which are designed to pick out targets based on temperature rather than sight. Finally, radio waves are what you listen to on your way to and from work. Every once in a while, the sun decides to emit a "burst" of one or more of these radiation types.

The sun also emits electrons and protons which stream continuously outward to form what is known as the "solar wind." These electrons and protons can also be released in bursts and, along with all that radiation, they slam into Earth's magnetic field. When radiation emitted from the sun interacts with atoms in Earth's atmosphere, things happen. X-rays cause ionization of molecules in the upper atmosphere. Radio waves can penetrate Earth's atmosphere and reach the surface. Electrons can cause both ionization of molecules as well as heat up the upper atmosphere. This is also the cause of aurorae (discussed below).

The solar flare is the main culprit that impacts our little corner of the Universe. You have likely seen flares on television or on imagery. If not, here's a pretty picture of a large flare which occurred on December 4, 2014.

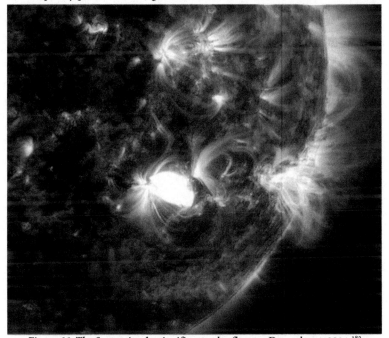

Figure 66. The Sun emitted a significant solar flare on December 4, 2014.[182]

Flares emit electromagnetic energy over a wide range of wavelengths. Although these flares cannot always be predicted, we do know of several events that are flare-induced. Solar flares are associated with shutting down radio communications, geomagnetic storming, loss of satellite control, manned spacecraft particle bombardment, and **aurorae**.

Aurorae

Of all solar stuff, I believe aurorae are the most awe-inspiring. Romantics (at least in the Northern Hemisphere) may call them the "Northern Lights" but the official term is **aurora borealis**. In the Southern Hemisphere, the same celestial feature is known as **aurora australis** or "Southern Lights." The sun is continually spitting out charged particles from its corona and creating a solar wind. When the solar wind slams into our atmosphere, auroras appear.

While it was Galileo who coined the term aurora borealis after the Roman god Aurora, the first recorded viewing was some 30,000 years ago (in a cave painting). Frankly that artwork could be a bunch of squiggles to my untrained anthropological eyes, but that's what the history books tell us. It also tells us that humans have been continually fascinated with these lights for thousands of years.

The earliest known writing of an aurora was in a Chinese text written in 2600 BCE. "Fu-Pao, the mother of the Yellow Empire Shuan-Yuan, saw strong lightning moving around the star Su, which belongs to the constellation of Bei-Dou, and the light illuminated the whole area."[183]

Aurorae appear as early as the Bible. In Ezekiel 1:4, he writes:

> As I looked, I saw a great storm coming from the
> north, driving before it a huge cloud that flashed with
> lightning and shone with brilliant light. There was fire
> inside the cloud, and in the middle of the fire glowed
> something like gleaming amber.

David has similar view in Psalms 19:1, although his is slightly less descriptive. "The heavens proclaim the glory of God. The skies display his craftsmanship."

In 1873, Henry Wadsworth Longfellow wrote a decent description of an aurora, and being the poet, a bit more imaginative.

> And now the Northern Lights begin to burn, faintly at
> first, like sunbeams playing in the waters of the blue

sea. Then a soft crimson glow tinges the heavens.
There is a blush on the cheek of night. The colors
come and go; and change from crimson to gold, from
gold to crimson. The snow is stained with rosy light.
Twofold from the zenith, east and west, flames a fiery
sword; and a broad band passes athwart the heavens,
like a summer sunset. Soft purple clouds come sailing
over the sky, and through their vapory folds the wink-
ing stars shine white as silver.[184]

To use descriptions of aurorae in your writing is to invite awe in the
reader. Literature and mythology is filled with fascinating stories and poems about these lights. The lights can also be anthropomorphized. Herman Melville personified the advance and retreat of the Northern Lights
like that of an army. Or perhaps, the end of the Civil War prompted Melville to use the Northern Lights as allegory (the poem was written in May
of 1865).

> What power disbands the Northern Lights
> After their steely play?
> The lonely watcher feels an awe
> Of Nature's sway,
> As when appearing,
> He marked their flashed uprearing
> In the cold gloom—
> Retreatings and advancings,
> (Like dallyings of doom),
> Transitions and enhancings,
> And bloody ray.
>
> The phantom-host has faded quite,
> Splendor and Terror gone—
> Portent or promise—and gives way
> To pale, meek Dawn;

The coming, going,
Alike in wonder showing—
Alike the God,
Decreeing and commanding
The million blades that glowed,
The muster and disbanding—
Midnight and Morn.[185]

There are caveats to including aurorae in your stories. Unless you're setting your story in higher latitudes, auroras will typically not be visible. I say "typically" because in 1989 the Northern Lights could be seen as far south as Honduras during a solar storm which temporarily knocked out electricity across all of Quebec.

With that in mind, consider this as a story idea: what if the Aztecs witnessed a similar event? How would they respond? It may not have been with awe at the sight, but perhaps unbridled fear that their gods were angry. After all, not all cultures saw aurorae as good things. The Sami, who live in northern parts of Norway, Sweden, and Finland, have feared the Northern Lights for centuries. Even today some of the elders will stay indoors if the lights are out as they believe those lights (which contain the souls of the dead) might notice them. If that happens, the lights will carry them away or even cut off their heads. Some also believed that the Northern Lights represented the victims of murder who were still bleeding or cutting themselves in the afterlife. Indigenous Greenlanders believed that the Northern Lights were made up of the spirits of children who had died in childbirth, while in Iceland, the lights could relieve the pain of childbirth provided the mother didn't look at them. If she did, a cross-eyed child would be born. To the Chinese, aurorae were the fiery breath of dragons doing battle. Same with ancient Russian cultures, but if the "dragon" descended to Earth when a village's men were away, they would seduce the women.[186]

Sometimes the color makes the legend. Oxygen atoms in the air around 62 miles up glow a yellow-green when excited by solar wind. At 200 miles or so, that same oxygen will be more red. To the English and

French doing battle hundreds of years ago, red skies were omens of bloodshed or ill fortune. Nitrogen, however, gives off blue or red-purple lights, and there is a case when aurorae may be pink. While rare, if the solar wind which produces aurorae reaches below 62 miles, nitrogen may be excited enough to glow a neon pink color.[187]

You're a writer, and when you're including descriptions of aurorae you can certainly paint the sky however you want. If accuracy is important to you, though, don't go chasing a rainbow of colors (or waterfalls). Think about your characters and their history. Would they fear or worship the lights?

The Carrington Event, 1859

Of course, that pretty light in the sky is not all that the sun is capable of producing. There is a flipside to space weather. In 1859, a geomagnetic storm was recorded by Richard Carrington and Richard Hodgson. The event has since been viewed as the strongest ever recorded and would be considered at the top range of National Oceanic and Atmospheric Administration's (NOAA) space weather scales had it occurred today.

The aurora was seen as far south as Mexico. In my neck of the woods, the Northern Lights were bright enough to wake miners who went about their morning business clueless to the time. Telegraph operators found they were able to send and receive messages *without* being connected to a power supply. As a Baltimore newspaper noted, in the middle of the night "the quiet streets of the city resting under this strange light, presented a beautiful as well as singular appearance."[188]

New York Railroad Storm, 1921

In May 1921, a solar storm caused a mass disruption in railways in New York. The *New York Times* reported on May 16th of that year that "the entire signal and switching system of the New York Central Railroad below 125th Street was put out of operation, followed by a fire in the control tower...This is the first time that a sunspot has been blamed for such a piece of mischief."[189] Interesting use of the word "mischief" here, but the flare which caused the problem was equal in strength (if not larger than) the flare in 1859.[190] Fires broke out in Sweden as well, and could be linked to surging electrical currents. Similar disruptions occurred at high latitudes around the world.[191]

From a review of the data, researchers found a wealth of evidence of adverse impacts in infrastructures, especially telegraph and telephone systems, around the world. In addition, spectacular displays of aurorae were visible in locations not normally visited. In Sinola, Mexico, at a latitude of 27°N, a report of northern lights were "very plainly visible from the mesa here—only a few miles from the tropics...The glow began about eight o'clock and the rays were first visible about fifteen minutes later."[192]

Canada, 1989

In the middle of March 1989, the electricity in Quebec, Canada went out and residents as far south as Texas and Cuba reported seeing the Northern Lights. Good for the Texans and Cubans, but the high temperature in Montreal on March 13, 1989 was 30°F (-1.2°C) and the low was 6°F (-14.4°C). The lights (and heaters) died at 2:45 a.m. Canadians woke up cold, and the outage lasted nine hours. Up in the air, satellites had difficulty maintaining operational altitude and orbital debris were "lost" temporarily by tracking systems set up to keep screws and lost hammers from puncturing the sides of expensive equipment. And a guy in Utah nearly lost his fish while starring transfixed at the Northern Lights.[193]

The culprit of this near piscatorial disaster turned out to be a magnetic storm caused by two coronal mass ejections linked to solar flares which were spotted by an observatory on Kitt Peak, Arizona on March 9th and 10th. The impact to the power grid was rapid, and within 59 seconds the system collapsed. A capacitor at the Chibougamau sub-station tripped, and the loss of voltage caused power swings and a reduction of power generation in the transmission network. A second capacitor blew and then five more. In less than a minute, Hydro-Quebec's La Grande Hydroelectric Complex was out and half of Quebec was in the dark.[194]

IMAGINE IF THESE same events happened now. Blackouts and damages to electrical grids would cause mass panic, and according to Lloyds of London, the estimated cost of such an event in the U.S. alone would be upwards of $2.9 trillion.[195] In a summary report by the Royal Academy of Engineers, a dire prediction can be found about this possibility and the predicted impact. In the report, it is estimated that up to 10 percent of satellites currently in orbit could be affected, passengers of airplanes in flight would be exposed to high levels of radiation, high frequency communication would be inoperable, and electrical grids would fail. When will this happen? "The general consensus is that a solar superstorm is inevitable, a matter not of 'if' but 'when?'...a Carrington-level event will occur within a period of 250 years with a confidence of ~95% and within a period of 50 years with a confidence of ~50%."[196]

In short, we will probably see at least one event, if not several, in our lifetime. By my pessimistic calculations, we're due. Perhaps Aristotle figured out that bad things could happen with the sun, as heralded by the aurora. In *Meteorologica*, that horribly wrong book about all things weather that only gets one or two things right, Aristotle writes:

> For we have seen that the upper air condenses into an inflammable condition and that the combustion sometimes takes on the appearance of a burning flame, sometimes that of moving torches and stars. So it is not surprising that this same air when condensing should assume a variety of colours. For a weak light shining through a dense air, and the air when it acts as a mirror, will cause all kinds of colours to appear, but especially crimson and purple. For these colours generally appear when fire-colour and white are combined by superposition.[197]

Yes...maybe the sky is on fire.

Space Weather and Fiction

TO FURTHER YOUR exploration into the impacts that the sun can have on your story, consider the table at the end of this chapter (reprinted in part from

NOAA's space weather website). Take your plot, whatever that may be, and thrown in a solar storm. If your story takes place *before* the Information Age, you might be able to conjure **fear**, **awe**, or **anger** in your readers by the reaction of the characters. If your story is set in the present (or future), then perhaps **awe**, **joy**, or even **love** might be the emotion your characters feel.

There is a plethora of stories which mention aurorae and an equal number that talk of the sun and its impact on weather. One of the first mentions of this solar meddling I had ever run across was in H.G. Wells' *The Time Machine*. Recall that our hero the Time Traveller jumped forward after escaping the Morlocks and ended up somewhere near the end of the world. He spends a good chapter describing how the sun changed during his speedy flight through time, and just before he begins to slow the machine to stop his forward motion, the sun has grown in mass.

> At last, some time before I stopped, the sun, red and very large, halted motionless upon the horizon, a vast dome glowing with a dull heat, and now and then suffering a momentary extinction. At one time it had for a little while glowed more brilliantly again, but it speedily reverted to its sullen red heat. I perceived by this slowing down of its rising and setting that the work of the tidal drag was done. The earth had come to rest with one face to the sun, even as in our own time the moon faces the earth.[198]

It's a chilling end to the world (irony intended), for soon when the Time Traveller stops, all he can see is "a sharp bright horizon against the wan sky" and extensively evolved life in an atmosphere that lacked oxygen. Wells' novel is more an extension of Charles Darwin's theory of evolution through fictional narrative, but he does not forget to wonder what might happen when the sun's impact on Earth becomes extreme as its stellar lifecycle runs its course.

We know that the sun has an effect and drives our weather. When it comes up, fog goes away, and the temperature (normally) rises. When it sets, the winds may decrease, and the dew has a chance to form. In literature, the sun is often shown to be "rising" indicating change or the advent of something new and a dispersal of the darkness, or "setting" to show the advent of the night, the end to a day. These are no more literal than they are figurative. It is not a stretch of the imagination to mark the rising and setting of the sun as you would mark elements of plot development. For example, the sun breaking the horizon may be an inciting incident, and as it rises, we may see the rising action. The climax and start of falling action could be when the sun has reached its apex or even when it sets. Marking the transition between plot elements by the position of the sun is but one way to queue your reader in subconsciously to what's going on.

Eclipses of the sun by the moon are also common. I didn't explore eclipses or their reasons, but there is plenty available if you're itching to know the science behind the motion of heavenly bodies. Eclipses can be used as a comparison of one to another (e.g., light to dark, good to evil, or husband to wife as in Daniel Dafoe's *The Family Instructor*) or as allegory (e.g., Stephanie Meyer's *Eclipse*). An eclipse, by definition, is "a forsaking, quitting, or disappearance. Hence the covering over of something by something else, or the immersion of something in something."[199] In Dafoe's case, "...the Moon was like a cross Wife, that when she was out of Humour, could Thwart and Eclipse her Husband whenever she pleased; and that if an ill Wife stood in the Way, the brightest Husband could not shine."[200] In the Meyer case, Bella may fear that her pending transformation would eclipse her true self.

In historical fiction, it is often wise to research when eclipses happen. It has been said that Homer included a description of an eclipse in the *Odyssey*, yet there is no historical basis for one having happened at this exact time.[201] Perhaps it would have helped Homer had he access to NASA's Eclipse website (https://eclipse.gsfc.nasa.gov/SEcat5/SEcatalog.html) where five millennium of solar eclipses are cataloged. You, however, have more tools than Homer. Therefore, if you intend to include an eclipse in your narrative, I recommend researching when and where they have occurred so that your editor or beta reader doesn't call you out. As a bonus to science fiction writers, the NASA website has also calculated all eclipses through 3000 CE.

With eclipses (the blotting out of the sun), the daytime temperature can decrease creating a "chilly" atmosphere. However, you can use the sun to "heat" up your story, either passionately as in a romance ("He took his wet shirt off under the steaming, hot, sweaty sun"[a]) or in a way suggesting a dystopian nightmare wherein the reader feels as if they are burning hot. In her novel that follows a solar engineer set centuries after anthropogenic climate change has ravaged Earth, S.Z. Attwell uses imagery of the sun to keep the reader embedded in a hot, claustrophobic, and uncomfortable world. Readers have stated that they have needed water. This works on both a literal level (it is hot) and on an allegorical level as the story revolves around vengeance, power, shifting loyalties, and survival. Throughout *Aestus, Book 1: The City*[b], the word "sun" is used 43 times, and many times with a simple modifier to remind the reader of the climate: "burning summer sun," "the sun beat down," "the sun was more dangerous than anything," "hide from the sun," "the sun was starting to get to her," etc. These phrases, used throughout, are reflective of the "heat" of the atmosphere and keep the reader grounded.[202]

While saying "space weather" may conjure images of science fiction writers, in reality this refers to all narratives which may include the sun (or moon). The sun has a rich history (several billion years, apparently) and deserves a little respect. We can write it as a character, its impact on Earth as an inciting incident, use it as a climax, or enhance our stories with allegory.

---

[a] This is an example of why I should never attempt to write a romance novel.
[b] "Aestus" is Latin for burning heat/turmoil.

A Handy Table of Solar Storms & Effects

Scale	Description	Effect
G 5	Extreme	**Power systems:** Widespread voltage control problems and protective system problems can occur, some grid systems may experience complete collapse or blackouts. Transformers may experience damage. **Spacecraft operations:** May experience extensive surface charging, problems with orientation, uplink/downlink and tracking satellites. **Other systems:** Pipeline currents can reach hundreds of amps, HF (high frequency) radio propagation may be impossible in many areas for one to two days, satellite navigation may be degraded for days, low-frequency radio navigation can be out for hours, and aurora has been seen as low as Florida and southern Texas (typically 40° geomagnetic lat.).
G 4	Severe	**Power systems:** Possible widespread voltage control problems and some protective systems will mistakenly trip out key assets from the grid. **Spacecraft operations:** May experience surface charging and tracking problems, corrections may be needed for orientation problems. **Other systems:** Induced pipeline currents affect preventive measures, HF radio propagation sporadic, satellite navigation degraded for hours, low-frequency radio navigation disrupted, and aurora has been seen as low as Alabama and northern California (typically 45° geomagnetic lat.).
G 3	Strong	**Power systems:** Voltage corrections may be required, false alarms triggered on some protection devices. **Spacecraft operations:** Surface charging may occur on satellite components, drag may increase on low-

		Earth-orbit satellites, and corrections may be needed for orientation problems. **Other systems:** Intermittent satellite navigation and low-frequency radio navigation problems may occur, HF radio may be intermittent, and aurora has been seen as low as Illinois and Oregon (typically 50° geomagnetic lat.).
G 2	Moderate	**Power systems:** High-latitude power systems may experience voltage alarms, long-duration storms may cause transformer damage. **Spacecraft operations:** Corrective actions to orientation may be required by ground control; possible changes in drag affect orbit predictions. **Other systems:** HF radio propagation can fade at higher latitudes, and aurora has been seen as low as New York and Idaho (typically 55° geomagnetic lat.).
G 1	Minor	**Power systems:** Weak power grid fluctuations can occur. **Spacecraft operations:** Minor impact on satellite operations possible. **Other systems:** Migratory animals are affected at this and higher levels; aurora is commonly visible at high latitudes (northern Michigan and Maine).[203]

EXERCISE: Using Space Weather as a Prompt

We've seen just how much of an impact the sun can have on our planet. Here are some possible writing prompts for you to try. Remember to focus less on the event and more on your character's **emotional** state during (and possibly after) the event.

- Write a **poem** that describes the emotional impact of a solar storm on a person or a community. Use vivid imagery and sensory details to capture the power and unpredictability of the storm.

- Write a **short story** where a space weather event, such as a coronal mass ejection or a solar flare, causes a technological disaster that affects the entire world. Explore the ways in which the characters respond to the crisis and the emotional toll it takes on them.

- Write a **scene** in a larger work where the characters must navigate a hostile environment on a distant planet during a space weather event, such as an ion storm or a magnetic substorm. Use the weather to create tension and danger in the scene, and explore the emotional impact of the characters' struggle to survive.

- Write a **character sketch** of a scientist who studies space weather and the impact it has on Earth. Use the sketch to create a story or scene that explores the character's relationship to their work and the ways in which their scientific expertise affects their personal life.

- Write a piece of **flash fiction** that takes place during a geomagnetic storm with aurorae present. Use the brevity of the form to create a powerful story that captures the emotional impact of the storm on the characters.

- Write a **memoir** or personal **essay** that reflects on a time in your life when you experienced an extreme weather event, such as a solar storm or a meteor shower. Use the essay to explore the emotional impact of the event and the ways in which it changed your perspective on the world.

[179] Matsuo Bashō (1644-1694), as translated by Timm Chilcott

[180] Taken during the total solar eclipse over Casper, WY in 2017. Credit: U.S. Air Force photo by Staff Sgt. Christopher Ruano.

[181] Crockett, C. K. (2021, September 20). *Just How Big Can Solar Flares Get, and Are We Ready?* https://science.thewire.in/the-sciences/just-how-big-can-solar-flares-get-and-are-we-ready/

[182] *Sun Emits a Mid-Level Flare on Dec. 4, 2014.* (2017, August 7). NASA. https://www.nasa.gov/content/goddard/sun-emits-a-mid-level-flare-on-dec-4-2014/

[183] *NASA - The History of Auroras.* (n.d.). NASA. Retrieved from https://www.nasa.gov/mission_pages/themis/auroras/aurora_history.html

[184] Longfellow, H. W. (1873) *The Poetical Works of Henry Wadsworth Longfellow.* J.R. Osgood and Company.

[185] Melville, H. (1865). "Aurora-Borealis: Commemorative of the Dissolution of Armies at the Peace" (poem) in *Battle Pieces and Aspects of the War.*

[186] Coble, A. (2020, October 31). *Aurora Lore: Myths of the Northern Lights.* Coldfoot Camp. https://www.coldfootcamp.com/blog/2018/11/28/aurora-lore-myths-of-the-northern-lights

[187] Baker, H. (2022, November 7). *Solar storm smashes hole in Earth's magnetosphere, triggering extremely rare pink auroras.* livescience.com. https://www.livescience.com/pink-auroras-solar-storm

[188] "The Aurora Borealis". *Baltimore American and Commercial Advertiser.* 3 September 1859. p. 2, column 2.

[189] SUNSPOT CREDITED WITH RAIL TIE-UP; New York Central Signal System Put Out of Service by Play of Northern Lights. (1921, May 16). *New York Times,* 2.

[190] Phillips, D. (2020b, May 14). *The Great Geomagnetic Storm of May 1921.* Spaceweather.com. https://spaceweatherarchive.com/2020/05/12/the-great-geomagnetic-storm-of-may-1921/

[191] Hapgood, M. (2019). The Great Storm of May 1921: An Exemplar of a Dangerous Space Weather Event. *Space Weather, 17*(7), 950–975. https://doi.org/10.1029/2019sw002195

[192] Douglass, A. E. (1921). The aurora of May 14, 1921. *Science, 54*(1383), 14–14. https://doi.org/10.1126/science.54.1383.14

[193] *Chapter 1 : A Conflagration of Storms.* (2017, April 17). Solar Storms. https://www.solar-storms.org/SWChapter1.html

[194] Boteler, D. H. (2019). A 21st Century View of the March 1989 Magnetic Storm. *Space Weather, 17*(10), 1427–1441. https://doi.org/10.1029/2019sw002278

[195] *Space weather: Storms from the Sun.* (2016, June 23). National Oceanic and Atmospheric Administration. https://www.noaa.gov/explainers/space-weather-storms-from-sun

[196] *Extreme space weather: impacts on engineered systems and infrastructure.* (2013). Royal Academy of Engineering.

[197] Goold, G. P. (Ed.). (1952). *Aristotle: Meteorologica (Loeb Classical Library No. 397)* (H. D. P. Lee, Trans.; Illustrated). Harvard University Press.

[198] Wells, H.G. (1895). *The Time Machine.* William Heinemann.

[199] Chambers, G.F. (1899). *The Story of Eclipses Simply Told for General Readers.* George Newnes, Ltd.

[200] Dafoe, D. (1715). *The Family Instructor.*

[201] Baikouzis, C., & Magnasco, M. O. (2008). Is an eclipse described in the Odyssey? *Proceedings of the National Academy of Sciences, 105*(26), 8823–8828. https://doi.org/10.1073/pnas.0803317105

[202] Attwell, S.Z. (2021). *Aestus, Book 1: The City.* https://szattwell.com/

[203] *NOAA Space Weather Scales | NOAA / NWS Space Weather Prediction Center.* (n.d.). Retrieved from https://www.swpc.noaa.gov/noaa-scales-explanation

THINGS TO KNOW ABOUT...

But it is in the darkest nights, when storms are blowing and the agitated waves are phosphorescent, that
the most impressive displays are made.
　　　　　—John Muir, *Wilderness Essays*[204]

METEOROLOGY IS A HUGE FIELD OF STUDY, AND AS SUCH THERE are thousands of things I have not mentioned in this book. The intent here was to focus on our common human experience (as Twain put it) and relate that to the other common human experience of emotions. That said, there are a few unique meteorological phenomena I have only briefly mentioned or skipped altogether which I've tried to capture here. In the SUGGESTED READING section at the end of this book, I have added in a few additional resources that may help you if you decided to use any of these weather elements in your stories.

Hurricanes and Other Tropical Systems

THE TROPICS TYPICALLY have two seasons: wet and dry. The wet season is usually the time of high sun (summer) when a majority of annual precipitation falls. The dry season is typically the time of low sun (winter) and is characterized by little or no precipitation.

Tropical areas have several definable common characteristics:

- An average annual temperature of 80°F (27°C) or greater
- Dew points of 65° to 80°F (18° to 26.6°C) in most places
- Drier air aloft, except in disturbances

- Clouds are mostly cumuliform
- Conditionally unstable lapse rates (temperature profile in the vertical)
- Predominately easterly low-level flow

Tropical waves are common weather makers in tropical areas. Sometimes called Easterly Waves in the Atlantic and Equatorial Waves in the Pacific, they are more common in the Atlantic. Atlantic (easterly) waves form over the Ethiopian Highlands from June to October. They move westward south of the Sahara and exit coastal Africa. Once they reach the Lesser Antilles, they increase in intensity.

These storms are generally steered by the flow around the oceanic high pressure systems. Eventually, this drift brings them to the limit of the tropics (i.e., the western side of the anticyclone where the flow becomes westerly and curvature toward the north begins).

Tropical systems are fed by warm water and live best under weak shear (meaning the winds in the upper atmosphere are not strong). Under the right conditions, the wave becomes a **tropical disturbance.** This is a loosely packed formation of thunderstorms without a lot of wind. If the disturbance lives long enough, it becomes a **tropical depression.** Here wind speeds are less than 33 knots (38 mph) and become more organized, circulating around the middle of the storm. Should the depression become stronger, it may become a **tropical storm.** Winds have increased to 34 knots (39 mph) but less than 63 knots (73 mph) and come with heavy rains. Once the speed reaches 64 knots (74 mph), the tropical storm becomes a **hurricane.** An eye forms in the center and the news is all over it.

There are five categories on the **Saffir-Simpson Hurricane Wind Scale**, the scale of hurricane strength used by the United States. Each of these categories increase the potential for damage, storm surge, tornadic development, and flooding. The following table is constructed from the National Hurricane Center.[205]

Category	Winds	Potential Damage
1	74-95 mph (64-82 knots or 119-153 km/h)	Very dangerous winds will produce some damage: Well-constructed frame homes could have damage to roof, shingles, vinyl siding and gutters. Large branches of trees will snap and shallowly rooted trees may be toppled. Extensive damage to power lines and poles likely will result in power outages that could last a few to several days.
2	96-110 mph (83-95 knots or 154-177 km/h)	Extremely dangerous winds will cause extensive damage: Well-constructed frame homes could sustain major roof and siding damage. Many shallowly rooted trees will be snapped or uprooted and block numerous roads. Near-total power loss is expected with outages that could last from several days to weeks.
3	111-129 mph (96-112 knots or 178-208 km/h)	Devastating damage will occur: Well-built framed homes may incur major damage or removal of roof decking and gable ends. Many trees will be snapped or uprooted, blocking numerous roads. Electricity and water will be unavailable for several days to weeks after the storm passes.
4	130-156 mph (113-136 knots or 209-251 km/h)	Catastrophic damage will occur: Well-built framed homes can sustain severe damage with loss of most of the roof structure and/or some exterior walls. Most trees will be snapped or uprooted and power poles downed. Fallen trees and power poles will isolate residential areas. Power outages will last weeks to possibly months. Most of the area will be uninhabitable for weeks or months.
5	157 mph or higher (137 knots or higher or 252 km/h or higher)	Catastrophic damage will occur: A high percentage of framed homes will be destroyed, with total roof failure and wall collapse. Fallen trees and power poles will isolate residential areas. Power outages will last for weeks to possibly months. Most of the area will be uninhabitable for weeks or months.

Terrain has a great effect on the strength, with landfall causing storms to break apart and decrease the wind speeds. As the storm loses the warmer water, it begins to also lose its tropical characteristics and eventually dissipates altogether.

There are **extratropical cyclones** which appear and act like hurricanes but are formed differently. Should a tropical system cross a certain threshold (e.g., 40°N), it may be labeled an extratropical system. These systems are no less dangerous.

Tropical systems in the Northern Hemisphere spin in a counterclockwise direction, while in the Southern Hemisphere, they spin clockwise. They also have different names depending on the region of the world.

- Hurricane: Atlantic and Eastern, Central Pacific Oceans
- Typhoon: Western Pacific Ocean
- Cyclonic storm: Northern Indian Ocean
- Tropical cyclone: Southern Indian Ocean
- Cyclone: Southwestern Pacific Ocean

What's In a Name?

For years, tropical systems that made landfall were named after the saint's day on which it happened. Hurricane Santa Ana, for example struck Puerto Rico in July 1825.[206] Clement Wragge, an Australian meteorologist, began naming cyclones in the 1890s by using Polynesian mythological figures and politicians who annoyed him.[207] In the novel *Storm* by George R. Stewart, the titular event is named Maria. Throughout the novel, Maria wreaks havoc from California to New York.[208] No, the storm wasn't a hurricane.

The United States began naming hurricanes in 1953 using female names only. It wasn't until 1978 when men's names were included. The naming convention is not American. The World Meteorological Organization has set up procedures to determine the names of all tropical systems within a specific region or basin.[209] As such, there are five different naming organizations for five different basins. Within each region, the members get together and write up a list of names to use for six years. If a particular storm becomes uniquely destructive or newsworthy, the name is retired. The names are alphabetical for the most part and are never named after a particular person. Unlike Wragge who named a cyclone after Australian politician James Drake, the names used are intended to be easy for people of that basin to remember.

Stopping Hurricanes

Tropical systems cause damage and death. They can leave behind a swath of destruction that is unequaled by any other type of meteorological phenomena. What if we could stop them? What if we could rip out the heart of a hurricane before it began so that our lives would be nothing but unicorns and rainbows?

While the stuff of fiction (and mad scientists worshiping alien lizard overlords in fiction), there have been numerous real attempts at this over the years. From nuclear weapons to altering the heat balance to cooling water with icebergs, the attempts to stop hurricanes reads like any good thriller novel. For example, Project STORMFURY, a research mission conducted by the U.S. from 1962 to 1983, involved seeding the clouds around an eyewall with silver iodide in the hopes that the increased convection would create an eyewall with a larger radius and therefore lower speeds (thanks in part to the conservation of angular momentum). As you might have guessed already, it didn't work.[210]

Floods

FLOODS ARE SOME of our earliest stories, finding their way into just about every religion in the world. Without a doubt, the story of Noah in the Bible is the one that comes first to mind.

> Now the earth was corrupt in God's sight and was full
> of violence...I am going to bring floodwaters on the
> earth to destroy all life under the heavens, every crea-
> ture that has the breath of life in it. Everything on
> earth will perish.[211]

In the *Epic of Gilgamesh*, the god Enlil decides to destroy the world with a flood because it has become too noisy. (I'm with Enlil on this.) A similar story is told in the 18th century BCE by the Akkadians. Other flood myth stories have been found in Sumerian writing, Hindu mythology, and in the west with the Cheyenne tribe of North America as well as in Navajo oral traditions.

Floods are, in a word, fascinating. They are also emotionally draining and for many bring up memories and horrors of losing everything. Even if one of your readers has never experienced a flood themselves, they can still sympathize with a character who is being swept away by rising waters or a town drowning as the nearby river overflows its banks.

In *The Mill on the Floss* by George Eliot, a flood changes everything in the last few pages. Maggie Tulliver's stream of thoughts of her travails through the previous 900 or so pages are interrupted mid-flow by another kind of stream, "a startling sensation of sudden cold about her knees and feet..."

> ...it was water flowing under her. She started up; the stream was flowing under the door that led into the passage. She was not bewildered for an instant; she knew it was the flood!

> The tumult of emotion she had been enduring for the last twelve hours seemed to have left a great calm in her; without screaming, she hurried with the candle upstairs to Bob Jakin's bedroom. The door was ajar; she went in and shook him by the shoulder.

> "Bob, the flood is come! it is in the house; let us see if we can make the boats safe."

> She lighted his candle, while the poor wife, snatching up her baby, burst into screams; and then she hurried down again to see if the waters were rising fast. There was a step down into the room at the door leading from the staircase; she saw that the water was already

on a level with the step. While she was looking, something came with a tremendous crash against the window, and sent the leaded panes and the old wooden framework inward in shivers, the water pouring in after it.

"It is the boat!" cried Maggie. "Bob, come down to get the boats!"

If you're wondering, Maggie struggles through the waters in a boat to find her brother Tom at the old mill. There they set out to rescue their cousin Lucy Deane and her family. Like many Victorian-era novels, all does not end well as "...brother and sister had gone down in an embrace never to be parted."[212]

When considering a flood in your story, you might want to look at how floods are formed. Most flooding that is not coastal (i.e., caused by a tsunami or a surge of water from a tropical system) is river-based.

By definition, a river is a natural stream of water emptying into a larger river, lake, or ocean. All rivers are formed by a series of tributaries, or branches. The source is the beginning of the river system—perhaps an area of melting snow or a glacier. It could be run-off from an overflowing lake, reservoir, or spring. About 70% of rainfall evaporates, while the rest flows into rivers or is absorbed into the ground (which may make its way into a river eventually). Without getting into too much hydrology, rivers have a current, depth (which is affected by tides), and waves or swells.

A not-so-fun fact: a **tidal bore** is a dangerous wave up to several feet high surging *upstream*. Tidal bores occur most often during spring tide which is when the tidal range (the difference between high and low tide) is the greatest. The largest known bores occur in China where wave heights have been measured up to 15 feet high and moved upstream 25 feet per second. Put your character on a raft in a river minding their own business and see what you can do to your narrative.

Apart from the tidal bore, there are four types of floods. The first is **rainfall**. It is the most common and can occur in less than one hour in a hilly, or a mountainous region. Rainfall floods can occur several days after the precipitation has stopped. Upstream lakes overflow into rivers and tributaries bringing water into the flood zone. Water begins to rise, and the river overflows its banks covering the surrounding area in water. There is no need for your characters ever see a drop of rain, either. On July 31, 1976, a thunderstorm miles away caused a major flash flood in Big Thompson River Canyon. One hundred forty four people died.

The second type of flooding is **snow melt**. This flood starts in the near-polar regions as large snowfields begin to melt. The resulting water flows miles downstream until it finally floods. Usually, the affected area is smaller than rainfall flooding, but it can be extremely dangerous when the temperatures rise quickly above freezing or if the runoff water mixes with rainfall as it flows downstream.

The third type of flooding is called **ice jam**. It only occurs in cold climates over a small geographical area. There are two sources for ice jam flooding. One is from glaciers and the other is from thick ice forming on a river during the winter months. In both cases, melting begins and the river water rises. The rising water breaks the ice into large chunks. Those chunks are carried downstream until they get stuck in bridges or along sharp river bends. The ice blocks the water and small-scale flooding occurs.

The last type is called **dam break**. As the name implies, it occurs most often as the result of a deliberate act. This is the most dangerous type of flooding since it releases millions of gallons of water in a short period of time and can destroy entire towns in minutes.

El Niño and La Niña

ONE OF THE most important sources of year-to-year climate variation in the United States (and around the world) is the **El Niño** and **La Niña** phenomena of the tropical Pacific Ocean. Under "normal" conditions, the tropical trade winds blow from east to west, building up warm water in the western Pacific. In the eastern Pacific, the trade winds pull up cold, deep, nutrient-rich waters along the equator from the Ecuadorian and Peruvian coasts to the central Pacific. The warmth of the western Pacific results in particularly vigorous convection with towering cumulus clouds and tropical storms that "radiate" atmospheric waves and disturbances across vast regions of the globe. Heat and moisture lofted into the upper atmosphere by the clouds and storms are distributed by high-altitude winds across vast regions of the globe.

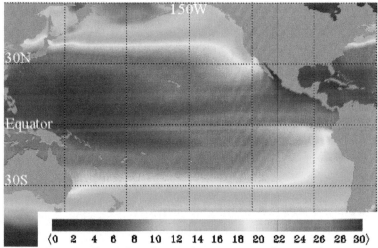

Figure 67. Climatological sea-surface temperatures for September.

During an El Niño, this situation is disrupted and the trade winds weaken, thus reducing the upwelling of cool waters in the eastern Pacific and allowing the pool of warm water in the west to drift eastward toward South America. As the central and eastern Pacific warm, atmospheric pressure gradients along the equator weaken, and the trade winds diminish even more.

These changes were identified as the "Southern Oscillation" of the global atmosphere by Sir Gilbert Walker in the early 20th century. A chicken-and-egg relation exists between the changes in ocean temperatures and changes in winds—the two sets of changes reinforce and drive each other, but neither is clearly "the" initiator of El Niño. Ocean temperatures and surface winds interact to form the complex process known as the El Niño-Southern Oscillation (ENSO). The interactions can be set off by subtle changes in one or the other, by buffeting from other parts of the tropics, or from regions beyond the tropics. Such a complex interplay and its uncertain (and variable) origins are the primary limitations on the ability to predict El Niño.

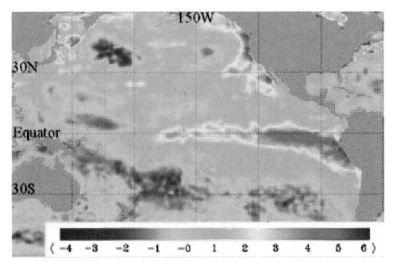

Figure 68. Sea-surface temperature anomalies during an El Niño event.

As the waters of the central and eastern Pacific warm, the powerful tropical Pacific storms begin to form farther east than usual. As the distribution of storms spreads east along the equator, their influence on global weather systems also changes. Most notably, the jet stream over the North Pacific Ocean strengthens and moves farther south than normal, where it collects moisture and storms and carries them to the southwestern United States and northern Mexico.

During an El Niño, the trade winds are too weak to cause upwelling of nutrient-rich waters off the coasts of Ecuador and Peru. Generations of South American fisherman have recognized these conditions by the disappearance of their standard catch, commonly during December and January, every three to seven years. Because of the near coincidence in timing between these conditions and Christmas, the fishing communities have called the phenomenon "El Niño", for the Christ child. The geologic record suggests that El Niño conditions have been a part of Earth's climate for at least several thousand years.

An El Niño event usually lasts for several months, and, along with its other effects, represents an interruption of the "normal" seasonal cycle of the tropical climate. After one to two years, and usually during springtime (in the Northern Hemisphere), the seasonal cycle reasserts itself and the tropical ocean cools back to normal east-to-west sea-surface temperature gradients. Sometimes the warm El Niño events give way to unusually cold sea-surface temperatures and unusually strong trade winds—a condition now called **La Niña**. On other occasions, La Niñas may begin on their own, without an immediately preceding El Niño. The effects of the El Niño and La Niña on global climate are, in part, mirror images of each other. For example, drought is a common occurrence in the southwestern United States during La Niña, in contrast to the wet years associated with El Niño.

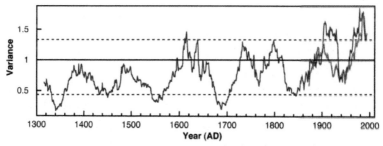

Figure 69. El Niño variability derived from tree rings (blue) and instrumental measurements (red). [213]

In *Dry Humor: Tales of Arizona Weather*, author James E. Cook describes the flooding that occurs in the desert southwest during El Niño events.

> Most weather-related deaths in Arizona result from someone driving in a mountain canyon or a desert wash. Inevitably, someone tries to outrun a wall of water running through a steep canyon, or ignores the warnings about crossing desert washes. Only a lucky few survive.

> Either desert washes are not as shallow as they appear, or they mischievously sink when they fill with water. One Good Samaritan was getting ready to throw a rope over the head and shoulders of a man struggling against the swift waters of a flooded river wash in

northwest Phoenix.

"How deep is it?" he called.

"Pretty deep. I'm standing on my pickup."

Within hours the water recedes. In a few days, the cemetery is dry enough to bury those who didn't take the flood seriously. Homes and businesses dry out, and streets are repaired. Bridges take a little longer.

Within a month, tourists are chuckling at the dry rivers and the signs that say, "Do Not Cross When Flooded."

And your average long-time Arizonan can't remember the last time it rained.[214]

Upper-Atmospheric Lightning

TRANSIENT LUMINOUS EVENTS (TLEs) are the stuff of coolness. Sometimes called upper atmospheric lightning or ionospheric lightning, TLEs are electrically produced forms of plasma that occur above cumulonimbus clouds. TLEs come in four flavors: sprites, blue jets, gigantic jets, and ELVES.[215]

Sprites are flashes of bright red light above storms. They can also be reddish-orange or greenish-blue and have been categorized as jellyfish, column, or carrots sprites. **Blue jets** come out of the top of a thunderstorm and last less than a second. **Gigantic jets** reach much higher than blue jets and may change from blue to red. **ELVES** (Emission of Light and Very Low Frequency perturbations due to Electromagnetic Pulse Sources) are ring-shaped glows that last a total of 0.001 seconds up to about 250 miles (400 km) in diameter.[216]

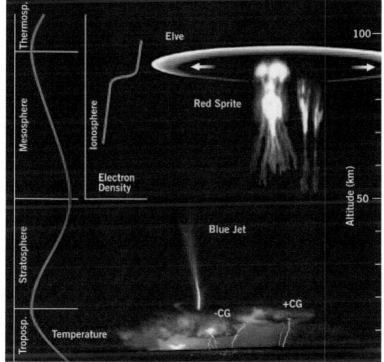

Figure 70. Transient luminous events (TLEs).[217]

Noctilucent Clouds

NOCTILUCENT CLOUDS ARE rare, thin, wispy high-altitude clouds that can only be seen under specific conditions. You may see them in the summer after sunset, but only if you're in higher latitudes and the sky is clear. The name is derived from Latin (like so much else in the scientific world): *nocto* meaning "at night" and *lucent* which translates to "they shine." Put those together and you get "at night they shine," which is true.

Noctilucent clouds are found in the mesosphere, the layer of atmosphere above the stratosphere (which is above the troposphere where we hang out). That puts these clouds about 47 to 53 miles (76 to 85 km) up. Like their lowly buddies, noctilucent clouds need water vapor, dust, and very low temperatures. The water vapor freezes on the dust created by tiny meteors or volcanic ash and the sun illuminates the ice crystals from below. Magical blue wisps appear across the sky like angels riding the surf of space.

Figure 71. Noctilucent clouds, June 25, 2018, Central Russia.[218]

There is evidence that these clouds are increasing in frequency thanks to methane emissions which have more than doubled the amount of mesospheric ice present.[219] In a statement, the author of the study that supports this states, "People living in the mid to high latitudes now have a good chance of seeing noctilucent clouds several times each summer. In the 19th century, they were probably visible only once every several decades or so."[220]

It has been said that the first recorded viewing of a noctilucent cloud was following the explosion of Krakatoa in 1883. As reported in *Nature* in 1884, painter Robert Charles Leslie saw "The sky around and above where the sun had set, looking almost ceiling-like in its opacity, upon which soon appeared numbers of weird small cloud forms, at times very regular, like ripple-marks in sand, or the bones of some great fish or saurian embedded on a slab of stone."[221] Yet there is also an argument to be made that many prior volcanic eruptions had been large enough to create the conditions necessary for noctilucent cloud development. In 1814, Russian poet Alexander Pushkin wrote:

> A gloomy night became a veil for sleeping heaven,
> A dale and groves keep silence in their dreams,

There is a wood in grizzled mist and
Gentle voice of stream, which running to the oaks
shadow,
The breeze is slightly breathing in the bed of
leaves,
And serene Moon – majestic swan,
Is swimming through the silvery clouds.
It swims and suddenly,
Its pale light illumes the landscape,
Discovering for eyes the alley of old lindens,
And hills and meadow come partly into view.

This poem is particularly noteworthy for the inclusion of "silvery clouds", which is the exact translation of the Russian word for noctilucent clouds (серебристые облака).[222]

Rainbows, Moonbows, and Sundogs

RAINBOWS HAVE A special place in literature. While they are nothing more than optical illusions caused by light refracting through water droplets, they are nonetheless magical. Hence the phrase I often use: "It'll be unicorns and rainbows from now on." I haven't found a unicorn, yet.

Aristotle wrote quite a bit about rainbows in *Meteorologica*. Again, he was wrong—kind of. To him, rainbows were reflections of the sun, where every droplet of water was a tiny mirror which was too small to reflect figures. "It is impossible that the figure of a thing should be reflected in them, for if it is the mirror will be sensibly divisible since divisibility is involved in the notion of figure."[223]

The science behind the magic of a rainbow is simple: sunlight hits drops of water suspended in the air, and a viewer at exactly 42 degrees sees the prismatic effect. The sun will usually be behind the person seeing the rainbow. Rainbows are created by the change in a light wave's direction through refraction and reflection. Light entering a water droplet is refracted (bent) and then reflected by the back of the droplet. As the light is reflected back, it is refracted again and magical colors of serenity are made.

The light that strikes a water droplet splits into the visible spectrum of light that we see as the colors of a rainbow: red, orange, yellow, green, blue, indigo, and violet. **Double rainbows** (double the serenity, double the magic) are created by light being reflected twice inside the raindrop. The secondary rainbow displays the colors in reverse order. The strength of the rainbow is dependent on the size of the water droplet. Therefore, **fogbows** (rainbows in fog) and **cloudbows** (rainbows in clouds) are fainter. As the moon has no light of its own but reflects the sun, **moonbows** are faint as well.

In Norse mythology, the rainbow is a bridge between Earth and the gods. This notion of a connection to the divine has also been found in Zulu, Navaho, Hawaiian, Japanese, Cambodian, Greek, Australian Aborigine, Chumash, and Hopi myths.[224] In the Hindu world, Indra uses a rainbow bow to shoot arrows of lightning.[225] Rainbows are also covenants, as in the *Epic of Gilgamesh* and the Bible. A promise is made by the deity who caused the flood that it would not happen again.

Rainbows are not all...um...rainbows and unicorns in some cultures. In Burma, rainbows are demons that threaten children. In the Amazon, rainbows are associated with illness. In the Amuesha language of central Peru, certain diseases are called *ayona'achartan*, meaning "the rainbow hurt my skin."[226] Of course, there is the pot of gold at the end of the rainbow, which is guarded by a leprechaun, and for those who have seen the first movie Jennifer Anniston ever starred in, you know that bad things can happen. "Try as they will, and try as they might, who steals me gold won't live through the night."[227]

Not all is so bad at the end of the mythical rainbow, though. The Rainbow Trail from Kayenta to Rainbow Bridge in northeast Arizona in the Navajo Nation was inspiration for Zane Grey who took the trip on horseback in 1913. While not a rainbow in the meteorological sense, In *The Rainbow Trail*, Grey's sequel to *Riders of the Purple Stage*, the author does not waste time connecting the idea of finding the treasure at the end of the rainbow to the journey the protagonist takes.

But just yet I can't tell you why I came to Kayenta,
what I want to do, how long I shall stay. My thoughts
put in words would seem so like dreams. Maybe they
are dreams. Perhaps I'm only chasing a phantom—
perhaps I'm only hunting the treasure at the foot of
the rainbow."

"Well, this is the country for rainbows," laughed
Withers. "In summer from June to August when it
storms we have rainbows that'll make you think
you're in another world. The Navajos have rainbow
mountains, rainbow canyons, rainbow bridges of
stone, rainbow trails. It sure is rainbow country."[228]

The refraction of light through ice crystals creates **sundogs**. These are
colored spots of light located approximately 22 degrees either left, right,
or both, from the sun. The colors typically go from red towards the sun
to blue away from it. Sundogs are also known as parhelia, a Greek word
meaning "beside the sun." Our buddy Aristotle called them "mock suns,"
and said of them that they are "a surer sign of rain."

The War of the Roses was supposedly won by the appearance of three suns,
as dramatized with emotion in *Henry VI, Part 3* by William Shakespeare.

EDWARD
Dazzle mine eyes, or do I see three suns?

RICHARD
Three glorious suns, each one a perfect sun;
Not separated with the racking clouds,
But sever'd in a pale clear-shining sky.
See, see! they join, embrace, and seem to kiss,
As if they vow'd some league inviolable:
Now are they but one lamp, one light, one sun.
In this the heaven figures some event.[229]

In 1461, King Edward was to go into the battle of Mortimer's Cross when he saw this phenomena. He took this as a sign that represented his two brothers and himself and told his army that they were prophesized they would be victorious.[230]

They were, but still. It's just an optical effect.

Climate Change

GIVEN THE IMPACT of climate change, it is no wonder that true anxiety can be instilled in a reader by describing a bleak and unforgiving future, one influenced by the 8 billion people on Earth. Climate change can be defined as "a long-term change in the average weather patterns that have come to define Earth's local, regional and global climates."[231] The impacts of human intervention are known as **anthropogenic** changes, or "environmental change caused or influenced by people, either directly or indirectly."[232] The Great Smog of London in 1952 discussed earlier in this book is one such example of an environmental change caused by people.

Climate change is a combination of the anthropogenic and the natural. There is no denying that climate change existed before people, and events like the Ice Age were caused by a chain reaction of changes in the orbit of Earth around the sun. Yes, Earth is constantly changing and has been for billions of years. However, anthropogenic impact has now augmented the natural. You cannot discount the influence that people might have on a fragile ecosystem. Media has had an impact in the way information is transmitted, as well, and the more you're made aware of something, the more you believe it to be out of control. There is a difference in reading about slight changes in the weekly paper you may have picked up on a 1900s New York street corner and hearing about it almost daily in today's information-rich landscape.

In 1953, John Wyndham published what is considered the first cli-fi—climate fiction—novel, *The Kraken Wakes*. In the novel, he predicted specific events half a century in the future, which is now two decades ago. Some of his predictions included: mistrust of the media contributing to conspiracy theories; political gridlock; and the outright rejection of scientific evidence without supporting arguments. Sound familiar? While the novel is more about aliens who live in the ocean, it has become influential in how cli-fi is written today.[233] From racial unrest, the disruption of the social order, to the repercussions of procrastination, *The Kraken Wakes* is a novel that begs the reader of today to think hard about what the next fifty years will be like.

Wyndham wasn't the only early pioneer of disastrous world-ending scenarios rooted in weather. Jules Verne wrote of climate change in 1889 in *The Purchase of the North Pole*, where the tilt of Earth's axis makes the arctic regions valuable real estate. In *The Man Who Awoke*, written in 1933, Laurence Manning writes about a man who puts himself to sleep for 5,000 years at a time and finds Earth's climate destroyed by anthropogenic climate change. (In the next 5,000 years, humans are dominated by an AI-like intelligence, which might be coming sooner than we think.) Frank Herbert's *Dune* written in 1965 is ripe with environmentalism.

More recently in 1993, Octavia E. Butler's *Parable of the Sower* takes Wyndham's dire predictions of society to a new level with an apocalyptic scenario enhanced by corporate greed and wealth inequality. Climate change in fiction is also often accelerated by the mad scientist trope. In *Category 7* by Bill Evans, a hurricane is augmented by a rogue scientist and billionaire and used as a weapon.

The U.S. Office of the Director of National Intelligence has brought climate change into the realm of military threats. In a 2021 report on annual threat assessments, the report states:

> We assess that the effects of a changing climate and environmental degradation will create a mix of direct and indirect threats, including risks to the economy, heightened political volatility, human displacement, and new venues for geopolitical competition that will play out during the next decade and beyond...The degradation and depletion of soil, water, and biodiversity resources almost certainly will threaten infrastructure, health, water, food, and security, especially in many developing countries that lack the capacity to adapt

quickly to change, and increase the potential for conflict over competition for scarce natural resources.[234]

Climate change—despite being seen by many as a political hot potato—
is not something that should be discounted in fiction. There is a lot that can
be written about the anthropogenic and natural impacts on the environment,
and without a doubt, most predictions of a future world would certainly
bring about feelings of **anxiety, fear,** and **sadness** in the reader. Even in the
survey on weather and emotions discussed early in this book, the image used
for heat could have been interpreted as "global warming," which may explain
why 23% of respondents chose emotions on the spectrum of **sadness** (to include grief, pensiveness, remorse, and disapproval).

It does not *have* to be a sermon, though. There are too may authors
who want to use their platform to promote environmental activism and
do so on a level that is akin to having your head beat in by a baseball bat
that says "DRIVE ELECTRIC OR DIE" written across the side. To me,
those authors proselytize and *tell* rather than *show*.

You can show the effects of climate change without telling the reader
that the whole thing is their fault and they should feel guilty. S.Z. Attwell
perfected this in *Aestus, Book 1: The City* by simply *showing* what life
would be like if the temperature were higher globally. People live under-
ground and work to harness the power of the sun through solar farms. In
other words, it's not preachy. The most the reader gets is a brief backstory
about the Founders and why they settled where they did. Thank you. I sat
through enough sermons when I was a child.

REVERSING THE ANTHROPOGENIC influence on climate change is an on-
going discussion that has netted several different possibilities. In the
"break in case of glass" category, the U.S. Government wants to fund a
research plan[235] to reverse the effects of anthropogenic climate change
using—as an example—what is known as solar radiation modification
(SRM). SRM is way to lower the heat absorbed by Earth by spraying fine
aerosols into the atmosphere which would theoretically reflect sunlight
away.[236] It's not entirely science fiction. In 1815, the Tambora Volcano in

Indonesia erupted and sent so much ash into the atmosphere to drop annual temperature averages by up to 5°F (3°C) the following year, known as "The Year Without a Summer."[237] The same thing happened with the explosion of Krakatoa in Indonesia in 1883, with Ksudach in Russia in 1907, and Bezymianny, also in Russia, in 1956.[238]

These attempts at reversal have a place in literature as well, although there are not (to my knowledge) many authors who explore it outside of saying if something isn't done, our children are going to die. Cli-fi does not have to be dystopian. It can look forward into a world that is better off than the one we have now. Novels take us places, and those places make us feel things. Why couldn't we escape to a utopian world where the climate is perfect?

Then again, what exactly is a "perfect" climate? Put an Inuit on the equator and they would curse you for years.

[204] Muir, J. (2011). *Wilderness Essays* (Revised). Gibbs Smith.

[205] *Saffir-Simpson Hurricane Wind Scale.* (n.d.). https://www.nhc.noaa.gov/aboutsshws.php

[206] Tannehill, I.R. (1945). *Hurricanes, Their Nature and History, Particularly Those of the West Indies and ohe Southern Coasts of the United States.* Princeton University Press.

[207] *How do tropical cyclones get their names? - Social Media Blog - Bureau of Meteorology.* (2016, January 14). https://media.bom.gov.au/social/blog/875/how-do-tropical-cyclones-get-their-names/

[208] Stewart, G.R. (1941). *Storm.* Random House.

[209] *Tropical Cyclone Naming.* (2022, May 6). World Meteorological Organization. https://public.wmo.int/en/our-mandate/focus-areas/natural-hazards-and-disaster-risk-reduction/tropical-cyclones/Naming

[210] Willoughby, H. E., Jorgensen, D. P., Black, R. A., & Rosenthal, S. L. (1985). Project STORM-FURY: A Scientific Chronicle 1962–1983. *Bulletin of the American Meteorological Society,* 66(5), 505–514. http://www.jstor.org/stable/26224358

[211] *New International Version.* (1973). Bible Hub. https://biblehub.com/niv/genesis/6.htm

[212] Eliot, G. (1860). *The Mill on the Floss.* William Blackwood and Sons.

[213] Staff, S. X. (2013, June 30). *El Nino unusually active in the late 20th century, study finds.* https://phys.org/news/2013-06-el-nino-unusually-late-20th.html

[214] Cook, J. E. (1992). *Dry Humor: Tales of Arizona Weather.* Gem Guides Book Co.

[215] *Proceedings Volume 10564, International Conference on Space Optics — ICSO 2012;* 1056404 (2017) https://doi.org/10.1117/12.2309048 Event: International Conference on Space Optics 2012, 2012, Ajaccio, Corsica, France

[216] *Transient Luminous Events (TLEs) | SKYbrary Aviation Safety.* (n.d.). https://skybrary.aero/articles/transient-luminous-events-tles

[217] FECYT - Spanish Foundation for Science and Technology (2010, June 10). *Storm elves and sprites recorded on video.* https://phys.org/news/2010-06-storm-elves-sprites-video.html

218 PhotoChur (Photographer). *Atmospheric phenomenon of noctilucent clouds (night shining clouds), June 25, 2018, Central Russia* [digital image]. Retrieved from https://www.shutter-stock.com/

219 Lübken, F.-J., Berger, U., & Baumgarten, G. (2018). On the anthropogenic impact on long-term evolution of noctilucent clouds. *Geophysical Research Letters, 45*, 6681– 6689. https://doi.org/10.1029/2018GL077719

220 American Geophysical Union. (2018, July 2). *Climate change is making night-shining clouds more visible.* https://phys.org/news/2018-07-climate-night-shining-clouds-visible.html

221 Leslie, R. (1884). The sky-glows. *Nature, 30.*

222 Dalin, P., Pertsev, N., and Romejko, V.: Notes on historical aspects on the earliest known observations of noctilucent clouds, *Hist. Geo Space. Sci., 3*, 87–97, https://doi.org/10.5194/hgss-3-87-2012, 2012.

223 Goold, G. P. (Ed.). (1952). *Aristotle: Meteorologica (Loeb Classical Library No. 397)* (H. D. P. Lee, Trans.; Illustrated). Harvard University Press.

224 Lee, R. L., Jr, & Fraser, A. B. (2001). *The Rainbow Bridge: Rainbows in Art, Myth, and Science* (1st ed.). Penn State University Press.

225 *rainbow | National Geographic Society.* (2001, August 31). https://education.nationalgeo-graphic.org/resource/rainbow/

226 Valadeau, C., Castillo, J. A., Sauvain, M., Lores, A. F., & Bourdy, G. (2010). The rainbow hurts my skin: Medicinal concepts and plants uses among the Yanesha (Amuesha), an Amazonian Peruvian ethnic group. *Journal of Ethnopharmacology, 127*(1), 175–192. https://doi.org/10.1016/j.jep.2009.09.024

227 Jones, M. (Director). (1993). *Leprechaun* [Film]. Trimark Pictures.

228 Grey, Z. (1915). *The Rainbow Trail.*

229 Shakespeare, W. (1992). *Henry VI, Part 3.* C. Watts & K. Carabine (Eds.). Wordsworth Editions. (Original work published 1623).

230 Young, J. (2011, October 2). *The Mortimer's Cross Parhelion: How a Meteorological Phenomenon Changed English History.* Decoded Science. https://web.ar-chive.org/web/20160306005627/https://www.decodedscience.org/the-mortimers-cross-par-helion-how-a-meteorological-phenomenon-changed-english-history/3437 (archived)

231 Shaftel, H. (2022, September 26). *Overview: Weather, Global Warming and Climate Change.* Climate Change: Vital Signs of the Planet. https://climate.nasa.gov/global-warming-vs-climate-change/

232 *EarthWord: Anthropogenic* | U.S. Geological Survey. (2015, September 1). https://www.usgs.gov/news/earthword-anthropogenic

233 *The First Climate Fiction Masterpiece: On John Wyndham's 1953 Novel "The Kraken Wakes."* (2022, October 15). Los Angeles Review of Books. https://lareviewofbooks.org/article/the-first-climate-fiction-masterpiece-on-john-wyndhams-1953-novel-the-kraken-wakes/

234 Office of the Director of National Intelligence. (2021). *Annual Threat Assessment of the US Intelligence Community.*

235 The White House. (2022, November 4). *Request for Input to a Five-Year Plan for Research on Climate Intervention.* https://www.whitehouse.gov/ostp/legal/

236 *Solar Radiation Modification.* (2022, November 2). C2G. https://www.c2g2.net/solar-radiation-modification/

237 Stothers, R. B. (1984). The Great Tambora Eruption in 1815 and Its Aftermath. *Science, 224*(4654), 1191–1198. https://doi.org/10.1126/science.224.4654.1191

238 Bradley, R. S. (1988). The explosive volcanic eruption signal in northern hemisphere continental temperature records. *Climatic Change, 12*(3), 221–243. https://doi.org/10.1007/bf00139431

ALIEN WEATHER

The exoplanet atmosphere is the only way to infer
whether or not a planet is habitable or likely inhabited;
the planetary atmosphere is our window into temperatures, habitability indicators, and biosignature gases.
— Sara Seager and Drake Deming[239]

A S AN AUTHOR OF SPECULATIVE FICTION, I DO DABBLE IN SCIENCE
fiction frequently. Even if a story is about life on another world,
weather still plays a huge part. In the start of the second novel of
my series *Transit*, the colonists experience the results of a theoretical shift
in the weather patterns on their new planet. While I intended this to be a
commentary on the political nature of climate change, its inclusion plays
a huge role in the further development of the human species on the
planet. The book starts with a flood that forces the relocation of the col-
ony. That, in itself, is not fiction. Societies throughout time have been
displaced by weather, and it is no stretch to pull the historical record into
science fiction.

There are, of course, physics which we must pay attention to, but atmospheres on other planets are *not* going to be like ours. Even on my
fictional planet, the atmosphere is slightly different (as is the size of the
planet and therefore the gravitational constant).

For those science fiction writers who might be reading this, consider
the following:

- Parcels of air are going to behave differently because the atmosphere on another planet will be made up of different elements

and have a different density. **Atmospheric buoyancy** is a function of density which is determined by gas laws. Change the gas, you change the buoyancy but not the laws.

- The gravitational constant may be the same (6.6743×10^{-11} m^3 kg^{-1} s^{-2}, if you're dying to know), but as it describes the attraction between two different masses, if your masses are different (e.g., a bigger or smaller planet), the attraction will be different. The **gravitational acceleration** of Earth is 9.81 m/s^2 (32.2 ft/s^2) but it will not be on other planets. Many of the formulas meteorologists have used to figure things out use Earth's gravitational constant.

- Those formulas are also used in **atmospheric modeling**, so it goes to reason if *any* constant changes, the output would change as well. New models would need to be developed if any hope of forecasting the weather on a different planet is possible.

- Weather on another planet will also have a big impact on the **evolution of whatever species of life exists**, too. For example, it has long been known that birds of the same species are smaller in warmer habitats.[240] Known as Bergmann's rule, warm-blooded species inhabiting colder climates have larger average body sizes than their warm-weather colleagues. Recently, however, it appears that anthropogenic climate change may be breaking that rule.[241]

- The **distribution of humans** has also been altered by changes in temperature and rainfall as ancient humans became global wanderers, adapting to different—and changing—climates.[242]

- **Alien chemistry on exoplanets** will also be influenced by the atmospheric conditions. *Methanoperedens*, unicellular organisms that look like bacteria, break down methane (CH^4) in soils, groundwater, and the atmosphere to support cellular metabolism. Perhaps other organisms "feed" off exotic chemicals found on other planets.[243]

Interesting fact: Blue eyes contain less melanin in the irises than brown, hazel, or green eyes. As a result, those with blue eyes are more susceptible to photophobia than those with darker-colored eyes. So, on a planet that may have a different atmospheric composition than Earth and therefore has a sky that reflects different wavelengths of the planet's star's light, would those with blue eyes have a major evolutionary advantage or disadvantage? I'm not making a guess here, but it's something to think about.

Diamond Rain?

DIAMOND RAIN SOUNDS like a song title (and probably is), but what I'm referring to here is all the weird stuff we might find on other planets. Apparently, research has shown that it may rain diamonds on **Jupiter** and **Saturn**.[244] Lightning in storms turns methane (of which there is an abundance on gaseous planets) into soot, which then hardens into balls of graphite. That graphite would compress into diamonds as it falls, which would mean diamond rain. Or hail. Whichever you prefer.

Along with Jupiter and Saturn, here are some others from our own backyard (solar system):

- **Neptune** has been found to have hurricane-like storms which last anywhere from two to six years.[245]
- While **Venus** is hot, it snows. Pyrite vaporizes at certain temperatures on our neighboring planet. This metal mist falls and covers mountains.[246]
- The average recorded temperature on **Mars** is -63°C (−81°F) with a maximum temperature of 20°C (68°F) and a minimum of −140°C (−220°F).[247] Talk about your need to wear layers.

It's easy to see how planets *outside* our solar system may also have different weather. On **HD 189773b**, for example, glass shards (silicate particles) are whipped through the air by thousand mile per hour winds.[248] Depending on your alien species, this might not make for a good vacation spot. And on **WASP-39b**, it was recently discovered by the James Webb Space Telescope, that the atmosphere of this gas giant contains carbon dioxide, water vapor, sodium, and carbon monoxide.[249] Companion research has also revealed that this exoplanet's sky is made up of broken clouds formed from silicates and sulfites—a metal sky.[250]

Currently, the best methods for detecting planets outside our solar system nets only fleeting atmospheric data. Yet there are over 5,200 planets which have been discovered as of late 2022 using a variety of techniques and tools from radial velocity to direct imaging.[251,252] As a planet moves in front of a star, its transit[a] allows light to pass through the atmospheres which can then be measured by high-precision instruments. And while we don't know the exact nature of the interaction between the ground of those planets (should they have "ground"), we can infer the weather and potential habitability through an examination of the atmosphere and chemical processes such as photochemistry, or photon-induced chemical reactions.[253]

Knowing what we do about how Earth's atmosphere behaves and things like the interaction of solar wind and the ionosphere, planetary circulation systems driven by rotation, the chemical processes within the troposphere, etc., it may be possible to infer Earth-like characteristics of relatively close exoplanets. As more of this information comes out, studies on the feasibility of alien life on those planets can be conducted. From there, it's a few more steps to understanding how aliens might view their own weather and, to really mess with Twain's words, uncover "the narrative of *alien* experience."[b]

Approaching Alien Weather in Fiction

WHEN WRITING A story which includes alien weather, the writer should consider the meteorology that might produce it. Here are some questions you might consider if you're writing a science fiction piece:

- Does the precipitation in the atmosphere pick up other particles or does it fall as pure H2O (water)?
- Is your planet Earth-like (i.e., within the habitable zone around its star which may support liquid water)?
- Is your fictional planet more gaseous?

---

[a] Incidentally, the science fiction series I have been writing is called *Transit*. While the original term uses the definition of moving from one place to another, its secondary term as defined here by astrophysicists, will also be brought up within the series.

[b] See INTRODUCTION.

- What is the terrain of your planet? As terrain has a modifying effect on the lower atmosphere, what mountain ranges or other geographical features exist?
- What is the gaseous concentration of your planet (on Earth, it's roughly 78% nitrogen, 21% oxygen, 0.9% argon, and 0.1 % other gases)?[c]
- Does your planet have an ozone? What is the atmospheric layering (e.g., troposphere, stratosphere, ionosphere)?
- What about tides? Does your planet have a satellite or two? Three? What is the effect of those moons on your water bodies (if your planet even has water bodies)?
- When the wind blows or storm systems move, are they doing so based on the rotation of the planet?

There's a lot to think about, and there are some readers who may question your atmospheric physics. I know I did when I saw clouds in space in a *Flash Gordon* serial from the 1930s. In *A Princess of Mars*, Edgar Rice Burroughs introduces us to the atmosphere of the red planet by saying, "It was midday, the sun was shining full upon me and the heat of it was rather intense upon my naked body, yet no greater than would have been true under similar conditions on an Arizona desert."[254] Recall that the actual temperature of Mars gets nowhere near the suggested temperature mentioned here. But we may excuse Burroughs as this was serialized in 1912 and published as a book in 1917...long before true meteorological observations were made on Mars.

I recently put a lot of thought into alien weather while world building a planet for a new series. The general makeup of the world—Minor Pales—is water. Imagine a certain Kevin Costner movie and *The Perfect Storm* put together. I had fun with it (and will need to update some things as the story progresses). Here is how the narrator describes "normal" conditions in my first draft.

---

[c] By the way, if you want to see a cool diagram that shows the gaseous composition of the atmospheres in the Solar System, take a look at this page from The Planetary Society: https://www.planetary.org/space-images/the-atmospheres-of-the-solar-system

The ship settled onto the surface of the sea after a good hundred-meter dive. Most of the *Amesware Pleasure Seven*, like all pleasure craft, was surrounded by a titanium and carbon-fiber shell, with only a few places to step out and enjoy the weather. Not that you could enjoy the weather on Minor Pales. There were a few days a year when the wind blew at over two hundred knots, the sky was covered with a thick blanket of dark, undulating green clouds, and the waves were around fifty meters. Most days, however, the atmosphere was relatively nice—two degrees centigrade, wind calmer at only fifty knots, horizontal acidic rain, and sea swells at five to seven meters. You could go out on the bow of your pleasure craft provided you were fully encased in an outersuit and tied to one of the support beams.

Alien planets *should* be weird. Seth Shostak, an astronomer with SETI says, "If you have biology on planets around such stars, it will be mostly confined to a thin strip along the terminator. That would be interesting, of course, and quite unlike most of the planets you see in films."[255] This isn't a film-writing book, but the same considerations could be made for fiction. Our planet is but one of an infinite number of biomes with an infinite number of possible atmospheres that may or may not support an infinite variety of life. You are a writer, however, so if you feel the need to fashion your world like Earth, go for it. The weirder your world, the more you will have to explain to your reader. I'm still thinking about Isaac Asimov's *The Gods Themselves* nearly 35 years after I first read it.

Using what you know about the weather on Earth, however, can help you craft similar events on other worlds. Atmospheres may be different, but there will still be wind, clouds may form even if they aren't made of water vapor, rain or snow may fall, lightning is bound to be produced, and extreme events like tornadoes and large hail are certainly within the realm of reality. Remember those multi-year storms on Neptune? Why couldn't your alien world have similar hurricanes that slowly move around its equator and the colonists (or aliens) must always be on the move?

Literary critics and Internet...um..."commentators" love to poke holes in the facts as presented in fictional narratives, be it film or the written word. How could those two planets appear so big on that screen? Why are there clouds on that desert planet without water? But unless you're writing a nonfiction book on the weather on Mars, I say *don't listen* to them. Again: there are infinite possibilities, provided your atmospheric physics are correct. But also remember that science evolves. As one of my characters in my *Transit* series says:

> Just because the physics make little sense, it's only confusing because *humans* interpreted those physical laws. Sure, they've been scientifically proven, but every day some new article or study comes out that rewrites something, whether it modifies the behavior of a quark at the quantum level or argues against Newton's Laws or Einstein's equations. Science is an ever-evolving thing, facts built from theory built from experiments which lead to more theories and more facts.[d]

You are the writer and that alien weather on that alien world is all yours. If you want it to rain diamonds, snow frozen methane balls, or have your thunderstorms reach 200,000 feet into the air, go for it. Or, if you want it to be more Earth-like, take a hint from Isaac Asimov who described the planet Erythro in *Nemesis* as "a planet of sea and land." Its atmosphere is "a little denser than Earth's and it contains free oxygen— 16 percent of it, plus 5 percent argon and the rest nitrogen."[256] Or Ben Bova, who described a newly found planet orbiting in the "Goldilocks" zone near Sirius as "almost the same size as Earth...where its surface temperature was not too hot, and not too cold for liquid water to exist."[257]

---

[d] This is from *Out of Due Season: The First Transit.*

You could also be more extreme, like David Gerrold's *Hella* where the weather is extreme enough to force the colonists to migrate twice a year.[258]

The possibilities for alien weather are endless, really. Sure, many writers will want to stick to physics as much as possible, and that's good. Sticking to meteorological principles will help establish validity as well. But you could also be a little more creative, if you wish. Do the "weird" thing. "Cosmologists speculate that a multitude of other universes exist," according to *MIT News*, "each with its own laws of physics...[and] when the masses of the elementary particles are dramatically altered, life may find a way".[259] If that's true, what's to say the world you built in your science fiction novel exists not in our universe but in another, with a completely different set of rules?

Nothing says that. Have fun with your world and keep on writing. There are *universes* of possibility.

---

[239] Seager, S., & Deming, D. (2010). Exoplanet Atmospheres. *Annual Review of Astronomy and Astrophysics, 48*(1), 631–672. https://doi.org/10.1146/annurev-astro-081309-130837

[240] Bergmann, C. (1847). Ueber die verhältnisse der wärmeökonomie der thiere zu ihrer grösse. *Göttinger Studien 1*, 595–708.

[241] See Juman, M.M., Millien, V., Olson, L.E. et al. (2022). Recent and rapid ecogeographical rule reversals in Northern Treeshrews. *Scientific Reports 12*:19689. https://doi.org/10.1038/s41598-022-23774-w

[242] Timmermann, A., Yun, KS., Raia, P. et al. Climate effects on archaic human habitats and species successions. *Nature 604*, 495–501 (2022). https://doi.org/10.1038/s41586-022-04600-9

[243] Al-Shayeb, B., Schoelmerich, M.C., West-Roberts, J. et al. Borgs are giant genetic elements with potential to expand metabolic capacity. *Nature 610*, 731–736 (2022). https://doi.org/10.1038/s41586-022-05256-1

[244] McKee, M. Diamond drizzle forecast for Saturn and Jupiter. *Nature* (2013). https://doi.org/10.1038/nature.2013.13925

[245] Jenner, L. (2020b, December 16). *Dark Storm on Neptune Reverses Direction, Possibly Shedding a Fragment*. NASA. https://www.nasa.gov/feature/goddard/2020/dark-storm-on-neptune-reverses-direction-possibly-shedding-a-fragment/

[246] Eveleth, R. (2013, June 12). *On Venus It Snows Metal*. Smithsonian Magazine. https://www.smithsonianmag.com/smart-news/on-venus-it-snows-metal-99154/

[247] Hamilton, C. J. (n.d.). *Mars Introduction*. Views of the Solar System Calvin J. Hamilton. https://solarviews.com/eng/mars.htm

[248] *Rains of Terror on Exoplanet HD 189733b*. (2017, August 6). NASA. https://www.nasa.gov/image-feature/rains-of-terror-on-exoplanet-hd-189733b/

[249] Alderson, L. (2022, November 18). *Early Release Science of the Exoplanet WASP-39b with JWST*

NIRSpec G395H. arXiv.org. https://arxiv.org/abs/2211.10488

[250] Ahrer, E. (2022, November 18). *Early Release Science of the exoplanet WASP-39b with JWST NIRCam*. arXiv.org. https://arxiv.org/abs/2211.10489

[251] Beichman, C. A., & Greene, T. P. (2017). Observing Exoplanets with the James Webb Space Telescope. *Handbook of Exoplanets*, 1–26. https://doi.org/10.1007/978-3-319-30648-3_85-1

[252] *NASA Exoplanet Archive*. (n.d.). https://exoplanetarchive.ipac.caltech.edu/

[253] Starr, M. (2022, November 26). *We Just Got The Most Detailed View of an Exoplanet Atmosphere Yet - And It's Active* : ScienceAlert. https://www.sciencealert.com/we-just-got-the-most-detailed-view-of-an-exoplanet-atmosphere-yet-and-its-active

[254] Burroughs, E.R. (1917). *A Princess of Mars*. A.C. McClurg & Company.

[255] Anders, C. J. (2015, December 16). *The Worst Blunders People Make in Inventing Fictional Alien Worlds*. Gizmodo. https://gizmodo.com/the-worst-blunders-people-make-in-inventing-fictional-a-1527153617

[256] Asimov, I. (1989). *Nemesis*. Doubleday.

[257] Bova, B. (2013). *New Earth*. Tor.

[258] Gerrold, D. (2020). *Hella*. DAW Books, Inc.

[259] *Life beyond our universe*. (2010, February 22). MIT News | Massachusetts Institute of Technology. https://news.mit.edu/2010/multiple-universes

CONCLUSION

I've found that it's of some help to think of one's
moods and feelings about the world as being similar to
weather.
  —Stephen Fry[260]

I'T'S CLEAR ENOUGH THAT SETTING MATTERS IN FICTION, WHETHER
you place your characters in a city, a countryside, the open ocean, or
on a different planet. To butcher a marketing phrase, "setting, setting, setting." While the focus in any fictional account should be on the
characters and the plot, the setting—the time, place, and circum-
stances—is arguably the thing that *allows* the characters to execute the
plot. The setting can also influence the characters and twist the plot in
unexpected ways. Weaving elements of weather into your narrative can
manipulate your readers by tapping into the common human experience.

When you go outside, what do you see? The trees, the ground, buildings, maybe a street or a path, a bush, grass. What do you hear? The sym-
phony of a city, children playing in a park, a dog barking. What do you
smell? What do you taste? Finally, what do you feel? Weather is indis-
pensable to the experience of setting, and when it is left out of fiction, it
robs the reader of your character's experience within the plot. You spent
a great deal of time crafting characters and building out your plot elements. Spend the same time working on the setting, building a world that
invites your reader in and begs them to ask for more.

As important as it is to include weather in your stories, it is just as
important to do so in a way that is as accurate as possible so as not to trip

up your readers who may be weather nerds. There are more out there than you think, and as you've probably noticed if you've been on social media for a least one day, people like to challenge everything. While accuracy is a hallmark need of nonfiction, it should not be discounted when the format shifts to fiction.

From Bad to Good

TAKE A MOMENT to look at the weather you may have already written into your narrative. If you're unsure of something (like if a hurricane spins clockwise or counterclockwise in the Southern Hemisphere or the name of a wind that's pummeling your character in Paraguay is correct), look at the previous chapters which mention that element. If it's not in this book, then a little research will be required. That tiny bit of research can make a big difference and will endear you to your fans a little more. Details matter.

Next, look at the *impact* your weather has. Is it just an aside (e.g., "it was a sunny day") or does it serve a purpose? Is your weather analogous to a plot element or the emotional state of your characters? Setting the atmosphere with atmosphere is more than just providing a weather report. It is tapping into the common human experience (weather) and connecting it to that other common human experience (emotion). If your weather is dry (no pun intended), then you might want to read through some of the examples in this book to find ways to give it more substance. Or try an exercise or two to see if you can't describe your weather in a way that will emotionally charge your reader. Let others read it with and without the weather and see if they notice a difference.

Your words are the conduit through which your world is imparted upon your reader. It is therefore important to make those words as effectual as possible.

Show, Don't Tell

AS WITH MOST things in fiction, it is best to show the reader any meteorological phenomena without mentioning it by name or being pedagogical in presentation. Climate change (and rainbows and El Niño and floods and noctilucent clouds, etc.) are more telling if they are shown. If you want to pull in your reader and get them to empathize with your characters, it is best not to beat them over the head with meteorological facts. Rather, present them in a way that elicits emotion on the sly. In other words, trick the reader into feeling through description and narration.

In the introduction to this book, I mentioned a Mark Twain quote that is more poignant than anything I could write. To end this book, I will repeat it, urging you all to create atmosphere with atmosphere.

> ...**weather is necessary to a narrative of human experi-**
> **ence**...to be put where it will **not be in the way**; where
> it will not interrupt the flow of the narrative...Weather
> is a literary specialty, and no untrained hand can turn
> out a good article of it.

---

[260] *It will be sunny one day.* (2021, January 5). Letters of Note. https://letter-sofnote.com/2009/10/08/it-will-be-sunny-one-day/

The Shipwreck by Claude-Joseph Vernet (1772)

EXERCISES, EXERCISES, EXERCISES

HERE ARE A few additional exercises primarily geared toward students. However, if you are an author, try out any of these as a writing exercise when you need a little inspiration. You can even challenge your writing group and see what they come up with. These are in no order, so skip around to find one that piques your interest.

A note to educators: Based on the level of complexity and skills required, the exercises listed here might be appropriate for students in middle or high school, depending on their level of proficiency. Some of the exercises may be more challenging and require more advanced skills, and thus might be appropriate for higher-level high school students in advanced classes. The objectives are included in case you need something for a lesson plan.

Emotional weather report: Ask students to imagine they are a weather reporter, but instead of reporting on the actual weather, they are reporting on the emotional climate in their community. Have them describe the emotional "conditions" in vivid detail, using metaphors and sensory language to create a vivid and evocative report.

Objective: Recognize the emotional and sensory associations of a given weather condition, and describe its impact on mood and atmosphere using sensory language and imagery.

Weather-based character study: Have students create a character based on a particular weather condition. For example, they could create a character who embodies the mood of a gloomy, overcast day or a character who exudes the energy of a bright, sunny morning. Encourage them to think about how the character's appearance, personality, and actions are influenced by the weather condition they embody.

Objective: Identify the emotional and thematic qualities of a given weather condition or element, and express those qualities through a character portrait using sensory language and characterization.

Weather and memory: Ask students to recall a vivid memory that is tied to a specific weather condition (e.g. the feeling of a warm summer rain or the sight of a crisp winter landscape). Have them write a narrative that captures the sensory details of that memory and explores the emotions and associations that the weather condition evokes.

Objective: Recall a personal memory or association with a weather condition, and describe the emotional and sensory details of that memory using descriptive language and narrative structure.

Weather-based dialogue: Have students write a dialogue between two characters who are experiencing a particular weather condition. Encourage them to think about how the weather might influence the characters' emotions, actions, and conversations. For example, they could write a dialogue between two people who are stuck in a rainstorm or two friends who are enjoying a sunny day at the beach.

Objective: Recognize the emotional and sensory impact of a given weather condition, and create a dialogue between characters that reflects that impact using sensory language and dialogue.

Weather Collage: Have students identify the emotions that they associate with different types of weather and use these emotions to create a collage that reflects their feelings. For example, they could create a collage that reflects their emotions on a sunny day, a rainy day, or a snowy day.

Objective: Identify different types of weather and use descriptive words to label and communicate associated emotions and feelings.

Weather and metaphor: Have students create a metaphor or extended metaphor that links a particular weather condition to a larger theme or concept. For example, they could write about how a stormy night is a metaphor for the tumultuous emotions of a character going through a personal crisis, or how a bright, sunny day is a metaphor for the hope and optimism of a new beginning.

Objective: Analyze the emotional and thematic potential of a given weather condition or element, and create a metaphor or extended metaphor that captures that potential using sensory language and imagery.

Cloud poetry: Have students write a poem that focuses on the imagery of clouds. Encourage them to experiment with different forms and structures (e.g. haiku, sonnet, free verse) and to use sensory language to capture the mood and atmosphere of the clouds. For an added challenge, have students try to personify the clouds and imagine what they might be thinking or feeling.

Objective: Express the emotional and sensory qualities of a given cloudscape through poetry, using poetic language and structure to create an engaging and impactful work.

Snow scene: Ask students to write a descriptive paragraph or short story that takes place in a snowy landscape. Encourage them to use sensory language to capture the atmosphere and mood of the scene, and to think about how the snow might affect the characters' emotions and actions.

Objective: Create a vivid and engaging description of a given snowscape, using sensory language and imagery to convey its emotional and sensory qualities.

Wind monologue: Ask students to write a monologue from the perspective of someone who is experiencing a strong wind. Have them explore how the wind might affect the character's thoughts, feelings, and physical sensations. Encourage them to use sensory language to convey the power and force of the wind, and to think about how the wind might be a metaphor for larger themes or concepts.

Objective: Describe the emotional and sensory associations of a given wind condition or element, and create a monologue that captures those associations using sensory language and characterization.

Temperature contrast: Have students write a short story that contrasts two different temperature conditions (e.g. a sweltering hot day and a freezing cold night). Encourage them to think about how the temperature conditions affect the characters' emotions and actions, and to use sensory language to capture the physical sensations of each condition.

Objective: Compare and contrast the emotional and sensory implications of two different temperature conditions, and create a short story or scene that reflects those implications using descriptive language and narrative structure.

Lightning dialogue: Ask students to write a dialogue between two characters who are experiencing a lightning storm. Encourage them to think about how the lightning might affect the characters' emotions, thoughts, and conversation. Have them use sensory language to capture the atmosphere of the storm, and to think about how the lightning might be a metaphor for larger themes or concepts.

Objective: Recognize the emotional and sensory impact of a given lightning storm or strike, and create a dialogue between characters that reflects that impact using sensory language and dialogue.

Rain reflection: Have students write a reflective essay or journal entry about how rain affects their emotions. Encourage them to think about the different types of rain (e.g. light drizzle, heavy downpour) and how each type might evoke different emotions or associations. Have them use personal anecdotes and sensory language to create a vivid and engaging reflection.

Objective: Recall a personal memory or association with a rainstorm, and reflect on the emotional and psychological effects of that memory using personal anecdotes and descriptive language.

Thunderstorm soundtrack: Have students create a playlist of songs that they think would capture the mood and atmosphere of a thunderstorm. Encourage them to think about the lyrics, instrumentation, and overall mood of each song and how it relates to the emotions and associations that a thunderstorm might evoke.

Objective: Select music that captures the emotional and atmospheric qualities of a given thunderstorm, and explain the rationale behind those selections using descriptive language.

Sun-inspired character sketch: Have students create a character who is inspired by the energy and warmth of the sun. Encourage them to think about how the character's appearance, personality, and actions are influenced by the sunny disposition, and to use sensory language to create a vivid and engaging portrait.

Objective: Identify the emotional and thematic qualities of a given sunny day or sunshine, and express those qualities through a character portrait using sensory language and characterization.

Foggy setting: Ask students to write a scene that takes place in a foggy setting. Encourage them to use sensory language to capture the atmosphere and mood of the scene, and to think about how the fog might affect the characters' perceptions, emotions, and actions.

Objective: Create a vivid and engaging description of a given foggy setting, using sensory language and imagery to convey its emotional and sensory qualities.

Heat wave diary: Have students keep a diary or journal during a heat wave, reflecting on their thoughts, emotions, and experiences. Encourage them to use sensory language to describe the physical sensations of the heat, and to think about how the heat might affect their mood, productivity, and social interactions.

Objective: Reflect on the emotional and psychological effects of a given heat wave, and record those reflections in a diary format using personal anecdotes and descriptive language.

Opposing weather conditions: Ask students to choose two opposing weather conditions (e.g. a sunny day and a stormy night) and write a short scene that contrasts the emotions and actions of characters in each condition. Encourage them to use sensory language to capture the atmosphere and mood of each scene, and to think about how the weather conditions might reflect larger themes or concepts in the story.

Objective: Differentiate and contrast the emotional and sensory implications of two opposing weather conditions, and create a scene or short story that reflects those implications using descriptive language and narrative structure.

Weather and memory: Ask students to recall a vivid memory that is tied to a specific weather condition. Have them write a narrative that captures the sensory details of that memory and explores the emotions and associations that the weather condition evokes. Encourage them to use sensory language and descriptive detail to create a vivid and engaging story.

Objective: Recall a personal memory or association with a weather condition, and describe the emotional and sensory details of that memory using descriptive and sensory language. Then, use those details to create a narrative that captures the impact of the weather on mood and perception.

Weather-inspired metaphor: Have students create a metaphor or extended metaphor that links a particular weather condition to a character's emotional state or journey. Encourage them to use sensory language and imagery to create a vivid and impactful metaphor, and to think about how it might evolve over the course of the story.

Objective: Analyze the emotional and thematic potential of a given weather condition or element, and create a metaphor or extended metaphor that captures that potential using sensory language and imagery.

Weather and setting: Ask students to write a short story or scene in which the weather plays a significant role in the setting. Encourage them to use sensory language to create a vivid and engaging scene, and to think about how the weather conditions might influence the characters' emotions and actions.

Objective: Describe the sensory and emotional qualities of a given weather condition or element, and create a vivid and engaging setting that reflects those qualities using descriptive language and imagery.

Nature and emotion: Have students write a reflective essay or journal entry that explores the connections between nature and emotion. Encourage them to use personal anecdotes and sensory language to explore how natural environments (such as mountains, forests, or beaches) affect their emotions and perceptions.

Objective: Recognize the emotional and psychological effects of a given natural element or phenomenon, and express those effects through personal reflection using descriptive language and personal anecdotes.

Misty landscape: Ask students to write a descriptive paragraph or short story that takes place in a misty landscape. Encourage them to use sensory language to capture the atmosphere and mood of the scene, and to think about how the mist might affect the characters' emotions and actions.

Objective: Describe the sensory and emotional qualities of a given misty landscape, and create a vivid and engaging setting that reflects those qualities using descriptive language and imagery.

Frosty character sketch: Have students create a character who is inspired by the cold and stillness of a frosty morning. Encourage them to think about how the character's appearance, personality, and actions are influenced by the frigid disposition, and to use sensory language to create a vivid and engaging portrait.

Objective: Identify the emotional and thematic qualities of a given frosty day or frost, and express those qualities through a character portrait using sensory language and characterization.

Hail and tension: Ask students to write a scene that takes place during a hailstorm, in which tension is high between two characters. Encourage them to use sensory language to capture the atmosphere and mood of the scene, and to think about how the hail might intensify the emotions and actions of the characters.

Objective: Differentiate and contrast the emotional and sensory implications of two opposing weather conditions (such as hail and calm), and create a scene or short story that reflects those implications using descriptive language and narrative structure.

Heat and character development: Have students write a short story that takes place during a heat wave, in which a character undergoes significant emotional and psychological development. Encourage them to use sensory language to describe the physical sensations of the heat, and to think about how the heat might trigger or amplify the character's internal conflicts.

Objective: Analyze the emotional and psychological effects of a given heat wave or high temperature, and develop a character whose emotions or psychological state are influenced by that heat wave or high temperature, using sensory language and characterization.

Snow and character conflict: Ask students to write a scene that takes place during a snowstorm, in which two characters are at odds with one another. Encourage them to use sensory language to capture the atmosphere and mood of the scene, and to think about how the snow might add layers of complexity to the conflict between the characters.

Objective: Create a scene or short story that features two characters in conflict, with a snowstorm or snowscape playing a significant role in the emotional and sensory impact of the conflict, using descriptive language and narrative structure.

Examples of Weather in Fiction

Objective: Understand the relationship between weather and emotion in fiction, and practice close reading skills by finding examples of weather in a work of fiction and analyzing its emotional and thematic implications. Use critical thinking and analytical skills to develop a deeper understanding of the literary significance of weather in literature, and express that understanding through a well-structured and well-written essay.

Instructions

Find examples of weather in fiction and analyze how it contributes to the mood and themes of the story.

1. Assign a short story or novel for students to read. Make sure the text contains examples of weather that play a significant role in the story.
2. Ask students to identify and record at least three examples of weather in the text. For each example, they should note the specific details (e.g. the type of weather, the time of day, the setting), as well as the emotions and associations that the weather evokes.
3. In a short essay, ask students to analyze how the weather contributes to the mood and themes of the story. They should consider questions such as:

- How does the weather reflect or amplify the characters' emotions?

- How does the weather contribute to the setting or atmosphere of the story?

- How does the weather function as a metaphor or symbol for larger themes or concepts in the text?

4. Encourage students to use specific quotes and examples from the text to support their analysis. They should also use descriptive and sensory language to create a vivid and engaging essay.

5. For an added challenge, have students compare and contrast the different examples of weather in the text and consider how they contribute to the overall mood and themes of the story.

This exercise asks students to engage in close reading and literary analysis, while also exploring the fascinating connections between weather and emotions in fiction. It can be adapted to work with a wide range of texts and grade levels.

Suggested Rubric

Category	Excellent (5)	Good (3)	Needs Improvement (1)
Content	Thoroughly and insightfully examines the relationship between weather and emotion in the work of fiction, and identifies multiple examples of weather that significantly contribute to the work's literary significance.	Adequately examines the relationship between weather and emotion in the work of fiction, and identifies one or more examples of weather that contribute to the work's literary significance.	Examines the relationship between weather and emotion in the work of fiction, but may not identify examples of weather that contribute to the work's literary significance.
Critical Thinking	Demonstrates a high level of critical thinking, analyzing the emotional and thematic implications of the weather examples in	Demonstrates some critical thinking, analyzing the emotional and thematic implications of the weather examples to some ex-	Demonstrates limited critical thinking, analyzing the emotional and thematic implications of the weather examples to a minimal extent, and

Category	Excellent (5)	Good (3)	Needs Improvement (1)
	depth, and drawing insightful conclusions about their significance in the work of fiction.	tent, and drawing conclusions about their significance in the work of fiction.	drawing only basic conclusions about their significance in the work of fiction.
Organization	Presents ideas in a well-structured and well-organized essay format, with a clear and engaging introduction, well-organized body paragraphs, and a thoughtful conclusion.	Presents ideas in a somewhat structured and organized essay format, with an adequate introduction, body paragraphs that could be more clearly organized, and a conclusion that could be more developed.	Presents ideas in a poorly-structured and disorganized essay format, with an unclear or rambling introduction, body paragraphs that are difficult to follow, and a weak or nonexistent conclusion.
Style	Employs clear and engaging language that effectively conveys the emotional and sensory impact of the weather examples, and demonstrates a strong command of grammar and style.	Employs language that is somewhat clear and engaging, but could be more effective in conveying the emotional and sensory impact of the weather examples, and may contain some errors in grammar and style.	Employs language that is unclear or unengaging, and does not effectively convey the emotional and sensory impact of the weather examples, and contains numerous errors in grammar and style.

Research-Based Creative Writing

Objective: Engage in research and critical thinking, and use that knowledge to inform a creative writing piece that explores the emotional and thematic implications of a specific weather element or phenomenon. Use descriptive and sensory language to create vivid and engaging characters, settings, and scenes, and practice using narrative structure to create impactful and engaging works. Develop analytical and creative skills by recognizing the cultural, historical, or literary significance of a weather element, and expressing that understanding through a well-structured and well-written piece of creative writing.

Instructions

1. Ask students to find an example of weather in a work of fiction,

either from a book or a short story. Encourage them to choose an example that is particularly vivid or impactful, and to take note of the details that make it memorable.

2. Have students research the cultural, historical, or literary significance of the weather element they have chosen. For example, they might research the symbolism of rain in literature, the historical significance of a particular type of storm, or the cultural associations of a particular type of weather.

3. Ask students to write a short essay or creative piece that explores the emotional and thematic implications of the weather element in the story. They should use the research they have conducted to inform their analysis, and to consider how the weather might function as a metaphor, symbol, or plot device in the story.

4. Encourage students to use sensory language to describe the weather element and its impact on the story. They should also use specific quotes and examples from the text to support their analysis.

5. For an added challenge, have students compare and contrast the use of weather in different works of fiction, or consider how weather is used in different genres or time periods.

6. This exercise asks students to engage in research and analysis, while also exploring the creative potential of weather in literature. It can be adapted to work with a wide range of texts and grade levels, and can be a great way to encourage students to explore the cultural and historical contexts of literature.

This exercise asks students to engage in research and analysis, while also exploring the creative potential of weather in literature. It can be adapted to work with a wide range of texts and grade levels, and can be a great way to encourage students to explore the cultural and historical contexts of literature.

Suggested Rubric

Category	Excellent (5)	Good (3)	Needs Improvement (1)
Content	Accurately identifies and analyzes the weather element in a work of fiction, effectively describing its emotional and thematic implications.	Adequately identifies and analyzes the weather element in a work of fiction, somewhat describing its emotional and thematic implications.	Minimally identifies and analyzes the weather element in a work of fiction, failing to effectively describe its emotional and thematic implications.
Descriptive Language	Employs rich and engaging sensory and descriptive language to effectively capture the emotional and atmospheric associations of the weather element in the story.	Employs somewhat effective sensory and descriptive language to partly capture the emotional and atmospheric associations of the weather element in the story.	Employs minimal or ineffective sensory and descriptive language that fails to capture the emotional and atmospheric associations of the weather element in the story.
Organization	Effectively organizes the essay with a clear introduction, well-developed body paragraphs, and a thoughtful conclusion. Transitions between paragraphs and sections are smooth and effective, contributing to the overall coherence and flow of the essay.	Adequately organizes the essay with an introduction, body paragraphs, and a conclusion. Transitions between paragraphs and sections could be more effective in creating coherence and flow.	Poorly organizes the essay with an unclear or rambling introduction, body paragraphs that lack coherence and development, and a weak or non-existent conclusion. Transitions between paragraphs and sections are ineffective and do not contribute to coherence and flow.
Critical Thinking	Analyzes the cultural, historical, or literary significance of the weather element in the story and expresses that understanding through a well-structured and well-written essay. Demonstrates a deep understanding of the literary significance of the weather element.	Adequately analyzes the cultural, historical, or literary significance of the weather element in the story and expresses that understanding through an adequately structured and written essay. Demonstrates an adequate understanding of the literary significance of the weather element.	Minimally analyzes the cultural, historical, or literary significance of the weather element in the story and inadequately expresses that understanding through a poorly-structured and written essay. Demonstrates a limited understanding of the literary significance of the weather element.

SUGGESTED READING

ASIDE FROM THE references found in the endnotes at the end of each chapter, below are some additional readings that I have found useful as both an obsessive weather nerd and a writer.

Clouds

International Cloud Atlas: Manual on the Observation of Clouds and Other Meteors (WMO-No. 407). Published by the World Meteorological Organization's (WMO), this atlas describes the classification system for clouds and meteorological phenomena other than clouds—hydrometeors, lithometeors, photometeors, and electrometeors. See: https://cloudatlas.wmo.int/en/home.html

The Cloudspotter's Guide: The Science, History, and Culture of Clouds by Gavin Pretor-Pinny (ISBN: 978-0399533457). A fun book that will have you looking at clouds like ornithologists look at birds.

The Invention of Clouds: How an Amateur Meteorologist Forged the Language of the Skies by Richard Hamblyn (ISBN: 978-0274881444). If you're looking for a little history into clouds and cloud names, look no further than this biography of Luke Howard, a 19th century Quaker who made cumulus a household name.

Fog

London Fog: The Biography by Christin L. Corton (ISBN: 978-0674088351). If you're as fascinated with the fogs of London as all those 19th century writers, look at this historical dive into how fog became a character all its own.

The Sky of Our Manufacturer: The London Fog in British Fiction from Dickens to Woolf by Jesse O. Taylor (ISBN: 978-0813937939). In the true form of literary criticism, the author uses the works of London's greatest writers to explore both the fog and anthropogenic climate change. From Dickens to Doyle to Conrad to Woolf, the book reveals the distinct relationship between culture and climate.

Mysteries in the Mist: Mist, Fog, and Clouds in the Paranormal by W.T. Watson (ISBN: 978-1954528253). This book will take you behind the veil (there's a pun in there somewhere) to give you glimpses of UFOs, cryptids, and ghosts that might be hidden in fog, mist, and clouds.

Precipitation

Rain, Hail, Sleet & Snow by Nancy Larrick (ISBN: 978-0692810477). Written in 1961, this book is more for elementary students interested in how weather forms. While it deals with rain, hail, sleet, and snow, the book also looks at tornadoes, hurricanes, thunderstorms, and more.

Washed Away: How the Great Flood of 1913, America's Most Widespread Natural Disaster, Terrorized a Nation and Changed It Forever by Geoff Williams (ISBN: 9781605984049). Specifically detailing a series of storms in 1913 which killed over 700 people, this book also looks at the governmental and societal impact that flood had over the years.

The West without Water: What Past Floods, Droughts, and Other Climatic Clues Tell Us about Tomorrow by B. Lynn Ingram (ISBN: 978-0520286009). While I did not get into droughts in this book, it is still related to (the lack of) precipitation. This book takes a historical look back to show what a "normal" climate should look like in the western United States.

Temperature

U.S. Standard Atmosphere, 1976 (NOAA-S/T-76-1562) published by National Oceanic and Atmospheric Administration (NOAA). Not for the faint of heart, but useful if you want to know more about the temperature profile of the atmosphere. Includes the basis for computation of the main tables of atmospheric properties, including values of physical constants, conversion factors, and definitions of derived properties.
https://www.ngdc.noaa.gov/stp/space-weather/online-publications/miscellaneous/us-standard-atmosphere-1976/us-standard-atmosphere_st76-1562_noaa.pdf

Skew-T Parameters, an online guide published by the National Weather Service (NWS). Are you dying to know how to read an atmospheric profile? Want to know what a weather balloon can tell you? This online primer can help the writer who, for whatever reason, might feel the need to include information about a Skew-T in their novels.
https://www.weather.gov/source/zhu/ZHU_Training_Page/convective_parameters/skewt/skewtinfo.html

Wind

Wind: How the Flow of Air Has Shaped Life, Myth, and the Land by Jan DeBlieu (ISBN: 978-1593760946). This book explores the effects of atmospheric flow across the United States from Oregon to Mount Washington. A highly detailed examination of society's response to wind written by a creative writing professor and conservationist.

Heaven's Breath: A Natural History of the Wind by Lyall Watson (ISBN: 978-1681373690). Watson describes the wind as the "circulatory system" of Earth. This book looks at the wind's role in history, geology, evolution, trade, health, mythology, art, literature, and language.

Thunderstorms & Lightning

The Thunderstorm in Human Affairs by Edwin Kessler (ed) (ISBN: 978-0806121536). This was one of the first books I picked up specifically devoted to thunderstorms. Perfect for the layperson, the student, and the researcher, the book includes helpful information on how thunderstorms, flash floods, tornadoes, and lightning have impacted society from the Big Thompson Canyon flood of 1976 to the tornado outbreak of 1974.

Storm Kings: America's First Tornado Chasers by Lee Sandlin (ISBN: 978-0307473585). Digging into America's fascination with severe weather, this book shows how chasing storms led to meteorology as we know it today. Sandlin provides vivid descriptions of some of the most devastating storms in the country's history and describes the evolution of tornado science and chasing.

All About Lightning by Martin A. Uman (ISBN: 978-0486252377). Written by an American engineer who is considered one of the world's leading experts on lightning and lightning modeling, this book answers multiple questions about lightning in an easy-to-grasp way so that it's accessible to all.

Space Weather

An Introduction to Space Weather by Mark Moldwin (ISBN: 978-0521711128). Definitely a textbook but written for non-science majors. I encourage you to look up this book if you're dealing with the interaction between the sun and Earth. Special attention should be made to how space weather affects our satellite, navigation, communication, and power systems.

Climate Change

Introduction to Modern Climate Change by Andrew E. Dessler (ISBN: 978-1108793872). Another textbook for non-science majors, but a great book that focuses on anthropogenic climate change and its impact on society, economy, and politics. Spend some time looking at the first part of the book which gets into fundamentals, like radiative forcing, blackbody radiation and the carbon cycle.

A Cultural History of Climate by Wolfgang Behringer (ISBN: 978-0745645292). Just as the title presumes, this book looks back at climate change (both natural and anthropogenic) over the centuries to show how small changes impact social, political, and religious beliefs.

Alien Weather

The Zoologist's Guide to the Galaxy: What Animals on Earth Reveal About Aliens—and Ourselves by Arik Kershenbaum (ISBN: 978-1984881984). You're probably wondering what this book has to do with weather. As I wrote in my review of Kershenbaum's book, when humans design aliens as part of science fiction, they do so based on certain cognitive biases. That is, authors tend to favor things which conform to their existing beliefs about the world, or they frame their imaginations within the confines of what they have been influence by. In this incredible book, Kershenbaum evolves the concept of aliens by devolving our own Earth-bound species. Each chapter of the book dives into things that make animals, well, animals. And guess what? Atmospheric conditions have guided our evolution, just as it would anywhere else in the universe.

Weather and Climate on Planets by K.Y. Kondratyev & G.E. Hunt (ISBN: 978-1483118376). Perhaps because the science is relatively new, there are not a lot of books specifically detailing weather on other planets. This textbook may be a good starting point for those writers who are interested in world building to the extreme. There are three chapters on the weather of Venus, Mars, and Jupiter.

Drifting on Alien Winds: Exploring the Skies and Weather of Other Worlds by Michael Carroll (ISBN: 978-1441969163). This book takes a look at the weather on other planets and their moons within our solar system through photographs and paintings. It starts off with a brief review of Earth's atmosphere and moves on to other worlds.

General Meteorological Awesomeness

Weatherland by Alexandra Harris (ISBN: 978-0500518113). This book examines English weather as it has been related through the arts. It is a highly detailed and dense examination of centuries of English literature, art, and songs which digs deep into finding those connections between weather and the human experience.

It's Raining Frogs and Fishes: Four Seasons of Natural Phenomena and Oddities of the Sky by Jerry Dennis (ISBN: 978-0989333139). Updated in 2013, this book investigates some of the more obscure meteorological phenomena, like why fish, reptiles, snails, and snakes have rained down from the heavens. Broken down by season, this book is a collection of curiosities written in very accessible and fun way.

A Golden Guide: Weather by Paul E. Lehr, R. Will Burnett, and Herbert S. Zim (ISBN: 978-1582381596). This is an updated version of the book that started it all for me, the one mentioned in the dedication. The 1965 edition I have is just as awesome and includes many illustrations and up-to-date facts to help you understand weather and forecasting.

Online Glossaries

The American Meteorological Society (AMS) Glossary of Meteorology. This searchable glossary is the definitive resource for all things related to weather. Constantly updated. *https://glossary.ametsoc.org/wiki/Welcome*

Glossary of Meteorological Terms by NovaLynx. This is a layman's version with short definitions for a variety of meteorological words. Worth a good bookmark for the writer. *https://novalynx.com/store/pc/Glossary-of-Meteorological-Terms-A-d9.htm*

The Government of Canada Weather and Meteorology Glossary. Not to be left out, the Canadian government has complied an extensive glossary of terms used in public forecasting and observation. *https://www.canada.ca/en/environment-climate-change/services/weather-general-tools-resources/glossary.html*

The Royal Meteorological Society Weather Glossary. For those writers who want a glossary that's not too long, this glossary of weather terms is smaller but a good stop if you want to find a quick definition. *https://www.metlink.org/resource/weather-glossary/*

A Comprehensive Glossary of Weather Terms for Storm Spotters. Maintained by the National Weather Service office in Norman, Oklahoma, this more technical glossary will be helpful for those writers looking to include severe weather (or storm chasing) in their narratives. *https://www.weather.gov/oun/spotterglossary*

UNTERM: The United Nations Terminology Database. If you need a local flair to your narrative, this searchable multilingual database includes terms and definitions used by the International Maritime Organization, the United Nations Educational, Scientific and Cultural Organization, the World Health Organization, and the World Meteorological Organization. *https://unterm.un.org/unterm/portal/welcome*

ACKNOWLEDGEMENTS

THIS BOOK WAS PROMPTED BY MY ACCEPTANCE (AND ATTENDANCE at) the 2022 Pikes Peak Writers Conference. If you're looking for the "friendliest writers conference" ever (according to *Writer's Digest*) look no further. The conference is typically held in late April.

As with everything I've written, I thank my wife, Jesse, for her support. Without her, I would not have been able to explore my creative side in so many ways. In the case of this book, she and I both worked as forecasters for the U.S. Air Force, so you could say I had an in-house quality check.

A special thank you goes to three Indie writers who appear in this book as examples. I read a lot and have found many great novels in the Indie scene, novels that don't get the attention they deserve. These authors stood out and I made plenty of notes on their work regarding the use of atmosphere to set atmosphere. When you get a chance, check out Raymond Beaman (http://www.awritestruggle.com/), S.Z. Attwell (https://szattwell.com/), and N.L. McLaughlin (https://www.nancylmclaughlin.com/), and give them a read.

INDEX

Printed in Great Britain
by Amazon

46135946R00185